THE WORKER
VIEWS HIS UNION

Joel Seidman

Jack London

Bernard Karsh

Daisy L. Tagliacozzo

THE WORKER
VIEWS HIS UNION

The University of Chicago Press

Chicago & London

Library of Congress Catalog Card Number: 58–5686

THE UNIVERSITY OF CHICAGO PRESS, CHICAGO & LONDON
The University of Toronto Press, Toronto 5, Canada

FOREWORD

In the logic of modern industrial society there is a functional distinction between the managers and the managed, which in turn requires the development of a system of rules governing the relationships between them. These rules encompass, among other things, the wages to be paid, the pace and quality of work to be performed, the assignment of tasks, the movement from one position to another, and the conditions governing tenure of, or discharge from, employment. In this relationship management wants three things from workers: subordination to managerial direction, loyalty to the enterprise, and efficiency in productive activity. Naturally, management would like to play the leading role as the rule-maker. But others also seek a share in the rule-making and rule-enforcing processes. In the United States the unions are the major contenders, and they have won in the organized shops a joint proprietorship with management over the determination of wages and working conditions through the process of collective bargaining.

In the factory the workers, of course, can serve only one master—the employer. But through their representatives they have some voice in the determination of policies which affect them. Their union leaders act as their advocates in the formulation of rules and as their policemen in the day-to-day administration of those rules in the shop. Thus the links between the worker as an employee in a particular establishment and as a member of his local union are tangible and intimate. In America, unions are not geared to the organization of a crusade to change the structure or the order of society; they exist primarily to regulate and to press demands upon the employer. To the American worker the union is, first and foremost, a service-rendering agency in the area of relationships with management.

Some people have assumed that labor in this country has no ideology. This is not true. As this study shows clearly, the American worker as a union member has a very definite philosophy. To be sure, he has many other interests—his family, church, ethnic group, club, fraternal order, or political party. The union touches only one aspect of his life—the relationship with management. And, even here, some of his relationships with the employer lie beyond the scope of union concern. It is true that most workers do not participate actively in union affairs, just as most citizens are not active participants in the government of the communities in which they live. Nevertheless, American workers believe strongly in the purposes of the union as an institution; indeed, in most cases, they are even quite willing to be "taxed" to support it. In this country the ideology of organized labor is not to overthrow the economic system but rather to get everything possible within it. And an important feature of labor's philosophy is a feeling of confidence, based upon actual performance, that it can and will get more and more from the system.

The labor movement, nevertheless, faces serious problems. As unions have matured and become more secure in the economy, they have lost much of their youthful imagination and vigor. As the years go by, the leaders appear to become farther removed from the rank and file. And as the employers, largely because of the impact of unions, have greatly improved human relationships in the plants, the "police-force" functions of the unions become more routine. The local unions are the grass roots of the American labor movement. As this volume shows, they are still alive and vigorous, but in many cases they are beginning to suffer for lack of nourishment. The dead rot of complacency and overconfidence which is so prevalent in many aspects of American life is also discernible in unions, and the cancers of corruption in a few organizations are an indication that parts of the labor movement are far from healthy. In the minds of workers there is room for improvement in unions, as there is a crying need for a fresh look at all our institutions in this time of ever deepening national crisis. The basic problems of developing worker interest and participation in union affairs are clearly presented in this volume.

This study of the American worker as a union member was launched almost ten years ago. At that time, those engaged in teaching labor and industrial relations were forced to rely largely upon "insights and hunches" in describing the attitudes of workers toward their unions. There were, of course, many books available on the function and structure of unions, the processes of collective bargaining, and the activities of the top men in the international unions and federations. But there was very little material about the people who make up the ranks of the union. As the authors of this volume correctly point out, "As one moves down from the national leaders through the ranks of paid local officers, and then of unpaid local leaders in the plants, the outlines grow increasingly dim, until, by the time the rank-and-file workers are reached, they are but a shadowy mass, about whom little systematic, reliable knowledge is available."

In 1948, a number of us in the Industrial Relations Center at the University of Chicago concluded that a definitive study of the attitude of union members was needed, and it was decided that such a study should focus on the local union. There were in the university a number of young graduate students who had also had rich experience as union members or leaders prior to or during the war. Professor Joel Seidman, a leading authority on American labor, was also on the campus, and we prevailed upon him to devote his energies to the organization and direction of the project. We had the human resources capable of doing the research and also the intimate contacts with the labor movement which were necessary to undertake it. The Carnegie Corporation graciously provided the funds to make it a reality.

Today, thanks to this study as well as to those of others which have appeared during the past few years, there is now a highway of knowledge about union members which is fairly well paved with objective and systematic research. Although this volume is not the first study of local unions in the American scene, it is certainly the most comprehensive and definitive. It enables one now to speak with reasonable confidence and authority about why American workers join unions and what they think is the appropriate role of the unions in representing their interests.

The coal miners, the plumbers, the steel workers, the metal workers, the knitting mill workers, and the telephone workers do not encompass all of organized labor; but they do represent very important and strategic segments of the working class in the United States. In this volume the authors give a view of six quite different local unions *in depth*, and from these depth studies they have drawn conclusions which unquestionably are valid for very broad categories of union members. They have focused their attention on patterns of experience rather than on statistical cross-sections and on qualitative rather than quantitative analysis. In this way they have been able to paint in full color, rather than merely to sketch roughly, the range and variation of workers' attitudes.

The authors of this volume were known at the University of Chicago as the "Seidman group." During the years 1949–54 they all worked together as a team in the Industrial Relations Center. They published a number of articles based upon their research, and they participated in countless conferences, seminars, and programs on the American worker as a union member. This volume is their final report. Like the visible part of an iceberg, it is an indication of even broader contributions to knowledge which they have made in this very vital area of industrial relations.

FREDERICK H. HARBISON

PREFACE

This is a study of the attitudes of union members. Six midwestern locals, of coal miners, plumbers, steel workers, metal workers, knitting mill employees, and telephone workers, were selected for study, and interviews held with samples of rank-and-file members as well as with the leadership group. Each local union was chosen so as to be different from the other situations yet representative of a broad segment of the American labor movement. We were concerned with the attitudes of workers toward the union and its leading activities as well as toward job and company; in each case we built our interview guides around the key problems with which each group of workers was faced, and we sought to interpret the results against the total social-economic background of the workers' jobs and lives. For the most part we did not study union performance, though in the course of our observations of the six locals we were alert to performance as well as to the attitudes of leaders and members. The six case studies are followed by five chapters containing our observations about the union member in America suggested by our research material.

Our interest lay in types of reactions and patterns of experience rather than in statistical relationships, in qualitative rather than in quantitative analysis. Nevertheless, we sought to use care in the selection of samples, in the construction of interview guides, and in the analysis of interview data, to permit confidence in our results. The way in which we conducted the study is described in the Appendix.

The research project on which this volume reports was sponsored by the Industrial Relations Center of the University of Chicago. We wish to record our indebtedness to the many people, both at the university and elsewhere, who helped us with the study. We are particularly indebted to Frederick H. Harbison, formerly an executive officer of the Industrial Relations Center and now associated with the Industrial Relations Section at Princeton, for assistance in launching the project and for help in guiding the work to its conclusion. The initial idea for a study of rank-and-file workers grew out of discussions that A. A. Liveright, who then directed the University of Chicago's union education project, held with local union officers. Albert Rees and Val R. Lorwin of the University of Chicago faculty and Chancellor Clark Kerr of the University of California at Berkeley read the manuscript and made valuable suggestions for revision. Others of our colleagues, including Ethel Shanas, have given us advice on methodological problems. Richard S. Hammett was a member of the research team through much of the life of the project, and we wish to acknowledge his important contribution both in the gathering and in the analysis of material. Annette Karsh helped with the interviewing in two of the local union studies, and Marie Klein, then executive secretary of the Industrial Relations Center, was helpful with clerical and other chores.

We wish to record also our debt to the many union leaders and management officials who opened up their records to us, patiently answered our questions, and pointed out our errors; we cannot list them, since we promised not to reveal the identity of the particular local unions studied. All of them gave generously of their time and deserve much of the credit for whatever merit the case studies may have. Finally we wish to thank the several hundred rank-and-file union members who consented to be interviewed; what we know of the American worker as a union member we have learned from them.

Some of the material included in this book first appeared in articles in various professional journals. We wish to thank the editors of the *American Journal of Sociology*, the *Journal of Political Economy*, the *Annals of the American Academy of Political and Social Science*, the *Quarterly Journal of Economics*, the *Public Opinion Quarterly*, and the *Journal of Business* for permission to reproduce material that first appeared in their pages.

The study was made possible by a grant from the Carnegie Corporation of New York. We wish to record our appreciation to its officers and staff for their generous support and for their understanding. However, the Corporation is not to be understood as approving by virtue of its grant any of the statements we have made or the views we have expressed.

THE AUTHORS

CONTENTS

1 *The Unions and Their Members*   1

2 *Coal Miners: Unionism as a Tradition*   15

3 *Plumbers: Craft-conscious Unionism*   42

4 *Steel Workers: Militant Unionism*   63

5 *Metal Workers: Factionalism and Conflict*   91

6 *Knitting Mill Workers: The Impact of an Organizing Strike*   114

7 *Telephone Workers: White-Collar Unionism*   138

8 *Leadership in Local Unions*   164

9 *Membership Participation and Union Democracy*   185

10 *The Scope of Union Activities*   220

11 *A Typology of Union Members*   241

12 *Some Problems and Policy Issues*   255

Appendix   277

Index   295

81685

THE UNIONS
AND THEIR MEMBERS

In the past quarter of a century the American labor movement has emerged as one of the powerful forces dominating American life. From a position little more than peripheral in 1933, when its three million members were largely confined to skilled trades in relatively isolated or protected parts of the economy, the organized labor movement has expanded until collective bargaining has become a recognized and well-established procedure in virtually every industry, with union influence either pervading the industry or concentrated in the key plants or areas which set the standards followed by the remainder. The strikes that periodically interrupt production, the collective bargaining agreements that determine wage rates and key fringe benefits, the influence of unions in political affairs—these and related developments testify to the increasing importance of the organized labor movement in American society. The businessman, the government official, the political boss, and the community leader are all aware that they now share their power with the union head.

In the 150-year history of the American labor movement there is no parallel to the rapid growth that occurred in the late 1930's and early 1940's. The fundamental change in our basic labor law, accomplished by the passage of the National Labor Relations, or Wagner, Act in 1935, laid the legal foundation for the organization of millions of workers in the mass-production and other less-skilled industries; and the organizing drives first of the CIO and then of the AFL, taking advantage of this opportunity, provided the impetus for the mass movement into unionism. The full employment of the war and postwar periods, combined with the rising level of prices and the ample profits earned by employers, provided an economic environment favorable to the growth of unionism, just as the conditions of wage settlement during wartime gave an advantage to experienced union leadership.

Yet perhaps an even more fundamental reason for the rapid growth of the labor movement during these years was the changing attitude of the American wage-earner. The fact that the worker had at last become receptive rather than hostile to the idea of labor organization reflected his acceptance of a long-term, perhaps permanent, status as an employee, combined with a belief that his security and progress were dependent primarily upon group rather than individual effort. Such beliefs, growing stronger over a century and a half, were themselves products of economic and social change. Attitudes alter slowly, but the sudden development of possibilities for organization brought a mass upsurge of unionism within a few years, sweeping millions of recruits into the labor movement. The assimilation of these formerly non-union workers insured the future of organized labor, for the wage-earners of the next generation would come for the most part from union homes.

The development of a labor movement in any country is determined by a number of important factors—the nature of the economy, the political habits and traditions of the people, the opportunity for social mobility, and the values and attitudes fostered by the culture. In the older European countries, with their rigid class barriers, it was hard for workers to rise into the ranks of employers, and, as a consequence, mass interest in and loyalty to the labor movement developed early. In addition, the state of industrial productivity and profit levels permitted only narrow gains through collective bargaining, and this factor, combined with a variety of social evils, turned workers' attention to political action and plans for a far-reaching reconstruction of society. Historical developments in each country determined whether the trade unions were to control or be subordinate to the party, usually socialist in philosophy, that represented the bulk of the workers in the political area. Consciousness of difference in social class was likely to form the basis of political alignments in those countries, where, in contrast to the United States, almost everyone was native-born.

In America a variety of conditions, including abundant natural resources, rapid population growth, availablity of education, absence of a feudal past and no tradition of rigid class distinctions, and internal free trade over a large area, encouraged social mobility and produced a dynamic capitalism and an expanding economy with ample bargaining gains available to well-organized workers. With a wide margin of benefits attainable through collective bargaining, a union movement that was conservative politically but aggressive in its economic actions was able to establish a dominant position; its success, in turn, helped eventually to foster attitudes among unorganized workers favorable to the type of labor organization that it represented.

During the Colonial period and the early years of their history as an independent nation, Americans were primarily an agricultural people whose energies were absorbed in the task of pushing back the frontier. To people so engaged, the virtues upon which economic success depended were self-reliance, initiative, and hard physical labor—traits characteristic of the individualism fostered by other aspects of our culture. In the towns, which comprised a smaller proportion of the population, the small size of the business unit made it relatively easy for an ambitious and hard-working man to accumulate or borrow the sum needed to launch a business venture. The mechanic of that day followed a traditional path that led through apprenticeship to journeyman status, with a business of his own as master craftsman within his reach as an enterprising workman.

In the early nineteenth century the beginnings of the factory system crowded hundreds of relatively unskilled laborers into individual manufacturing enterprises and brought about sharp changes in the lives of workers and in their relations with employers. For such workers, who were paid much less than craftsmen, it was impossible in a lifetime of effort to accumulate the large sums needed to open a business of the type in which they worked, even if they could have acquired the necessary business and managerial skills. Yet these workers, whose working conditions should have led them to seek permanent group organization to solve their problems, usually found themselves powerless in the face of opposition from financially, socially, and politically powerful employers, backed by the influence of other dominant members of the community and the power of the state. Not surprisingly, the unions that did emerge were composed primarily of craftsmen, who were far more difficult to replace and whose employers were often not too far above their own level in financial resources and social status.

Successive streams of immigration brought new arrivals to the bottom of the economic and social order, forcing them into the hot, heavy, and dirty jobs in industry. With the shutting off of mass immigration from Europe the ranks were filled in large numbers with Negroes, most of them freshly arrived from rural areas in the South, who streamed into the industrial centers of the North and Middle West to get the better paying jobs now open to them. Along with them came southern whites, who, like the Negroes, sought the higher incomes that industrial employment afforded. Even more recently, Mexicans and Puerto Ricans have swelled the industrial as well as the agricultural labor force in some portions of the country, taking their places, as did those who arrived before them, at the bottom.

As industry expanded and as fresh recruits moved in, the older groups of immigrants, by now at least partially acclimated, moved up into the better paying, more highly skilled, more desirable types of employment. Many of their sons and daughters, who enjoyed far greater educational opportunities, entered white-collar occupations, the most rapidly expanding portion of the economy. Social mobility, blocked for most immigrant workers by the conditions of modern life, became a hope for their children, with upward movement taking place from one generation to the next rather than within a single lifetime. To many of the younger generation, white-collar employment, even though one remained permanently an employee, represented an escape from the conditions of factory life. Thus, while it might promise economic benefits, to join a union might also pose a psychological threat to middle-class status so painfully and recently won. For the factory worker also, the social mobility possible in the larger society was matched by greater opportunities to rise inside the factory as the business unit expanded and the ranks below were successively filled by new arrivals from abroad or from the farm. The American dream, exemplified in political life by the advance from log cabin to White House, had its economic parallel in the rise of the immigrant lad to the position of captain of industry, and its more modest counterpart within the factory in the rise of the skilled employee to superintendent or works manager. Once established, the tradition tended to persist, coloring ambitions long after the ranks of the higher supervisory employees had begun to be filled primarily with college-educated engineers and administrators.

The needs that the earliest unions served, and that unionism continues to serve today, were social as well as economic. The disparity in bargaining power between an individual worker in a large enterprise and its management is readily apparent. Students disagree on the extent to which group action operates to raise the level of real wages under the economic conditions prevailing in the enterprise and in the industry as a whole. Most observers agree, however, that such action will be effective within limits, which are difficult to define precisely, in raising wages and living standards as well as in reducing the hours of labor and in bringing about a variety of other changes in the employment relationship.

There is general agreement that unions have served to call attention to the human factor in industry, to make management conscious of the need for enlightened handling of its employees. A union that is properly administered tends to give its members a sense of belonging, a feeling of security and of worth as individuals that workers might have possessed in an earlier age but that has largely been lost under the impersonal conditions of large-scale production. To the factory worker of modern times, his union, besides winning higher wages and improved working conditions, insures that he will be treated with consideration and provides machinery through which his problems may be brought to the attention of responsible management officials.

Importance of the Local Union

The powerful men of the American labor movement—the presidents of the labor federations and the leading national unions—have long enjoyed the spotlight of publicity, and their organizations have been the object of considerable study by social scientists. Yet such study has largely been focused on organizational history or on problems such as union structure or collective bargaining relationships, for which documentary material has been available. Much less has been attempted with regard to the human material that makes up union membership. As one moves down from the national leaders through the ranks of paid local officers, and then of unpaid local leaders in the plants, the outlines grow increasingly dim, until by the time the rank-and-file workers are reached they are but a shadowy mass, about whom little systematic, reliable knowledge is available. It is the purpose of this study to help make a beginning in this very important direction.

Until recently little study has been attempted with regard to the local union,[1] the basic structural unit in which the membership is

---

[1] One of the first good studies to appear in this area is that of Leonard R. Sayles and George Strauss, *The Local Union: Its Place in the Industrial Plant* (New York: Harper & Bros., 1953). For interesting studies of the local union and its relations with management see Theodore V. Purcell, *The Worker Speaks His Mind on Company and Union* (Cambridge, Mass.: Harvard University Press, 1953), and Fred H. Blum, *Toward a Democratic Work Process: The Hormel-Packinghouse Workers' Ex-*

found. Yet this is the only union world that the rank-and-file member knows. The national president of his union may be a powerful person who negotiates the contract that sets the pattern for the industry, but he is distant and legendary, not part of the real world in which the worker moves. In that real world, where the general manager or the superintendent is the source of authority and one takes daily orders from the foreman, a worker who has a problem on the job may complain about it to his fellow workers or to his wife, he may speak to the foreman in an effort to get satisfaction himself, or he may take his problem to the union steward or grievance committeeman. The general level of wages is something beyond his control, but if he thinks his job should pay an extra nickel an hour, or if he fails to get his share of overtime work or is passed over unfairly on a promotion, he knows that he is most likely to get favorable action if he takes his case to his local union officials. In the world in which he moves the local union is the important agency, and the most important union official he is ever likely to know is the president of his local, who, like himself, may be a worker in the plant; or, especially if the worker is a skilled craftsman, the official may be a full-time business agent on the payroll of the local union.

From the point of view of the rank-and-file union member, the well-publicized union head, the William Green or John L. Lewis or Walter P. Reuther, is almost as far removed as General Eisenhower was from the buck private during World War II. The rank-and-file member goes through life at a humble level, seeking in his own way the livelihood, the security, the necessities, and small comforts that our civilization makes possible. He is caught up, as all of us are, in the mass society that technology has fashioned. Usually he lives in an urban community near the job that is his economic base, in a small town or metropolitan center created by forces beyond his control. A less-advantaged member of the community, he has had limited education and enjoys little prestige; he has a relatively small income and seldom gets to own property more substantial than his modest home or car; he never makes a speech or gets his name in the papers; he rarely makes important decisions, except in his own little world. He becomes an unskilled, semiskilled, or, if he is fortunate, a skilled worker, gets a job

---

periment (New York: Harper & Bros., 1953). See also Arnold M. Rose, *Union Solidarity: The Internal Cohesion of a Labor Union* (Minneapolis: University of Minnesota Press, 1952).

and holds on to it, joins a union, and eventually dies as anonymously as he has lived.

Even though his union may become a powerful force in the larger society, the rank-and-file member is likely to remain as nameless within his organization, if it is a large one, as he is in the society as a whole. He holds no office, attends no conventions, rarely if ever attends a meeting of his local union, and almost never speaks there. Often he is poorly informed about his local union, while the international union with which his local is affiliated is ordinarily but a shadowy, though perhaps powerful, organization far in the background. To him unionism may be a force designed to secure social justice, or it may be merely a policeman who need not do anything but whose mere presence keeps the employer honest. In his eyes the union may be symbolized by the national president, if he happens to be a highly publicized figure; otherwise he is likely to identify the union with the local business agent, or even the unpaid shop steward working in the same department.

Yet this rank-and-file worker, anonymous and unimportant though he may seem, is at the base of American society, and unless one knows what he is like one cannot fully understand the society. In the last analysis his voice, so seldom heard, is the decisive one. He may seem unimportant politically until one recalls that the impressive political landslide is made up of the votes of millions like him. At NLRB elections he decides which union, if any, is to represent him for purposes of collective bargaining, just as his responsiveness to the efforts of union organizers determines whether an election is to be held at all. When a strike is called it is his morale that largely determines whether the effort will prove successful. He elects the local union officers and the convention delegates who help to determine the policies of the national union; the national union head, however he obtains office, is unlikely to remain long in control unless he enjoys some degree of confidence and support from the rank-and-file member. Union leaders and company managers base many of their decisions on what they believe to be true about him. The union that is unresponsive to his wishes is unlikely to organize successfully, or to develop much strength if it is able to establish itself. One will never understand the labor union until one knows more about the millions of persons who make up its membership, a nameless mass until one singles out an individual and tries to find out what he is like and how he views his union.

The worker brings to his first job the prejudices and opinions, favorable or unfavorable to the labor movement, that he has absorbed from his environment—from his family, friends, school, and church, from the local newspaper, the movies and radio, and other agencies of mass communication. Thereafter, his attitude toward unionism will be influenced by his experiences on the job, including his hopes to rise in income and status, the extent to which these hopes are realized or frustrated, the security that he enjoys, and the way in which he is treated by his supervisors. His experiences within his local union, in turn, may affect to a large extent his attitude toward the entire labor movement, as he generalizes from the only local that he is likely to know; his views of unionism may be colored by his relations with his union officer or departmental steward, the disposition of the occasional grievance that may have affected his personal interests, or the way he was received the very few times he attended a union meeting.

Diversity of Background and Attitudes

Just as workers differ in background, in point of view, and in the aspirations that they bring to employment, so they find varying conditions awaiting them there. Some find themselves employed by progressive firms in expanding, high-wage industries, enjoying good working conditions, regular employment, and fair treatment. At the other extreme, workers may find wages low, working conditions undesirable or even unsafe, employment irregular, and job tenure insecure. In some cases ample opportunities may exist for the ambitious and qualified worker to rise in skill and responsibility, perhaps into supervisory ranks, whereas elsewhere upward channels may be blocked by forces beyond the individual worker's control. He may find management responsive to his desires and complaints, or aloof and dictatorial. He may find union-management relations co-operative or marred by suspicion and distrust.

Within the union, in turn, he may find authority monopolized by national officers or shared with the officials of the locals, just as he may find his local officers conducting their business in democratic or dictatorial fashion, at a high or at a low level of competence. He may feel attached to the company, the occupation, and the union on a relatively permanent basis, perhaps for the duration of his working life, or he may be anxious to change at the first opportunity. Whatever he finds, in his employment as in his local union, will condition his attitudes toward unionism. The meaning of unionism to him will be the product of the particular but highly complex social situation in which he finds himself, as he discovers problems in his employment relationship and sees the union either address itself to these problems, successfully or unsuccessfully, or ignore them.

It has already been suggested that the rank-and-file union members in the United States do not in any sense form a homogeneous group, save for the fact of union membership. There are differences of skill, age, sex, race, and national origin to divide them, along with differences of religion, politics, personal philosophy, and economic and social goals. In their attitude toward their one common bond—union membership—they vary from profound loyalty through indifference to unwilling membership. A worker may think of himself primarily as a member of the open-hearth gang, or as an electrician on the maintenance crew; or he may view himself as one of the younger workers, with little seniority in his department, on the night shift, or as one of the Negroes in the foundry. In no single respect, except for union membership and the fact that they are employees, are union members alike. Some are members despite their opposition to unionism; others may not know to what national union they belong, and still others may be uncertain whether or not they are union members at all.

The man who is the primary breadwinner of his family will look upon his employment and all aspects of the work relationship differently from the woman, who may or may not remain permanently in the labor force but whose orientation is primarily toward marriage, homemaking, and the rearing of a family. To her the plant experience may be merely an interlude between school and marriage, and the union meeting a poor competitor with "dates" for her free time. The young worker, eager for new experiences and adaptive to change, is different from his elderly fellow worker, who is set in his work routines and his outlook upon life, waiting out his years until retirement, primarily concerned with security and perhaps apprehensive of change. Similarly, the skilled—the elite of the labor force in terms of income, importance to the work process, and prestige among their fellows—differ from the less-skilled. Other differences exist because of personality, family background, or work experiences.

In any union, moreover, there is likely to be a striking difference between those who originally formed it, who turned to unionism in an effort to solve by group action the problems that had baffled or frustrated them as individuals, and the workers who later followed them into the industry, who found unionism and collective bargaining well-established institutions, and who learned of the earlier non-union conditions only by hearsay. As these differ from their older co-workers in their experiences, so they may well differ in their attitudes, loyalties, and degree of emotional involvement, tending to view the union with detachment even when convinced of its value as a protective institution.

The cleavages within the work force in terms of race, religion, and national origin may impress the workers more than their common experiences and interests. The highly skilled tool-and-die maker, of northern or western European descent, whose family has resided here for several generations, may feel more closely identified with his employer than with the unskilled immigrant from eastern or southern Europe, or with the American Negro, freshly arrived from a rural area, who punches a time clock in the same factory. The high-school graduate holding a white-collar position in the firm's office, working in physical surroundings that more nearly resemble the employer's, and dressing more like him than like factory workers, may feel closer to the employer psychologically as well as physically. This identification is more likely to occur where both white-collar worker and employer are of the same race, religion, or national origin, and where the factory workers are primarily of other strains or come from other backgrounds.

Important as are these differences of race and national origin, however, the passage of years is bringing greater homogeneity to the work force, as immigration has lessened and as barriers of language and different traditions have been overcome. The immigrants from many lands who found communication with each other difficult or even impossible have for the most part died or retired, their places taken by native-born sons and daughters who speak the same language, share common experiences, and are the products of the same public schools.

Though this study is focused on the worker as a union member, we are dealing with only an aspect of the worker's total personality and behavior pattern. Union membership is an incident of the work relationship, a result of the fact that one earns one's living as an employee; vastly more, obviously, could be said about the work experience as a whole, in terms of social relationships, satisfactions, productivity, and the like. The work experience, similarly, is only a part of life; the worker is also a family man, a citizen, a churchgoer, a home owner or renter, and so on, with his individual family background, his hopes and fears, his ambitions and aspirations, his disappointments and frustrations.

In the complex of interests, activities, and loyalties that make up the individual, union membership is but one ingredient, of great importance to some workers, of little consequence to others. To some workers the unity that appears most compelling may be that with his fellow employees in a conflict of interests with the employer; to others it may be the unity of his craft as against less-skilled workers, of whites as against Negroes, of Americans of the older stocks as against the newer immigrants, of Protestants as against Catholics, or of Christians as against Jews. It may even embrace the wider unity of all Americans as against the outside world. To some the cleavages within the ranks of workers are to be regretted, whereas to others their status as employees may be viewed as temporary or as unimportant in the light of ambitions and loyalties that shape their goals and give meaning to their lives.

Objectives and Methods of the Study

What is it important for us to know about the American worker as a union member in order that the labor union as it exists and functions in this country may be better understood? There is not the space within the confines of a single volume to discuss more than a few of the most important problems. The particular topics that we have selected are the ones that, in our judgment, are crucial for an understanding of the American worker as a union member. Accordingly, we have inquired into the circumstances under which workers have joined unions and their expectations regarding membership; the workers' attitudes toward their union, including the degree of loyalty they feel toward it; the extent to which they participate in the life of their union and the degree to which their organization is democratic and responsive to the wishes of the membership; the attitude of workers toward the use of the strike as a weapon; the extent to which they look to the union to solve their problems, and the range of problems that they regard as properly within the scope of the union's activity; the circumstances under which leadership develops and the ways in which union leaders differ from rank-and-file members; and the aspirations of the worker, for himself or his children, in terms of occupation and

11

social status. Reliable knowledge in these important areas should help us understand better the operations of the local union and the ways in which union officers and union members are related to each other and to management.

We are keenly aware of the limitations of our methods and materials; we are conscious that we can offer not conclusions but only hypotheses, on the basis of interviews with a few hundred out of sixteen to seventeen million union members, organized into six of the eighty thousand to one hundred thousand local unions that make up the American labor movement. Since we could not hope to study intensively all aspects of even the few local unions investigated, we have chosen to focus upon the attitudes or orientation of the membership, treating the more formal functioning of the union, its structure, activities, collective bargaining relationships, and the like, as background material, valuable in its own right but secondary, for our purposes, to the views of the members. Our material is little more than fragmentary on some of the topics touched upon, and our remarks in these areas are therefore intended to be merely suggestive. We hope that this volume will help to stimulate other investigators to undertake more precise and comprehensive work in related areas.

How does one go about studying problems such as those here posed, so that reliable information may be gathered and even tentative generalizations advanced? The American labor movement is large and complex, and its tens of thousands of local unions differ widely in size, structure, type of membership, location, tradition, national union affiliation, and type of bargaining relationship with the employer. To study any substantial number of these local unions within the confines of a single research project was manifestly impossible, and yet, somehow, particular locals had to be singled out for observation.

It was our belief that more was to be gained by an intensive study of a small number of locals than by a more cursory examination of a larger number. The accident of geographical location and limitations of finances restricted us to the Midwest, and particularly to the area within fairly easy reach of Chicago. In selecting local situations we sought to make each as different as possible from the other cases, yet to have each one representative of a broad tradition within the American labor movement, in order to increase the likelihood that the findings would be typical within limits, rather than unique. We felt that more was to be gained by selecting wholly different situations than by attempting to hold most elements constant and vary just a single factor in the hope of more precisely determining its impact. The way in which we conducted the study is described in the Appendix on methodology. For the present purpose it is enough to say that we relied primarily upon interviews, rather intensive and fairly well structured, with workers whose names were chosen by a random sample method of selection, and that we supplemented the interview material with observations of the locals and their activities. We sought not merely to ascertain workers' views but to discover the respondents' degree of involvement in the problems under investigation, and the emotions affecting their estimates of unionism.

The pilot project was that of a large and militant industrial union, affiliated with the United Steelworkers of America, CIO, representing the workers in an integrated steel plant in the Chicago area and bargaining in an atmosphere of suspicion and hostility with a powerful corporation. The second case, again in a midwestern industrial center, was that of a moderate-size local of the UAW-CIO, organized in one of a series of plants operated by a leading manufacturer of farm and heavy construction equipment; in this case bargaining was carried on through a national council on which the local was represented, and the bargaining relationship, as in the steel case, was one of conflict. The third case study was that of a local of highly skilled craftsmen in the construction industry in a major city. Here jobs were usually of short duration; the powerful Plumbers' Union of the AFL confronted a large number of employers, most of them small, and was without question the dominating influence in the trade.

For the fourth case study we went to a small and fairly isolated town in Wisconsin, where a group of workers in a knitting mill, most of them middle-aged women of relatively low skill, had recently been organized by the International Ladies' Garment Workers' Union of the AFL. We arrived in town just after a protracted and bitter organizing strike had ended in a limited victory for the union, and we were particularly interested in the meaning of unionism to previously unorganized women workers in a small town and the effect on them of their strike experience. The fifth case study was that of miners in the central Illinois coal fields organized into a local of the United Mine Workers, in an area where unionism was part of the tradition, where few other occupations were available, and where, until recently, the strongly unionized groups of miners lived in isolated settlements exposed to a minimum of outside influences. The sixth and final study, in the telephone industry, was that of a white-collar group, including women operators and clerical workers, and male equipment technicians, organized into the Communications Workers of America of the CIO. Here one of the primary concerns was with the relationship of status and prestige to union membership.

It was our hope that these six local situations, each different from the others and yet each typical in its own way, would permit a maximum of contrast, suggest hypotheses that could serve as a starting point for further investigation, and yield tentative generalizations that would be significant for an understanding of the American worker as a union member.

2

COAL MINERS
Unionism as a Tradition

Underlying the prairie land of Illinois are extensive seams of soft coal that have made the state one of the principal bituminous producers in the country. The southern and central portions of the state, particularly, are dotted with mines; and in some areas coal mining, except for some rather indifferent farming land, offers the principal—in certain instances, virtually the only—means of livelihood. At its peak in 1923 the Illinois coal industry gave employment to more than a hundred thousand miners. Long the third bituminous coal mining state in the country, ranking behind West Virginia and Pennsylvania in volume of production, Illinois in recent years has been surpassed also by Kentucky. The Illinois fields remain, however, one of America's important sources of coal.

Nature's generosity in scattering coal deposits widely under more than thirty states has prevented centralized control of the industry. Instead, except during periods of war demand or government regulation, intense and ruthless competition has been the rule. The vast deposits in this country and the ease of opening new mines have helped productivity to outrun demand; in an industry in which wage costs traditionally have comprised about 65 or 70 per cent of total cost, it was inevitable that operators, faced with vigorous price competition for limited markets, should seek first to reduce the level of wages. Much of the history of unionism in the bituminous coal fields has been concerned with the efforts of miners to raise or preserve their standards in the face of wage cutting in the non-union areas of the industry.[1]

---

[1] The economic problems of the industry are analyzed in *Report of the United States Coal Commission* (Washington: U.S. Government Printing Office, 1925) and in Walton H. Hamilton and Helen R. Wright, *The Case of Bituminous Coal* (New York: Macmillan Co., 1925). For a review of collective bargaining in the industry see Waldo E. Fisher's chapter, "Bituminous Coal," in *How Collective Bargaining Works* (New York: Twentieth Century Fund, 1942).

Unionism in the Illinois Mine Fields

Illinois diggers took a prominent part in the various attempts to organize the expanding coal fields in the early 1860's and in the decades following the Civil War; and they were covered by the first interstate wage agreement negotiated with the operators in 1886, four years before the miners' assembly of the Knights of Labor and the National Federation of Miners and Mine Laborers combined to form the United Mine Workers. From the Illinois coal fields came a number of the leading figures of the UMW, including John Mitchell, still a hero in many of the coal patches, who led the union to its first great victories during the period of his presidency from 1899 to 1908. From that day to this the Illinois district has been one of the bulwarks of unionism in the coal fields, participating in struggles with operators and strikebreakers as well as in the violent internecine warfare that, along with low wages, widespread unemployment, and occasional mine disasters, has characterized much of the history of the coal industry of this country.

When John L. Lewis, himself a veteran of the Illinois mining fields, became president of the United Mine Workers in 1920, Illinois District 12, with eighty thousand experienced and disciplined unionists, formed part of the backbone of the organization. The years that followed brought difficult times to District 12, whose heads—in some cases tainted with scandal—were in frequent conflict with Lewis and whose members found their standards undermined by the non-union miners in southern West Virginia and Kentucky. In the dark depression years of the early 1930's, when unemployment and wage cuts plagued the lives of the Illinois miners, a rebellion against Lewis' autocratic use of his powers led to the formation of the Progressive Miners of America, whose members carried on an unequal struggle against an alliance of the United Mine Workers, leading operators, and local government officials. Supporters of the Progressive Miners, unable to obtain work in the mines, left the industry in large numbers, while others, though retaining some loyalties to the PMA, rejoined the UMW in order to earn a living in the mines. Two decades later they still comprise a substantial, though a diminishing, percentage of the miners in central Illinois, and a number of them appeared in our sample.

At the bottom of the depression little was left in Illinois, and less in most other mining states, of the once powerful union of the diggers.

In the mid-thirties, however, a combination of New Deal legislation and a moderate economic recovery provided an organizing opportunity of which Lewis took full advantage. There was a resurgence of United Mine Workers' strength throughout its old territory, coupled with a victorious march through the former non-union areas of the South, re-establishing the union in the forefront of the American labor movement. Lewis went on to help create the CIO and to lead that organization in its successful organizing drives in the mass-production industries. His aggressiveness and bargaining skill, backed by the solidarity of the miners, led to successive improvements in wage scales and fringe benefits, though the frequent stoppages of coal production during the World War II period brought a chorus of angry denunciations throughout the nation of Lewis and the men he led.

When our interviews were conducted the miners were earning a daily wage of $15.00 to $19.75, depending on their particular jobs. These were high daily rates, by comparison with miners' wages in the past or with the wages paid to men of comparable skill in other industries. Annual earnings were low, however, since the mines were working very irregularly—though only a few of the miners saw a connection between the limited amount of work available and the high daily wage scale. No men were still being paid on a tonnage rate in the Illinois fields.

As an incident of the UMW-PMA struggle, District 12 gave up its charter in 1933, accepting provisional officers appointed by Lewis in place of its elected officials.[2] Today, a quarter of a century later, the important powers in the district are still in the hands of provisional officers appointed by Lewis and subject to removal at his will. Even these officers have relatively little to do with collective bargaining, since the important decisions are made in nationwide negotiations dominated by the leading spokesmen of the union and the operators. The local's concern with collective bargaining is limited to grievance work,

[2] For an account of these and subsequent events in Illinois see Harriet D. Hudson, *The Progressive Mine Workers of America: A Study in Rival Unionism* (Urbana: University of Illinois Press, 1952). An able, critical biography of Lewis is James A. Wechsler, *Labor Baron: A Portrait of John L. Lewis* (New York: William Morrow & Co., 1944). A more recent and more sympathetic study of Lewis is Saul Alinsky, *John L. Lewis: An Unauthorized Biography* (New York: G. P. Putnam's Sons, 1949). The best account of unionism in the coal fields is McAlister Coleman, *Men and Coal* (New York: Farrar & Rinehart, 1943). For a briefer survey of coal unionism see the chapter, "A New School of Political Economists: The United Mine Workers' Union of America," in Herbert Harris, *American Labor* (New Haven: Yale University Press, 1938), pp. 97–148.

a function exercised in the local we studied through a grievance committeeman who devoted perhaps an hour daily to union business.

Though the miners' union has remained strong since its revival in the mid-thirties, its membership has dropped as employment opportunities in the industry have declined. Improved coal-cutting and coal-loading equipment in the mines has been matched by more efficient means of getting power from coal; and other sources of fuel and power—oil, natural gas, hydroelectric power—have cut deeply into the coal market.[3] Recurrent strikes in the coal fields, moreover, have helped to persuade some users to turn to alternative fuels. The coal industry, in consequence, can no longer furnish employment to the young men growing up in the mining camps, and most of them go off to the expanding industrial cities. Though there were some younger men in our sample, the coal mines are worked predominantly by men of middle age or beyond.

Solidarity in the Mining Towns

Before the automobile gave the miners mobility, the coal digger almost always lived within walking distance of his pit. This meant that, whenever a shaft was sunk at too great a distance from existing settlements, houses had to be erected if the operator wanted to be assured of a labor supply. In the mining towns that grew up in the shadow of the tipple,[4] there was seldom any way to make a living other than by working in the mine, except for an occasional storekeeper with whom the miners traded. In the shabby mine patches there was no public opinion except that of the miners; the cities, with their variety of occupations and social classes, were far away, and neither the newspaper nor the radio—outside voices that were heard sporadically in the coal

[3] Between 1920 and 1953 the annual production of bituminous coal in the United States declined from 568,000 to 457,000 tons. During the same period the average number of men employed fell from 639,000 to 293,000, while the average number of tons mined per man per day rose from 4 to a little over 8 (see U.S. Department of Commerce, *Statistical Abstract of the United States, 1955*, p. 743). In Illinois the number of coal miners grew steadily until a peak of 103,000 was reached in 1923; since then a steady decline has set in, reducing the number of miners to 31,000 in 1950 (see State of Illinois, Department of Mines and Minerals, *Sixty-ninth Coal Report of Illinois, 1950*, p. 98).

[4] For an excellent pictorial representation of life in mining communities see U.S. Department of the Interior, Coal Mines Administration, *The Coal Miner and His Family: A Supplement to "A Medical Survey of the Bituminous-Coal Industry"* (1947).

camps—made much impression with regard to problems that concerned mines and miners.

Instead of the heterogeneity, the anonymity, and often the isolation of factory workers who live in a metropolitan center, one finds in a mining community a closely knit group of people who have a feeling of solidarity that city factory workers can rarely, if ever, develop. Whereas factory work is a way of earning a living, mining is a way of life, with a set of distinctive traditions and loyalties. This feeling of solidarity and of separateness from the outside world must have been even more strongly pronounced in an earlier age, when miners lived in an isolated village that clustered around the tipple. Though the automobile has ended the isolation, permitting miners to live over a more widespread area, most of them continue to live in communities composed primarily of miners, in which alternative means of employment are relatively few. In these communities the miner is influenced by memories and traditions that reflect the distinctive experiences of his occupational group and by the reciprocal relations that bind him to his fellow workers. In contrast to the factory worker in a large city, the miner's definition of his work is not limited to on-the-job experiences in isolation from the rest of his life.

One can understand the feeling of unity that has developed in the coal patches if one bears in mind that virtually every wage-earner in the community is an employee of the same company, sharing the same working conditions and the same economic and physical hazards. This solidarity, which made the union possible, was in turn increased by the fact of organization, by the struggles with mine operators and strike-breakers, and by the sense of accomplishment and power associated with union success. Where the union was almost synonymous with the adult male population, it was not surprising that the union president should often be, in addition, the mayor of the town. In the small town nearest the mine that we studied, not only the mayor but virtually all other officials were union members, and the same was true of county officers. Solidarity and union strength, combined with the harsh conditions of work and of life, have bred powerful leaders, who have risen readily to positions of influence and leadership within the larger labor movement. It was no accident that John L. Lewis, William Green, and Philip Murray, the leading union figures on the national scene in the decades of the 1930's and the 1940's, were all products of the coal patches and the miners' union.

The Company

The company whose employees we chose for study is an old, large, and successful concern, an efficient producer operating a series of mines in the state. Periodically it closes down a mine when the expense of maintenance and of underground transportation becomes too great, and sinks a shaft at a fresh location, transferring its employees gradually as the new operation expands. With only rare exceptions the miners thought highly of their company, most of them pointing to fair treatment as the factor that they liked. "They treat you like human beings" was a common remark. As one put it, "The company is a pretty nice company to work for. You can talk to the bosses and they don't snub you off. Like I've seen some jobs where the boss won't even answer your question." Unlike factory workers, who tend to change employers several times before settling down as permanent employees, most of the miners had never worked for another coal company, although some of them had left the mining community during slack times to obtain work in other industries.

Miners and Mining

Well over half the men had been raised in coal mining communities and most of the others were the sons of farmers. Perhaps an eighth of them had been born abroad, most of them in southern or eastern European countries. Protestants predominated, with a substantial minority of Catholics. On the average they were forty-two years of age and had had eight and a half years of schooling; among the younger men there were a few who had graduated from high school.

It is a common saying among miners that "mining runs in the family." Most of those to whom we talked were themselves the sons of miners. Many represented a third generation in the industry and some even a fourth, while even those whose fathers had followed other occupations usually had close relatives in the mines. The response of a thirty-seven-year-old welder who had worked for this company for four years was far from unusual: "Dad was a miner from the time he was thirteen years old till he was sixty-two. He's on pension now. His dad was a miner and my mother's dad was a miner. I don't know about their folks, but most of them have been that way for years back. My brother has been a miner since he was seventeen or eighteen. Another brother of mine worked in the mines, but lost an arm in the war and couldn't come back." It was the general expectation in a mining community that a father would bring his sons into the mine at an early age; indeed, alternative occupational choices hardly existed in many of the towns. A boy grew up with the expectation, often bordering on the inevitable, that he would become a miner. The way in which a driller, now forty-one, entered the industry was fairly typical: "I was fifteen years old. There was nothing else in the town to do. I come from a large family and Dad just took me into the mines."

The peculiar characteristics of the occupation contributed to the common understandings that developed. Isolated from the rest of the world during working days and subjected to occupational hazards that strengthened their dependence upon each other, the miners developed close friendships, feelings of mutual responsibility, and a sense of security found in ties to the work group. A thirty-five-year-old machine operator who had been with the company for nineteen years put it this way: "You live underground and the men down there stick together closely. They're all the same down there. It's funny—when you come back on top and see them on the street or in town, they're almost different men. When you're down below you all have one thing in common: you are working down below." Their common experiences in the mines give miners a never ending topic of conversation after working hours. Miners' wives commented that their husbands "always talked mines," and the men, similarly, pointed out that "we always have something to talk about—we talk mines." Since almost all the men in the community are miners, they have a set of common interests, a feeling of identification with each other, and of belonging to the community, that are hardly possible in a larger urban setting.

During the interviews miners reacted with unusual sensitivity to the assumed superior or hostile views of the general public toward their occupational group. Statements such as the following were made frequently: "They [other people] don't know if a coal miner is an elephant or a monkey. One fellow tells a story that is supposed to be true, about a fellow worker who tells his wife that he is bringing home a coal miner for dinner. She says that it's OK, but to be sure to tie him on a leash in the yard. I'm not kidding—that's a true story. Some people don't even know if a coal miner is a human being. In the mine we say to each other, 'Get out of here, you underground savage.'" A number of factors, including the character of the work, the history of mining communities, the notorious poverty associated with them in the past, the violent conflicts between union and management, and the unfavorable publicity given the miners' union during the World War II period, may help to explain such marked feelings of inferiority and defensiveness.

When they feel called upon to defend their occupational group against the assumed critical views of the public, miners may emphasize the danger inherent in their work, though in other contexts they may deny that danger exists, emphasize the possibility of avoiding it, assert that one gets used to it as to anything else, or assume a fatalistic attitude. "I guess you're gonna get it anyway if it's your time." Most often the miner asserts that danger is an integral part of the job, which one accepts as a matter of fact: "I think that after you work there you don't think much about danger. You get accustomed to it. You look up at the loose ends of rock and just walk under it."

However fatalistic the miners might profess to be with regard to mining accidents, most of them admitted that they were affected, if only momentarily, by major disasters such as the mine explosions at Centralia and West Frankfort, Illinois:[5] "It kinda makes you leery for a day or two. You have a funny feeling . . . but then it wears off." Yet even in this connection other factors were stressed: "It's just one of them things. It makes you think, though. It's like a car wreck—but you don't stop driving a car. It gets into your system like race driving. There's been lots of guys around that quit and go up to Detroit and the next thing you know they are right back. You don't feel right at something else." Though miners adjust to the dangers associated with underground work, they consider safety along with job security their major occupational problems and look to their union for physical protection as well as for economic benefits.

Despite the danger to which they are exposed, the declining employment opportunities in the industry, and the belief that they are looked down upon by other occupational groups, a surprisingly small number of miners leave for other types of employment. Most of those who leave are forced to do so by immediate pressures—slack times, the closing of mines, or, in a few cases, internal union strife. Of those who

[5] In March, 1947, an explosion in a Centralia mine killed 111 miners, and in December, 1951, there were 119 fatalities in a mine explosion at West Frankfort. Both explosions could have been prevented, had coal dust been kept down and other precautions taken. For an excellent treatment of the Centralia disaster see John Bartlow Martin, "The Blast in Centralia No. 5," *Harper's Magazine*, CXCVI (1948), 193–220.

leave, a sizable proportion eventually return, despite the small number of jobs available, because they find factory work more burdensome or less satisfying than work in the mines. A thirty-six-year-old repairman who had worked in the mines since he was seventeen left in the hope of raising his income but returned because "that job [in the city] was long hours and the responsibility of the job was greater than I was used to and didn't pay as much money. Or it paid as much and your expenses sapped your wages."

Others preferred mining to work aboveground because the temperature was constant and pleasant. The absence of close supervision in the mines, moreover, doubtless prevented many of the tensions that are so common in the factory and contributed to the satisfaction of the miners. In addition, the upbringing and experiences in a small mining community made it difficult for some miners to adjust to the insecurities, the impersonal environment, and the tempo of urban and factory life. Some of those who left the mines returned because they missed the interpersonal relationships of the small mining community. Others, unable to verbalize the impact of common experience and of the security found in primary groups, said that "mining just gets into you," "once a miner, always a miner," or "it gets into your blood."

The Miners and Their Union

For most of the miners unionism was a normal and natural part of the environment in which they grew up, an institution to be accepted and identified with almost in the way that one's church is accepted. Loyalty to the union developed much as did loyalty to one's country, as a result of accepting and internalizing the standards of behavior, the values and the ideals, to which one is exposed in one's family and community. In the mining areas a boy grew up expecting to go into the mines when he reached the appropriate age, and going into the mines involved joining the union, which he had already learned to accept. It was not a choice to be made, as many factory workers may make a choice, but a step to be taken automatically and inevitably.

The typical miner, raised in a union miner's home in a community in which almost every man was also a miner and a union member, had heard a great deal about the union from a very early age. He had heard his father talk about the union, he had also heard strike stories from other relatives and friends, he had witnessed union-management conflicts or fights between members of rival unions, and he had attended burial services at which union leaders officiated. "All my life I heard about unions," a miner in late middle age said. "I would always hear speeches about how our forefathers lived and died and fought for unions." For men such as these there is an emotional quality to their attachment to unionism that stories of non-union days, or even personal experience of non-union conditions, can seldom bring to factory workers. For such miners, moreover, their union is part of an identification that includes the community and the occupational group, a view that can have no counterpart in the case of a worker reared in a metropolitan area. Workers who have gone through a bitter strike to build or maintain their union may have something of the emotional attitude toward unionism that so many miners exhibit, but there is a special quality to childhood attachments that adult experiences seldom attain.

Since a union-shop clause has been in effect in this mine field for more than a generation, those who wished to work in the mines had no choice but to join the union. Yet it is of interest that very few responses stressed the compulsory aspect of joining, in terms such as "You were forced to" that might suggest an action with which the worker was not in sympathy. The miners, on the contrary, were more apt to emphasize their support of unionism, their desire to join the organization. "If I had a choice, I would have joined anyway" was the usual response. The sons of union miners had little doubt as to the value of unionism. As one put it, "My dad was a member of the Knights of Labor and the union was just a natural thing for me." There were many, of course, who entered the mines at a very early age and gave hardly any thought to unionism until later.

Occasionally, a miner who had been raised in a farming area was forced into the union against his will, but even he soon became a loyal supporter of unionism. As one said: "I didn't think it was any good. I thought the union was just to rob the miner, take his money; that's all I thought about it. Even after I joined the UMW, I didn't think much about it. After a bit, I got me a book, our contract, and read up on it. The longer I worked at it the better I liked it. It was about three or four months before I got on to it and it was one of the most wonderful things we got. That's the reason why I hung on to it. It gives us good working conditions and good pay. If it wasn't for the UMW we would be working for nothing today."

The emotional attachment of the miners to unionism is apparent when the question of working in a non-union mine is raised. While factory workers usually respond to such a question in a matter-of-fact manner, whether or not they have worked in non-union plants, miners tend to react as if their fundamental principles are being doubted: "No. And I never aim to either. I don't think it's right. If it wasn't for the union, we wouldn't be getting anything. I am not a radical, mind you . . . but I think the union is the workingman's salvation."

Provisionalism in the UMW

It has been two decades since the miners in this district have had the right to elect their district president. Despite this long history of provisionalism, and the spirited debates about it at successive UMW conventions, the issue is of relatively limited consequence to the rank-and-file miners. It is not likely, however, that workers would be so little concerned with the lack of democratic rights if their union failed to produce the economic benefits with which the UMW leadership is credited.

Most of the miners did not know how the president of their district obtained his office. Only a fourth were aware of the policy of provisionalism and were critical of it. A much smaller number knew that the district president was appointed, and approved of this procedure, either on the ground that appointed officers are more efficient than elected officials or on the ground that only the national officers have a view of the entire industry and the competence to administer the affairs of the union and all its districts in a businesslike fashion. Those who are ignorant or misinformed with regard to the appointment of district officials tend to be younger miners who have entered the industry subsequent to the factional strife and dual unionism conflict in Illinois or older miners who have come recently from other regions. Those who are fully informed and critical of the policy of provisionalism are for the most part older men who were involved in the factional conflicts of the late twenties or early thirties. The bulk of the membership consists of inactive members who are concerned with the economic gains that the union achieves but who are relatively indifferent to organizational problems such as autonomy.

Typical of the misinformed, younger members was a twenty-four-year-old driller, who had been a member of the union for only four years. He asserted that the district president was elected, adding,

"Don't ask me who he is; I wouldn't know." Others stated that, though the district president had been appointed at one time, he was now elected, and some of them insisted that they had voted for district president on several occasions. This represented a confusion with other offices; in Illinois local and subdistrict officials are elected, as are some district officers, but the president and three other key officers of the district are appointed.

Those who were critical of the policy of provisionalism ordinarily argued that the right of self-organization was a basic principle of union organization. Some of these asserted, however, that the original loss of autonomy had been justified in view of the corruption of certain elected district officials and the Progressive split, and admitted that the miners had made greater economic advances under appointed than under elected leaders. Thus a thirty-five-year-old miner with nineteen years of experience in the mines declared: "It's true that autonomy ruined the miners around here before by getting men in office that just threw the money around. . . . It might wreck us again, but it's a free country and we should have the right to vote for our district officers. We've gotten more with no autonomy than we ever did with it. It wouldn't make any difference except for the democratic principle. We have good leaders on top and they know what they're doing. We had a taste of self-government before and it didn't work out. But that was a long time ago."

Some of those who favored the restoration of autonomy admitted that the system of appointment might produce better union officials: "Maybe John L. can get the best man by appointing him although there is always the problem of back-scratching and favoritism . . . I think he should be put in there by vote, but I think the men should know a good leader and pick him out to vote for. . . . But even if you can get a better man in office by appointing him, I don't think it's good to give the International Union which is really John L. so much power."

There was agreement, among most of those who supported autonomy, that little popular support for democratic principles could be aroused in the face of the improvements that Lewis had won and the influence that he exerted at conventions. One member argued that the situation had changed substantially since the district lost autonomy, and that democratic rights should be restored, though he had no fault to find with the performance of the provisional officers. He did not want autonomy enough, however, to risk conflict for it. Other critics of the policy of provisionalism asserted that full democratic rights were not restored because a majority for autonomy could not be found at union conventions; when enough miners wanted autonomy, they were sure that they would get it.

A number of miners defended the policy of provisionalism on the ground that better officers were selected that way, reflecting an argument that Lewis has often used in convention debate. In the view of a miner with thirty-two years of experience in the union, provisionalism was simply more efficient than autonomy: "If the President of the United States can appoint his cabinet, why can't the President of the United Mine Workers? . . . Not that I'm against the rank and file electing a man. But Lewis can pick a man who is competent and move him out if he isn't good. But if he's elected it would be hard to get rid of him." Other miners declared that provisionalism must be working out in satisfactory fashion, since they so rarely heard it criticized. Occasionally, a miner argued that a real element of democratic control existed despite the appointment of key district officers, since the latter were influenced by the resolutions adopted by the local unions. There were others, however, who found democracy troublesome and who preferred having decisions made for them. Thus one miner who had had considerable experience in other industries declared that he preferred the UMW to any other union to which he had belonged, adding: "Some unions have the business agents coming around, and with the CIO you have the International people coming around to tell you what to do. But with the miners, it's all done on top and there's no trouble—no fights like in the CIO."

Although two-thirds of the districts of the UMW were governed by provisional officers, a majority of the miners held a predominantly democratic view of their national union, often pointing to the convention as the ruling body and frequently asserting that the majority could force the adoption of any policy they wanted. Several who had been delegates to conventions of the UMW insisted that democratic procedures prevailed within the union. As one said, "They accuse John L. . . . of strong-arming at the conventions and I attended two of them and I never seen it. He just had the support of the miners. Autonomy is always discussed and put on the floor and the vote is always pretty much against it."

On the other hand, more than a third of the miners held an autocratic concept of the UMW, believing that it was impossible to bring about changes by either individual or collective action. Those who held this view, moreover, tended to be the active and better-informed union members, many of them veterans of the factional conflicts two decades earlier. Some of the miners differentiated in this respect between their local union on the one hand and the district or the national union on the other, asserting that they could make changes in the former but not in the latter.

Union Achievements

The miners listed pay increases and improvements in working conditions high among the union's accomplishments and pointed to the unusual achievements of the UMW in the health and welfare field as well. Miners fear the impersonal forces that produce economic instability as much as or more than they fear the visible power of the coal company, and in the past they have seen enough crippled and aged miners dependent upon their relatives to make them highly appreciative of the benefits now furnished through the health and welfare fund. Miners became most positive and enthusiastic when they spoke of this union achievement, which promised them a peaceful old age in relative security.

Almost all the miners credited the union with winning pay increases for them. As one said, in a typical response, "I started in 1932 at $4.75 a day and now I'm making $18.84 a day; that shows what the union did on wages." Another asserted that the UMW "kept to the top with regard to wages per hour. . . . No other common labor job pays as much as coal mining."[6] A veteran of thirty-four years in the mines who now earns $19.75 a day, after mentioning the welfare fund, listed the following other achievements of the union: "They have been able to accomplish higher wages, although they raised the price of coal. I have a nice home, two automobiles, and a tractor. Protects you if you

---

[6] Average gross weekly earnings in bituminous coal mining, $25.72 in 1929, fell to $13.91 in 1932 and rose to $95.19 by 1955, an increase of 270 per cent over the 1929 figure. During the same period the comparable figure for manufacturing rose from $25.03 to $76.52, an increase of 206 per cent, while the consumer price index rose 56 per cent. While other factors were at work, this suggests that the UMW has had an important part in raising miners' real income faster than the real income of other groups of workers. These figures on gross weekly earnings are taken from *Economic Report of the President Transmitted to the Congress January 24, 1956* (Washington: U.S. Government Printing Office, 1956), p. 192. Current trends in miners' income are collected by the Bureau of Labor Statistics of the U.S. Department of Labor and reported in the *Monthly Labor Review*.

get fired and gets your job back . . . maybe gets your job back with pay. That's what a union is for, to protect you if the boss don't like you." The high daily earnings were almost universally considered a leading union achievement, and served as one of the factors that kept workers attached to the industry despite the frequent shutdowns of the mines.

Yet a few of the more sophisticated members recognized that the high daily wage had a close relationship to the limited amount of work available. A miner in his late thirties, a high-school graduate who had worked eighteen years in the industry and who had a high regard for the union's other accomplishments, felt that its high wage policies had been a mistake: "I feel they made a mistake by raising miners' wages, and it has in turn raised the price of coal, although they were entitled to it because it's one of the most dangerous jobs a man can have, and it's seasonal work, and a miner has to make more to lay some money aside when he isn't working. On the other side, the high price of coal forced people to turn to oil and gas, and forced the operator to go on mass-production methods to raise the production of each man. . . . It would have been best if we could have kept the cost of living down, but that's a country-wide problem and maybe the UMW couldn't do anything about it. But coal affected most other industries first. All these small raises we got may not do us much good and may do us much harm."

Because of the danger of mine explosions, the term "working conditions" has taken on an unusual meaning for the miners; the lives of the entire work force are endangered if safety precautions are not rigidly observed. For mines to be safe, proper laws must be passed and enforced—and the miners credit their union with achievements in this vital area, as well as in enforcing safety conditions in direct dealings with management. The term "working conditions," in addition, had all the other meanings common to other groups of employees as well. As one miner, still in his thirties, said: "When I went to the coal mines there was no toilets or bathing facilities. Like in the ——— mine [an abandoned one near which he lived] the men came out sweating and walked a block to the washhouse." Other miners asserted that the union "keeps the company from making slaves out of us," or that the union, besides bringing better conditions, had improved relations between miners and supervisors: "There seems to be a better feeling between the boss and the men that never existed before. They respect you because you are a member of the union, and you respect them because they are boss."

Some of the miners, particularly the older ones, recalled past company abuses such as payment in company scrip instead of in cash and overcharging at company stores, giving the union credit for ending such practices: "They used to pay in scrip. The coal miner in those days didn't know what money was. You got your house from the company and the rent was checked off your statement; you got your food at the company store, and had to pay for your equipment like blasting powder and they checked that off. It was seldom you had anything coming—usually you owed the company. Then you got an advance in scrip that you could only spend in the company store, and they had you going round again. And stuff cost more there than anyplace else, but it was the only place that would give a coal miner credit. In some parts of Kentucky and Pennsylvania, it's still that way, in your non-union fields."

Appraisal of the Union and of Lewis

It is difficult to distinguish between members' appraisal of the UMW and their estimate of Lewis. Overwhelmingly, the miners expressed enthusiastic support of their union and its accomplishments—not a single member disapproved of the union. One of the leaders characteristically asserted that the UMW was "one of the best organizations of all countries all over the world. It is the father of all unions." With few exceptions, moreover, those interviewed expressed an intense admiration for and loyalty to their president. They referred to him in superlatives: "He's the greatest labor leader in America"; "Everything the miners have, we owe to Lewis"; etc. Even those who were deeply involved in opposition to Lewis in former years, and very critical of the current lack of autonomy, almost invariably coupled their criticism with praise for Lewis' economic achievements.

Typical of the younger miners was the driller who balanced the shortcomings of Lewis against the results which he achieved: "Maybe John L. is a little bit crooked, but by God he's got the miners with him and he gets things. He's pulled a few fast ones but, hell, look what conditions and wages he's got us. I'm all for him. There's lots of things you have no voice in and you're told what to do, but what he does, he does for your benefit. . . . Of course, he gets his and he's entitled to it. But look what he's done for us!"

An older member pointed to the high wages, the improved underground conditions, and the welfare and pension programs as adequate measures of Lewis' successful leadership. "It means something when you have to go to the hospital and just sign your name and it's paid for. John L. was responsible for this." Another miner with thirty-one years in the union, after praising Lewis' foresight and courage, added: "I don't like his strong-arm methods and power in the union. But we don't want to change him because he can get more for the miners than anybody else and he's done just that."

This widespread praise of Lewis was not always without an undertone of bitterness. For example, a sixty-year-old timberman with forty-five years of service complained about the power which Lewis wields: "When I went to work in the mines, the companies were rich and had power. Now it's the union president who is rich and has power. That's no good either." When this miner was asked if it were possible for anyone to run against Lewis for the presidency of the union, he declared that, though it was possible to run, no rival candidate could be elected. "The majority of the men are for him because they know what he has done," he explained.

Very few (about 8 per cent) wanted to see Lewis deposed as president, and even they usually expressed high regard for his achievements. Being mostly younger men, many of them were opposed in principle to long tenure in union office. As one put it: "It isn't good practice for a man to stay in office all his life. It's more like a monarch rule that way. He shouldn't have it forever even though he's a good man. No man is entitled to continuous rule, no matter how much he helps and does good. That tends to go against democratic principles. If a man stays in too long, he's bound to get crooked." Others who shared this general point of view argued that it was time that some younger men in the union had a chance to show what they could do. Only one, however, found nothing favorable to say about Lewis. This miner, with more than forty years of experience in the union, has had no use for Lewis since 1919, when he called off a strike under government pressure.

Though very few miners would like to see Lewis replaced as their leader, they felt that others were capable of carrying on the affairs of the union. As one put it: "There will be nobody who could take

John L.'s place like there was nobody who could fill Roosevelt's boots when he died. But there are good men up there and the union will stay strong." An old-timer expressed concern about the possible successor to Lewis, remembering that in the past some of the UMW leaders had embezzled union funds or had accepted payments from operators: "We'll have to get another leader and hope that he has enough money that he won't have to sell out. John L. has been in there long enough that we know he isn't there for the money. . . . If he's gonna get something, he's got it by now. Of a new one, we'd be fearful." Whatever the appraisal made by members of John L. Lewis as an individual or as a leader, the general feeling of the miners is typified in the words of another veteran who greatly admired Lewis but said: "No matter how much John L. has done for the miners, the union will go on because the union is bigger than John L. It might be tough for a little while but the union is here to stay."

Strikes in the Coal Fields

Coal miners are among the most strike-hardened veterans in the American labor movement. The general public never ceases to be amazed at the disciplined manner in which hundreds of thousands of miners respond to a strike call from their union—or, even more startling, to the simple word that the contract is expiring. Nor, with relatively few exceptions, has picketing been necessary in the unionized fields of Illinois during the past half-century to keep mines shut down. The men do chores around the house, tend their gardens, go fishing, or pass the hours in the streets or on their porches, but the mines remain tightly shut until the union tells its members to return to work. The solidarity of the mining community is never shown more clearly than in its support of a strike; even those miners who disapprove of a particular strike give it support, not through physical fear, but because they have accepted a code of behavior that values union solidarity as a prime virtue.[7]

The public has a concern with coal strikes other than as a demon-

---

[7] In all countries miners tend to be among the leaders in frequency of strikes. For an interesting effort to explain the relative incidence of strikes in various industries in terms of the location of the worker in society and the character of the job and the worker, see Clark Kerr and Abraham Siegel, "The Interindustry Propensity To Strike—An International Comparison," in *Industrial Conflict,* ed. Arthur Kornhauser, Robert Dubin, and Arthur M. Ross (New York: McGraw-Hill Book Co., 1954), chap. xiv, pp. 189–212.

stration of union solidarity, however. No other industry, with the exception of railroads and possibly of steel, has had as immediate an impact upon the lives of the general public. Until recently, once stocks of coal aboveground were used up, transportation and power were both affected, with repercussions upon the movement of goods and people, industrial production, and lighting. There was, likewise, a shortage of fuel for homes and other buildings. The development of alternative sources of fuel and power in recent years has substantially lessened the country's dependence upon coal. How quickly a nationwide coal strike becomes an emergency depends, needless to say, upon the available stocks aboveground; and the industry seeks to anticipate a labor stoppage by stepping up production in advance. Since there is chronic underemployment in the industry, except in time of war, the miners must be idle part of the time, so that the losses due to strikes tend to be exaggerated. Let a coal strike last long enough, however, and there is an inevitable effect upon the production and movement of goods and upon the comfort, convenience, and health of the general public.[8]

Overwhelmingly, the miners, rank and file as well as leaders, defended strikes as essential for winning improvements. Their general attitude can be summed up in the words of a fifty-four-year-old laborer who had worked thirty-nine years underground: "Without strikes, we would have no organization. Everything the miners got they got by striking—every cent, every condition, mining laws. I don't like strikes but they have to be."

Perhaps the greatest test of the union's strike solidarity occurred during World War II when the UMW, the only large American union to call national strikes during wartime, stopped coal production throughout the nation three times in the single year of 1943. These strikes posed the conflict between union loyalty and national patriotism, and afforded an additional index of the miners' general attitude toward the authority of their national leadership.

Most of the miners supported their wartime strikes, either on the ground that sufficient cause justified a strike in wartime as in peace-

[8] See the study of the impact of coal strikes in Neil W. Chamberlain and Jane Metzger Schilling, *The Impact of Strikes: Their Social and Economic Costs* (New York: Harper & Bros., 1954), chaps. 4–6; see also Irving Bernstein and Hugh G. Lovell, "Are Coal Strikes National Emergencies?" *Industrial and Labor Relations Review*, VI (April, 1953), 352–67; and C. Lawrence Christenson, "The Theory of the Offset Factor: The Impact of Labor Disputes upon Coal Production," *American Economic Review*, XLIII (September, 1953), 513–47.

time, or on the ground that there was always enough coal aboveground to take care of essential military needs. A veteran miner was among those who believed that John L. Lewis' tactics, without injuring the war effort, were necessary in order to win improvements for the men: "The way I felt about it, Lewis knows about the condition of coal and the shortage of coal, and he knew he could take the miners out for a few days and it wouldn't harm the war effort. . . . He knew what he was doing. You have to in order to get your demands. The companies are awfully tough." Others asserted that the operators were attempting to take advantage of a national emergency to weaken their union and to demand sacrifices which the operators themselves were unwilling to make. Some insisted that the radio and newspapers were biased against them; that only another coal miner, such as John L. Lewis, could understand the character of mining as an occupation; and that miners were entitled to all that they might gain in the light of their adverse working and living conditions.

Several were in military service at the time of these national coal strikes, and even they defended the union's actions: "I remember when I was in the Navy. Once I was sitting in the Chicago Theater in Chicago and John L.'s picture was flashed on the screen during a newsreel. Why you couldn't hear yourself think for all the boos. I sat there and admired the man. I've often thought what I would have done if the lights went on suddenly and I could get up and tell all those people what I thought—what it was like to be a coal miner." Another young miner recalled an experience he had had in 1943 while in service: "I was sitting next to an officer and he told me how much he was making and how he was going to retire after so many years. Then he got going on the miners' strikes and how terrible they were. I told him that he was just looking out for himself and they had the same right to look out for themselves."

There was a substantial minority, however, that had been opposed to the wartime strikes, even though, like the others, they had followed the union's call. A middle-aged miner with twenty-two years of experience in the union was one of these: "It was the wrong thing to do. There were boys fighting for us across the ocean and we should support them. . . . If you had a brother fighting, how would you feel about striking during the war?" Another admitted, "I didn't feel very good about it . . . those guys up there fighting and me on strike. The country needed the coal pretty bad." To most of the miners, however, whether or not they felt uneasy about wartime strikes, the call of the union, and the attainment of benefits considered just, took precedence over the country's need for coal.

In the miners' union centralized control exists over the cessation and resumption of work and over the terms of the agreement, a centralization of power that was generally defended by the miners as necessary. They generally agreed that such authority needed to be centralized in the hands of the national leadership. Some asserted that only the national officers had the over-all view required to know when strike action was necessary, while others pointed out that local union strikes, usually called "wildcats," were self-defeating. A mine carpenter declared that the local knew only its own affairs; when a nationwide strike was called, he argued, all miners should participate even though they had nothing to gain directly in their own local situation. "That's what makes us strong. We all stick together to benefit each other and the whole organization. It's majority rule with us. When I was in Kansas, we had a problem in that state and it was just a local problem in that state alone. The state went out while all over the country they were still mining coal. Why we could have stayed out for twenty years and not gained a thing. They should all pull together and pull them all out when there's trouble anywhere, and then there's no cutting one another's throat." Most miners asserted that centralized authority to call strikes did not represent autocracy, since the authority was freely delegated to the International Executive Board by convention action.

There were some who preferred not to have to make decisions. One such miner who had had experience in a CIO union preferred the concentration of authority in the UMW: "It comes down from the International. . . . It's good like it is. There's no trouble this way. In a factory where I worked, somebody had to get up and argue about going on strike, and there were fights about it. In the CIO you vote to go on strike or not and to accept contracts or not. But here it's all done by higher-ups and there's no trouble. It's better this way—the men don't argue with one another . . . and you never hear the men say anything about it."

There were several miners who, while approving of the control of strikes by the national officers, felt that the latter should make greater efforts to inform the men of the reasons for striking when such action was in order. As one said, "You are just told that there is a strike, but you don't know why. That's no good."

It is interesting to note that, while the word "strike" was often interpreted to mean an unauthorized work stoppage over purely local issues, nationwide production stoppages which occurred at the termination of agreements were considered to be legitimate and not strikes in the true sense of the word. National strikes or work stoppages were viewed as orderly efforts to get satisfactory contracts, but local strikes were generally looked upon with widespread disapproval. A miner with more than three decades of union experience expressed a typical dislike of them: "Wildcats are a radical business. I never approved of them. Some worthless miner wouldn't do right: they would try to discharge him, and the rest would strike. If I was a boss I would try to get rid of him, too." There were a few miners, however, who seemed to regret the decline of the wildcat strike. The minor local issues that usually gave rise to wildcats, it should be noted, would be handled through the grievance procedure under most union contracts; the prevalence of such strikes in the past might be related to the relative weakness of the grievance procedure in the mining industry.

Nevertheless, the principle of "no contract—no work" was fundamental and was not to be confused with striking. General work stoppages were almost always justified on the ground that miners did not work without the protection of a contract. A third-generation miner asserted that the union never called strikes: "When the contract expires, we just don't work. The company is responsible for that by not agreeing to a new contract. I'm not going down there with no representation. You've got to have a contract . . . and you automatically stop work if there's no contract. It's just good business. You wouldn't hire yourself out to make a suit of clothes if you didn't know what you were going to get paid for it, would you?"

Another miner who has been working underground for almost half a century insisted that the union hadn't called a strike in many years. When the interviewer mentioned a recent general stoppage, he replied: "That wasn't no strike. The men just refused to go to work without a contract; naturally we want a contract so we know what we are going to get." The majority of the miners insisted that they were never ordered to stop work. "We get telegrams when the contract expires. Say a contract expires on midnight on such and such a day.

Well, a telegram comes from Washington that says so. It doesn't tell us to shut down, but we know we don't work without a contract. Maybe we'll get one saying 'pending such and such, continue work.' But they never tell us to shut down."

The "no contract—no work" idea, deeply rooted in the miners' culture, marks them off from most other groups of workers in this country. Unionized factory workers would probably also refuse to work if their contract expired and was not extended temporarily during negotiations, but undoubtedly they would consider themselves on strike, not making a distinction that seems so obvious to the miners.

From time to time, usually in summer months preceding the expiration of a national agreement, the UMW leadership has called upon its members to work only three-day weeks. Often this has occurred when miners had been working full weeks and when no collective bargaining matter was at immediate issue. The overwhelming majority of the miners expressed no criticism of this union policy. On the contrary, the action was justified on the ground that the leaders have a commanding perspective of the conditions in the industry as these relate to the aboveground supply of coal, and act to protect the bargaining power of the union. Miners characteristically remarked that such actions are never demanded by their leaders unless "there'd be a purpose to it." For example, a miner who had been working a full week at the time the last three-day week was ordered said: "When the contract is coming up, the operators will get all the coal out they can before the contract expires and then sit there for three or four months and do nothing. . . . I'd rather see us work three days a week for four or five months if it can strengthen the union as a whole in a fight than see us go idle for four or five months due to the reason that we worked every day and produced millions of tons of coal. In any case . . . John L. wouldn't ask that if there wasn't a reason for it." Others supported the three-day week on the ground that this distributed the work, permitting everyone to make a living.

There were a number of miners, on the other hand, who reacted with a good deal of resignation, who accepted a three-day week because they felt powerless to do anything else. Some pointed out that, though they might personally disagree with such action because of the resulting loss of earnings, nevertheless, the collective will, as determined by their leadership and approved by most of their fellow workers, would prevail: "If the majority of my buddies working with me see the reason for it and I didn't, I'd still go out with them and help. Belonging to an outfit like this, you can't do what you feel as an individual. You have to do what the majority wants."

Hopes for the Future

Most of the miners planned to remain permanently in the occupation, despite the low status, the chronic underemployment, and the danger associated with it. Mostly a middle-aged group, they had an understandable reluctance to start afresh in some other area and industry, and to sacrifice their pension rights and whatever security their job provided for the uncertainties of life elsewhere. Indeed, many of the miners felt that they had little choice, since their skills were not transferable. "Mining is all I know" was a typical response, and others simply said that they were too old to consider a change in occupation. The high daily pay and the welfare and pension plans all appealed to the miners, the younger men doubting that they could earn the same rate in a factory, and the older men stressing the importance of their pension rights. Very seldom, however, did anyone say that he planned to stay because he liked his job, and only infrequently was any desire expressed to remain in the community—though the discipline of the factory and the impersonality of life in metropolitan areas are sources of great dissatisfaction to miners who leave, often resulting in their return to the mines.

Among the younger men there were a number who hoped to leave the industry in order to obtain steadier work and more regular income. Usually this was a vague hope rather than a definite plan, a readiness to leave "if something better turns up," combined with a growing realization as the years passed that this was very unlikely to happen. Some were aware of the practical difficulties in the way of change: "I don't plan to be a miner all my life, but I imagine I will. I'd take the first opportunity to get out of the mines; it would have to be something steady and good. Once a miner settles down in a small town like this and buys his home, it takes a lot to move him." A few miners, apprehensive because of the dangers of underground work, hoped to find something safer. Men who possessed a transferable skill such as carpentry could leave the mines most readily and find employment at acceptable wages elsewhere. Some of these, who had had work experience before entering the mines, preferred their earlier type of work and identified with that occupation or occupational group rather than with mining. There were several miners, in addition, who said that they would leave if they failed to receive a promotion to foreman, a consideration that seemed of relatively little importance to most of their fellow workers.

Although most miners, despite their dislike of some aspects of their occupation, were resigned to staying in it permanently, they hoped that their sons could get into something better, on the basis of a better education than they themselves had received. Occasionally, one talked about the professions or an independent business as a goal for his children, and some hoped vaguely that their sons could "improve themselves" or "get ahead." Usually, however, they considered and preferred factory employment in a city as the likely alternative to mining for their sons. Each father hoped that his son would escape those aspects of his occupation that he disliked most—the hard work, the low income, the lack of security. Many placed great emphasis on danger when they talked about their sons, though they usually minimized it in relation to themselves. Often danger was combined with one or more of the other disliked aspects of mining: "My son worked in the mines and liked it for a while. But I didn't exactly want him to continue. It's dangerous and youngsters don't know how to handle themselves like we old ones do. I know my work and know when there's going to be trouble. I've worked around mines so many years I ought to. But those young fellows don't and I didn't like worrying about him. It's true, you don't make so much in a factory, but he's better off there. And the work is more steady. Coal mining is an off-and-on job."

In a number of cases miners whose sons had established themselves in other occupations expressed satisfaction in their sons' improved status, in their escape from the low income and insecurity traditionally associated with mining. For example, one said with evident pride that his son was an army instructor and added: "I always told him, 'Never go to work in the mines, never go to work in the mines.' I pounded it into his head all the time. He saw that we always had to struggle to keep our feet on the ground and how hard life was when you work so hard and you're always poor." Though not clearly verbalized, there may also be a feeling here that the son's entry into another occupation represented an escape from a means of livelihood generally considered socially inferior.

Disappearance of the Union

The meaning of the union to the miners is revealed most clearly in their responses to the question, "Would it make any difference to you if the union disappeared?" Many of them could only visualize the disappearance of their national union as complete chaos and the loss of all protection; often their feelings were expressed in rather emotional terms: "That's like asking what would happen to us if the atomic bomb was thrown at you." "It would put our country in a pretty bad condition. It would put us all back to slave work again." "I would just feel like quitting work. . . . You wouldn't have no security at all. You would be a slave to the company."

The miners generally had two great fears of the consequences of the union's disappearance—that wages would deteriorate and that the companies would exercise autocratic power. Typical of those who stressed the downward pressure on wages was an electrical repairman with ten years of union experience: "It would be an open shop then, wouldn't it? I'd probably be competing with other guys for my job. If he could work for two dollars a day I would have to, too. Just to make a living I'd have to take a wage cut."

A thirty-eight-year-old driller with twenty years of union membership emphasized the deterioration of working conditions and the loss of job security: "I'd quit coal mining. We wouldn't have good working conditions. We'd have a job for one day and the next we wouldn't. If we wouldn't produce enough, we'd be told they had someone to take our place." Other responses showed the great fear of the miners that employers would abuse their authority—although the estimate of their particular employer, it must be remembered, was very favorable: "Everything would fall apart. They'd fire you right off the bat if they wanted to. Right around here there are fourteen hundred men out of jobs and if there was no union some of them are hard up for a job and would work cheaper and cut the conditions down to nothing."

Whereas the miners saw the national union in terms of power and protection, they visualized the local's contribution primarily in terms of administrative efficiency. Without the local, they asserted, grievances could not be handled as quickly or as effectively, and consequently it would be difficult or impossible to maintain working conditions. In the absence of the national union, on the other hand, there was general recognition that the local would be powerless.

The coal miners' loyalty to their union can be understood only in the light of the conditions under which the industry has operated, the history of its labor-management relations, and the nature of the mining communities. The isolation of the mining towns in the past, the belief on the part of the miners that they were unfairly treated by their employers and looked down upon by the public, the unpleasant conditions and physical danger involved in underground work—all these helped produce the solidarity that is a leading characteristic of the miners, a solidarity of which their union is an organizational expression and to which it owes much of its strength.

The high wages won by the miners' union do more than contribute to everyday comforts; they also symbolize achievements which have enabled the miners to escape the notorious poverty of the mining towns and to demonstrate that they are not much different from other people. Though irregular work keeps down their yearly income, miners have, at least in part, achieved a standard of living which enables them to share in some of the culturally valued symbols of status—a house, a car, education for the children, a chance to live like "respectable" people. The high hourly income, along with the union's achievements in the health and welfare field, gives the occupation some points of attractiveness and helps to balance the irregularity of employment, the danger, and the low status associated with it.

3

PLUMBERS
Craft-conscious Unionism

When one thinks of industry in the United States, the assembly lines
of Detroit or the vast steel works of the Chicago or the Pittsburgh
area come readily to mind; one thinks of large-scale production and
efficiency, of mechanical inventions and the use of vast amounts of
power, and of precise engineering methods. One of the largest of American industries, however, has experienced little of this industrial revolu-
tion; in building construction the small business unit is still typical, the
rule-of-thumb method still in effect, and the craftsman still supreme.
Among the craftsmen none is prouder of his skill than the plumber, or
more alert to protect its dignity. Among the craft-conscious unions
that dominate the industry, few can surpass the plumbers' union in
the control that it exercises over its portion, or in the jealousy with
which it guards its jurisdictional rights.

Economics of the Industry

Despite the development of some large construction companies in
the United States, a number of factors have combined to keep the
typical business unit small, particularly in the residential construction
field. So long as most people prefer to live in homes that differ from
those that surround them, custom methods will continue in the building trades long after they have yielded to mass-production techniques
in other areas of the economy. By its nature, moreover, the industry
is a local one; despite the development of prefabrication in recent
years, the industry continues to be a decentralized one, satisfying
the demand for its products separately in each community. In each
locality, moreover, the demand for housing shifts with changes in
prosperity and population. The housing industry is perhaps unique in

that new houses constitute a very small proportion of the total available on the market at any given time; since the number of old houses is fixed, however, a relatively slight fluctuation in the total demand can cause a very sharp change in the demand for new housing. In addition to these factors, the effects of weather and climate also contribute to the degree of uncertainty in the industry.

The system of contracting in general use adds its quota of instability by reducing to a very low level the amount of capital necessary to enter the business. The general contractor, while performing certain operations with his own employees, farms out other types of work to specialists, each of whom employs his own craftsmen. Since the capital outlay for these subcontractors may be little more than for office space and tools, it is a relatively simple matter for an ambitious worker to go into business for himself. The result is a highly competitive industry that tends to form associations to "regulate" the trade and restrict competition, with a high rate of failure on the part of new firms that prove inefficient or that bid too low in order to get jobs. If only one craftsman of a particular type is needed on a small job, the subcontracting system can become merely a disguised form of competitive wage bidding, undermining the established scale. In this respect, as in others, the building trades unions, along with their other functions, bring a measure of stability into a highly volatile business environment.

Since the job is ordinarily of short duration, and since the contractor's need for labor varies from job to job or even over the period of a single job, employment in the building trades is highly unstable. In each contractor's employ there is likely to be a group of men who remain with him steadily, supplemented by short-term workers who help meet the peak needs. Usually the contractor gets his extra help by calling the union, which functions as an employment service for its members and for the industry. The worker's concern is not that there be no layoff—a hazard always present in the construction industry— but that there be a job with another contractor available when his present employment runs out. The union seeks to insure this objective by a variety of devices, some designed to limit the number of available workers and others to enlarge the volume of work to be done.

Because the pay of plumbers has been high and employment steady in recent years, large numbers of young men have been eager to enter the trade. Becoming a plumber is not easy, however, since the number of apprentices is limited, and sons of members or other young men sponsored by those already engaged in plumbing are given preference by the union over outsiders. While the primary function of the apprenticeship system is to train skilled mechanics, it also provides the controls necessary to prevent flooding of the trade. Most members of the union speak only of the training aspect of the apprenticeship system, though there is a minority, among whom master plumbers, supervisors, and union officials are well represented, who see also its restrictive aspects.

The young man wishing to become a plumber must not only serve an apprenticeship of five years but also pass a state board examination to get his license. The license is justified on the ground that competent plumbers are essential to proper sanitation and public health. It has the additional effect, most plumbers recognize, of protecting their craft against the competition of related craftsmen and handymen.

The plumber, along with other building tradesmen, is in a protected position in still another respect: his work must be done in conformity with a city building code—a code, incidentally, that union officials help to write and that is enforced by city inspectors appointed from among the union's members. Plumbers emphasize that the purpose of the code is to protect public health. Some in the trade—particularly the master plumbers and supervisors, who could save money if "short cuts" were permitted—recognize that the code also serves to set work standards, and, therefore, makes work for the plumber.

In addition, the building trades unions seek to increase the volume of work that must be done on the job by rules that limit the use of prefabricated products or that reduce the amount of work that can be done in the shop—such as, in the case of the plumbers, the cutting and threading of pipe. Each union also seeks to set and enforce jurisdictional boundaries so as to keep disputed work in the hands of its members rather than allow it to be performed by members of a related craft or by handymen. The plumbers have carried on chronic jurisdictional disputes with the steamfitters, who are organized into a separate local of the same international union, and whose members can perform a fair percentage of plumbing work, and also, from time to time, with other craftsmen, such as sheet metal workers, with whom they conflict over the carrying and placing of sinks.

The apprenticeship system, licensing regulations, building code, union rules, and jurisdictional claims together form a network of devices, some private and some public, through which the union seeks to affect both the amount of work to be done and the number of men available to do it. Many of these devices, since they operate to increase costs, are opposed by contractors; others are not, where the cost may be passed on readily to the building purchaser or owner, and they may even be welcomed, as in the case of building code restrictions, where the contractors also profit as a result.

Conceptions of union-management relationships formed in other contexts may need substantial modification before they can be applied to the building construction industry. Here the union, far from being the weaker party, is a giant in size and economic power when compared with the typical small contractor, whose business could literally be snuffed out if the union chose to do so. The contractor, moreover, is usually a former union member in the organized centers of the industry, who may retain friendly associations with union members and officers. The relative ease of starting a business, together with the high incidence of failure, makes for a two-way flow between the union membership and the ranks of the employers. The union, though it may raise each contractor's labor cost, provides a valuable service by assuring him that all his competitors will have the same cost. In its efforts to promote the interests of its members, the union may regulate the trade in other ways as well; and since the employers seek ways of restricting the rigors of competition, there may be collusion occasionally between the employers and the union that runs afoul of antitrust legislation.

Union power is increased by the predominance of craftsmen in the industry—three-fourths of the work must be done by skilled men—and by the fact that in new construction the contractor may have obligated himself to finish the work by a particular date and may suffer a substantial loss if he fails to do so. Though hourly wages are high, the cost of a wage increase to a particular group of craftsmen may be a very small percentage of the total cost of the building. Besides, those for whom the building is erected have no interest in labor-management relations in the industry beyond their concern to have the structure finished by the expected date. Consequently, it may be desirable from the point of view of both the contractor and the owner to pay the additional wage demanded rather than risk a strike with its consequent expenses and delays.[1]

In the repair section of the plumbing industry the typical unit is a small neighborhood shop, employing several craftsmen at the most. The relationship here between employer and employee is likely to be a close personal one, with the economic and social gap between them at a minimum. The master plumber may or may not join the contractors' association that carries on collective bargaining negotiations with the union; whether he is a member or not, he is required by the union to accept the same terms. The union scale is the same, whether a craftsman is engaged in new construction, repair, or maintenance work. The repair shops are able with little difficulty to pass the cost of wage increases on to the home owner, who has little choice but to call a master plumber when he is faced with a task, often of an emergency nature, that calls for skill or tools that he does not possess.

Union Structure and Collective Bargaining

The building trades have traditionally been among the most powerful in the American Federation of Labor. The plumbers are one of the more important, in terms of size and influence, of the nineteen unions affiliated with the Building and Construction Trades Department, which embraces virtually all the unionized building tradesmen in the country. The desire of each union to assure employment to its membership in the face of constant changes in materials and methods and conflicting claims of other unions has led to almost constant quarreling over jurisdictional problems, problems that have absorbed

[1] For an excellent analysis of the economic factors underlying the building construction industry, and also of the role of the unions and the nature of collective bargaining, see William Haber, *Industrial Relations in the Building Industry* (Cambridge, Mass.: Harvard University Press, 1930); see also Haber's chapter on "Building Construction" in *How Collective Bargaining Works* (New York: Twentieth Century Fund, 1942), pp. 183–228, and William Haber and Harold M. Levinson, *Labor Relations and Productivity in the Building Trades* (Ann Arbor: Bureau of Industrial Relations, University of Michigan, 1956). For a good survey of building trades developments in a single center see Royal E. Montgomery, *Industrial Relations in the Chicago Building Trades* (Chicago: University of Chicago Press, 1927). See also the monograph by Gordon W. Bertram and Sherman J. Maisel, *Industrial Relations in the Construction Industry: The Northern California Experience* (Berkeley: Institute of Industrial Relations, University of California, 1955); Milton Derber, "Building Construction," Case Study No. 5 in *Labor-Management Relations in Illini City* (Champaign: Institute of Labor and Industrial Relations, University of Illinois, 1953), I, 659–785; and Stephen P. Sobotka, "Union Influence on Wages: The Construction Industry," *Journal of Political Economy*, LXI (April, 1953), 127–43.

a disproportionate share of the time of the national officers of the unions and of the department.[2]

As is appropriate to so decentralized an industry, power within each of the unions tends also to be decentralized, with each local union or district council much in control of affairs within its jurisdiction. Most of the employers in each local craft, in turn, federate into an association to bargain with the union, with those contractors who fail to become members of the association accepting the terms that it negotiates. The existence of a large number of building jobs in scattered locations, most of them employing a small number of craftsmen for a short period of time, requires constant policing if the terms of the agreement and the union rules are to be observed. As a result, the unions select a corps of business agents, each of whom is empowered to call his men off the job if the employer persists in a violation. This power of the business agent, in turn, has led to the graft and corruption that from time to time has disgraced unions in the building trades, particularly in cities governed by dishonest political machines.[3]

The Local Union

The local union that we studied operates in one of the metropolitan centers in the Middle West. It is an old local, tracing its existence back to the Knights of Labor, before it affiliated with the national union of plumbers some sixty years ago. Its membership comprises about four thousand journeymen and four hundred apprentices employed in building construction, city departments, neighborhood repair shops, or plant maintenance. The local encourages master plumbers to retain

[2] For an analysis of jurisdictional disputes in the construction industry and a review of the various efforts to establish machinery for their settlement, see John T. Dunlop, "Jurisdictional Disputes," *Proceedings of New York University Second Annual Conference on Labor* (Albany, N.Y.: Matthew Bender & Co., 1949), pp. 477–504.

[3] The legislatures in the states of New York and Illinois both established committees in the early 1920's to investigate abuses in the building construction industry. For the reports of these bodies, known respectively as the Lockwood and the Dailey committees, see State of New York, *Final Report of the Joint Legislative Committee on Housing* (Legislative Doc. No. 48) (1923); and *Report of Illinois Building Investigation Commission* (1923). For a general study of union abuses of these types, involving unions in building construction and also in other industries, see Harold Seidman, *Labor Czars: A History of Labor Racketeering* (New York: Liveright Publishing Corp., 1938). Labor racketeering has occurred most frequently in the building industry and in some of the service trades, where somewhat comparable economic conditions have permitted their development.

union membership, and a minority of the five hundred who operate within the local's area of operations do so. Once predominantly Irish and German, the local now embraces a variety of ethnic groups. Only in recent years has the local accepted Negroes, several dozen of whom are now included in its membership.

In order to police jobs within its territory, the local maintains a staff of five business agents, each assigned to a specific geographic area, who work under the supervision of the business manager. Some years earlier, within the experience of the older members, there had been a dishonest and dictatorial business manager who stamped out dissent with the aid of strong-arm methods. The present business manager, however, is an unusually able and enlightened leader of considerable prominence in the local building trades and in civic affairs generally. The decentralized character of the plumbers' national union gives him pretty much of a free hand within the local's jurisdiction, and the size and strength of his local union, in turn, make him a power within the national union. Though the local's elections, held every third year, are open and are honestly conducted, the popularity and prestige of the business manager are so great that the slate of officers that he heads is usually re-elected without opposition.

Within the plumbers' local union, at the time the study was made, there were no active political groups. Members were organized, however, into several clubs which had engaged only in social activities in recent years but which had their origins in factional groupings and could readily take on political functions again should the members feel the need. One of the social clubs had an ethnic base, having been organized by Jewish plumbers in order to increase their work opportunities outside the area in the city in which Jewish residents were then concentrated. A member of this club recalled the situation that led to its formation: "Years ago the business agent had much more power than he has now. That was when the union was run by crooks. I remember when the only place a Jew could work was in his own district, the ghetto. . . . If you got a job with a plumber or contractor who had work outside of the Jewish district, the business agent would come around and ask: 'How many Sheenies on this job?' And if there was more than one or two, he'd tell the boss to fire them and put some of his own people on the job. . . . That's why we organized the Jewish club inside the union—the Social Club. It was started originally so that we could have a block of votes at the meetings and get rid of the officers that set up and controlled that practice. Now they know we have an organization and could get active if that ever started again."

Another organization within the union, which had the unusual name of the Pot and Ladle Club, had been organized by rank-and-file plumbers to oust a set of officers who were thought to be allied with gangster elements in the city; and still another group, the Craftsmen's Club, was composed of members belonging to the Masonic order. Though to their newer members these organizations may mean little more than friendly card games accompanied by beer and sandwiches, to the older members, with their memories of successful campaigns against union abuses, the social clubs still signify a nucleus of political organization always available in case of need. Their existence, institutionalized within the union, constitutes a force for responsible leadership.

When our field work was conducted, in 1952–53, the pay scale of journeymen plumbers was three dollars an hour, with highly competent men earning somewhat above this figure. There was, in addition, a recently negotiated welfare fund, financed by a 3 per cent of payroll payment by contractors.[4] This high scale of payment had been achieved through the collective bargaining power of the union, operating within the favorable framework set by the economic conditions of the industry. The union leaders, knowing what could be achieved, had not needed to call a strike in support of their bargaining demands for more than three decades, although a strike did in fact occur a few months after the field work had been completed. There had been full employment in the trade for a dozen years through the defense and war emergencies and the postwar boom, and there was every expectation that high levels of prosperity would continue in the trade, for contractors and journeymen alike.

Under the contract subforemen or lead men were paid $3.20 an hour, foremen $3.30, and superintendents $3.55. The narrow differential in pay between journeymen and foremen was typical of the building trades, reflecting the limited nature of the foremen's supervisory duties. Whereas the foreman in an industrial plant usually has authority over the work of a large number of men at various levels of skill, the foreman in the building trades may work alongside several men, nominally

---

[4] About the time the interviewing was being completed, the employers' contribution to the welfare fund was raised to 5 per cent. Pensions to elderly plumbers began to be paid from this fund in 1955.

under his direction, each of them his equal in craftsmanship. The building trades foreman, moreover, is a union member, responsible to the union for observing its rules as well as to the employer for carrying out his orders. The foreman who violates union regulations may be brought on charges before the local's executive board, which may fine him or have him removed from the job.

The Plumbers and Their Work

The plumbers resembled the miners in their strong attachment to their occupation and their high degree of group solidarity, although they lacked the strong family tradition, the degree of community identification, and the well-defined subcultural background so typical of the miners. With a few exceptions the plumbers had been reared in an urban environment; about a fourth of them[5] had followed their fathers' trade, and many others had plumbers among their relatives. Most of them came from families of skilled workers. Almost all were native-born, of a variety of ethnic backgrounds; half of them were Catholic, with the remainder almost equally divided between Protestants and Jews. They were a mature group, averaging forty-eight years in age, with an average of nine and a half years of schooling. Unlike the miners, the plumbers had found a variety of occupational choices open to them.

There were some among the plumbers who, finding the occupation a family tradition, followed it with as little conscious choice as the young man in a mining community gives to his entrance into the mines. As one plumber said: "My whole family are plumbers and I just followed along, although my father didn't want me to be a plumber because he said that I was too small. I have four brothers and a father who were plumbers. I like the business[6]—my oldest brother was in it at the time and I don't know why, but I had a craving for it." More typical were those who, far from entering the trade automatically, made a conscious choice of it, attracted by the high pay that plumbers earned. In many

[5] Thirty-four rank-and-file plumbers were interviewed. A larger sample, containing ninety-three names, had been selected, but the plumbers proved to be so homogeneous that interviewing was stopped at a fairly early point.

[6] This manner of referring to the trade is typical of the occupational group. Whether they are masters or journeymen, they regularly speak of their occupation as the plumbing "business." This choice of phraseology may reveal the plumber's conception of himself as almost an entrepreneur, as well as his identification with the trade.

cases, lacking relatives who could get them admitted to the apprenticeship program, they experienced difficulty and delay before they found an opportunity to learn the skill.

For the plumber there are intrinsic rewards in the work he does, work that he finds interesting and satisfying. Plumbers assert that their work gives them a sense of accomplishment and that they gain great satisfaction from the variety of interests and experiences which the trade has to offer. Most of them stress, in addition, the importance of plumbing and the demands placed upon those who practice the trade. A thirty-five-year-old superintendent in a remodeling shop held a typical view: "Definitely, I like my work. To my honest belief, if a guy gets into it and believes in it with all his heart and soul, it grows on you just like anything else. My personal feeling about plumbing is that it does something to better the human race; it gives them better living conditions, more sanitary living conditions in the home, and that leads to better health." Emphasis on the social importance of the work is often combined with the assertion that the plumber has to "use his brains," is "always learning," or has to be able to meet the demands put on his ability and ingenuity: "I really love my work. . . . It's a challenge—it taxes your knowledge and skill and ingenuity to the utmost. Every job is a problem in itself and you get a real satisfaction out of doing a good job. And you are pleasing the housewife—don't discount the importance of that. We perform a useful service to the public and in recent years we're respected more and more all the time."

Most of the plumbers asserted that they liked their work very much. Some statements, such as "it's my whole life," "I eat and sleep it," and "I have my heart and soul in it," reflected a rather emotional approach to the work. While some pointed to the high pay, the opportunities for advancement, or the fact that the trade was not overcrowded, most of the plumbers emphasized the less materialistic aspects of their employment. There was no other work that they would rather do: "No, there's nothing else. I have my heart and soul in it. I've been in plumbing business since I've been sixteen years old. This is the work I like better than anything else." Only a small proportion of the plumbers, about one-sixth, would have preferred a different occupation. The types of work they mentioned, such as engineering and architectural drawing, reflected the occupational prestige hierarchy in their environment.

Despite their generally high regard for their occupation, the plumbers recognize that it requires them to perform unpleasant tasks from time to time. No one likes "dirty work"—work with sewage, ditches, clogged toilets, and the like. It may be significant that plumbers who have done both types of work tend to mention new construction, which is cleaner, first, adding that they may also do remodeling and repair. Nevertheless, they argue that a good plumber should always be ready to do all kinds of work; however unpleasant, the work is necessary for community health and it is part of the plumber's trade.

Plumbers, like miners, are sensitive to the view of them held by the public, but in a different way. Much of the plumbers' emphasis is on the criticism aroused by their high rate of pay and their alleged failure to give full return for their wages. As one plumber put it: "I think the public is under the impression that they don't get full value of dollar for dollar out of a plumber, but they don't realize how foolish they are in their thoughts. To me, plumbing is a very honorable industry and I don't think that it is overpaid. Of course, there is a lot of jokes about going back to the shop to do five minutes of work, but actually I don't think that the public is cheated by the plumbers. . . . You talk to people and they say, 'Well, plumbing is a vicious racketeering.' . . . People don't realize how long it takes to go from a shop into a home and see what is wrong and go back and get what you need, and maybe it's only a five-minute job, but somebody has to pay the freight and the fellow that owns the business isn't going to."

A large minority, while admitting that there might be public criticism, emphasized the growing popular respect for the plumber: "The old story is that the plumber always forgets his tools and has to go back to the shop. They never realize that the plumber has to be a walking supply house to meet all the conditions he might run into. But the public is more and more accepting the plumbers all the time. They know that he provides them with real service when he comes into a house." Many felt that the public was beginning to realize that good plumbing was necessary to prevent sickness and the spread of contagious diseases. This touches upon one of the plumber's favorite themes: as the person charged with protecting public sanitation he is as important to the community's health as the medical practitioner. The enthusiasm with which plumbers have adopted this view is evidence of the defense it provides against their basic insecurities; if, like doctors, they are vital to the health of the community, then their high income is amply justified and the respect accorded them ought to be greatly increased.

Though his status is working class, the plumber's high hourly rate of pay, combined with regular employment, gives him a lower middle-class income. This discrepancy between status and income may partly explain the eagerness with which he seizes upon a status factor like the vital contribution to community health. Where the status of a group is evident and accepted, emphasis upon it is unnecessary; the insecurity of the plumbers can be inferred from both the tone and content of their repeated references to the importance of their work.

Relationship to Master Plumbers

The plumber is in a remarkably independent position in regard to his employer. Since for many years the supply of journeymen in the city has been less than or, at best, equal to the demand, the plumber has felt free to change employers whenever he wished, although instances of long service with a particular employer are also quite frequent. As a result, the plumber is hardly concerned about such problems as discharge, layoff, and seniority, problems that bulk so large in the thinking of many other groups of employees.

Since the volume of work of any contractor or repair shop is bound to fluctuate, layoffs are inevitable. Plumbers accept uncritically the employers' practice, widely in effect, of laying off the least capable man, without the resentment or the demand for a seniority system that such a policy would be likely to produce among factory workers. In some shops the practice is to dismiss the last man who was hired. Whichever system is in effect, it is recognized that exceptions may be made for friends—a tendency that journeymen accept as legitimate. The question of layoff is approached casually by the plumbers, reflecting their economic basic security as suppliers of needed services.

Often the plumber has a very high regard for the master plumber who employs him, remaining in his employ for many years, developing a close personal and social relationship, and working with him on terms approaching social equality. There is likely to be no difference in status between the two in terms of dress, associations, residential neighborhood, or the like. The two men work side by side, many of the masters still holding union cards, and all of them having had their point of view shaped by years of experience as journeymen. Should the master's venture into business fail, he would expect to return to journeyman status. There are numerous cases where a journeyman who has worked many years for a master "inherits" the business when the latter retires. Both tend to identify with the trade rather than with employer or employee groups. All these factors provide a basis for a close relationship between the two, characterized by friendship and mutual respect. Unlike the factory worker, the plumber see his relationship with his employing master plumber as one of mutual dependency: "There are very few trades where the boss and the journeyman are as close as in our trade. Every master was a journeyman first and went through the whole business. . . . After all, the journeyman is in a position to hurt the master, not the other way around. . . . There are a lot of masters and there is a lot of competition between them, and the journeyman can get on the job and ruin a master by being destructive or wasteful with materials or time, or alienate customers and lose clients for the boss. . . . The master is at the mercy of the journeyman—all he does is sell the journeyman's labor."

As a result of this general attitude toward the relationship, there were few complaints of being unfairly treated. The usual view of the plumber was that the boss could not make trouble for him: "Unless the journeyman does something radically wrong, the boss is only interested in getting a good day's work. All he could do is fire you, and that isn't trouble because it is easy to go out and get another job." Many of the responses suggested that the journeyman must have been at fault if there were difficulties with the boss: a man might be disciplined, and properly so, for getting drunk, being lazy, or loafing on the job.

The major complaint, ordinarily hedged with qualifications, was that masters wanted work done too quickly; often the plumber promptly added that not all masters were like that, or that he had never had a personal experience of that sort. Asked what was the plumber's chief complaint about the boss, a fifty-four-year-old journeyman with twenty-eight years in the trade gave a typical response: "Well, gee, I don't know. . . . it would be that he says the work is behind and you know it isn't. If they hurry you they can make money. No matter how hard you work, you cannot satisfy them. But that's rarely the case. Most of them treat you like a brother and you have no gripes on them. They want your advice and you want theirs; it works out swell—hand in hand." Other occasional complaints were that the boss was unsociable, that he interfered with the work too much, that he didn't allow enough time for coffee breaks, that he preferred some men to others, or that he provided bad tools. Again, most plumbers emphasized that they personally had not had such experiences, and many of them could think of no complaints at all.

The plumber, in common with many other craftsmen, has an important advantage over the average factory worker in that he himself largely determines the speed at which he works. Plumbers emphasize that the man on the job knows best how to allot his time, that he knows as well as the contractor how long the job should take, and that he will not tolerate any pushing. "Generally the contractor don't succeed in speeding you up," one plumber pointed out; "the minute they crack the whip, you're bound to find ways of slowing down." Another pointed out the circumstances under which the men might work faster on request: "Lots of times there is only an hour and the boss says, 'Let's try and finish it so we won't have to make the trip again in the morning.' He makes a buck that way if the fellows co-operate with him. If he asks us to work a little faster, we usually go along with him. But generally we set our own pace."

Whereas the factory worker who has independence on his job is likely to emphasize it as a special privilege, the plumber takes independence for granted. He feels it his right, even his duty, to refuse to follow instructions if they involve lowering the accepted standards of the trade. The authority of the employer over the manner in which the work is to be done is accepted only so long as his demands are considered legitimate: "That's the way I'm gonna do my work. I don't care whether the employer likes it or not. Many times we have employers who like to do some cheating. . . . Well, if the plumber knows his stuff and believes in his unionism and believes in the code he'll stick to his point." In many responses of this type the plumber emerges as the defender of a professional code. Supervisory authority loses its legitimacy when it conflicts with trade standards. Master plumbers and foremen are as clear about this as journeymen are; as a small contractor expressed it: "It's the journeymen on the job that should have the say. Sometimes as a boss I'll tell a man to do it this way just to save time and materials, and he goes along; but the journeyman should have the say and tell me 'no' because he has to protect the trade and keep up the standards. He should tell me 'no—they'll catch me if I do it that way.'"

The Plumbers and Their Union

Most of the plumbers praised their union in glowing terms, with frequent use of superlatives. "I think it's wonderful," "one of the best," and "outstanding" were expressions that often appeared in the comments made by rank-and-file plumbers. Other responses, less enthusiastic, were still very favorable, such as, "it's a good local," or "I think it's done its job." The occasional neutral reactions or critical appraisals tended to come from supervisors or master craftsmen rather than from journeymen.

Particularly noticeable was the high praise spontaneously given to the officers of the local, particularly to the leading official, the business manager. The plumbers were appreciative of his honesty and efficiency, as well as of his friendly relations with them. The responses were studded with references to the "old days" when the leadership was autocratic and corrupt:

We have a good organization now. We have democracy there. You can get up and speak without fear of reprisal and that's always done. I've known steamfitters who had to leave the city because they became marked men who spoke against the leadership. That couldn't happen in our union. He [the business manager] is a different kind of fellow compared to what we had in the old days. . . . He believes in running the union with brains, not brawn. . . . He's cleaned up the union a long way from what it used to be.

We all got a voice now; we can say what we like. It's not like the old days. If a guy tried to argue back with the leaders in those days, he'd get conked on the head with a spittoon. We didn't know how the money was spent and when you'd ask you'd more than likely get a beating in the alley behind the hall. Now it's not like that; we have our arguments and disagreements, but we discuss it and after it's decided we're all friends again.

In a trade in which the union business manager is far more powerful than the employer, able and honest leadership is a real asset, not to be taken for granted nor to be lightly regarded.

The leadership was also credited with having avoided strikes for more than thirty years. Indeed, the view was widespread among the plumbers that a good union officer was one who was able to settle difficulties without resort to strikes; strikes could be avoided if the parties negotiated in a reasonable spirit. A minority, however, did feel that the weapon was vital to the union's bargaining position, however much they may have disliked going on strike. Whatever their view of the desirability or undesirability of strike action, all agreed that "If the union tells me to go on strike, I'll have to go." There was unanimous acceptance of the union's power to call a strike and to make it effective; this was a matter not merely of the power of the union to control the conduct of its members but of the legitimacy of its authority as well.

Most of the plumbers attributed the long absence of strikes to the high quality of the union leadership or the co-operative relations between journeymen and master plumbers. A number pointed to the reasonableness of the union's demands, and several emphasized the fact that the contractors had formerly been journeymen themselves. A few found the explanation in specific characteristics of the trade, particularly the fact that the masters could readily pass higher wage costs on to the householder.

The plumbers were also concerned with the union's concrete achievements. The level of wages, working conditions, protection from unfair treatment, and the welfare fund were mentioned by many; the good training program, the protection of trade standards and job opportunities, and the settlement of jurisdictional disputes also received attention. The younger plumbers tended to refer more frequently to these concrete achievements, while the older plumbers placed greater emphasis on the quality of the leadership.

Occasionally, officers were criticized for giving special protection to their friends or for spending the local's money too freely; and a foreman was critical of the officers for being overly concerned with benefits for journeymen and indifferent to the welfare of supervisors. But these were definitely minority responses in interviews for the most part high, sometimes extravagant, in their praise of union activities.

Most of the plumbers had joined the union automatically when they became apprentices. When entrance controls were relaxed following the great depression, however, those who had learned the trade under non-union conditions had also been permitted to join on the basis of competence. These men emphasized the greater security and protection they enjoyed as union members, the greater ease of obtaining employment, the higher wages they received, the feeling of belonging that they enjoyed, and the status they acquired as union members whose skill as craftsmen could no longer be questioned. Some, looking back upon their non-union days, described the long hours, low pay, and lack of security. One of these compared the difference between non-union and union conditions to that between night and day. "You feel better working with a code and a card," he asserted. "You know you have a body with you; you feel more secure."

The plumbers' attitude toward their union was also revealed in their reaction to plumbers who might not wish to join. This was a new concept to most of them, who had never met such a person. Many, unable to think of any reason why one would not wish to join, suggested that "the guy must be crazy": "I think a guy who doesn't want to join is a psycho. If he stands on his constitutional rights and doesn't want to join, then I think he is un-American because a good union organization is an asset to the country and not a detriment. A guy is crazy to refuse to join." Others thought that the reason for not joining was due to lack of information about the union. Still others suggested that an additional motivation might be the desire to avoid paying the initiation fee and dues.[7] The benefits of unionism appeared so great to these men, however, that the qualified plumber who preferred to remain non-union was a phenomenon difficult for them to understand.

Though the plumbers showed no resentment against the man who, for whatever reason, might not wish to join their union, they clearly would refuse to work with him. For this, three general reasons were advanced: self-interest, union principles, and obedience to their local's rules. Those who stressed self-interest pointed out that exceptions might lead to a general practice, with the result that they would soon be competing against handymen. "It would be cutting your nose off to spite your face. You pay dues to a union and then work with a man who doesn't pay dues. You spend time learning the trade and then work with a man who probably didn't spend any time but just picked up a wrench. It's bad for the morale. You pay dues to the union to uphold your rights and a non-union guy will come in and get the same benefits." Others argued that union principles, with which they agreed, required them to work only with union men, while still others were simply afraid of violating union rules lest they be caught and brought up on charges before the executive board.

A similar mixture of acceptance of union principles and fear of violating union rules was shown in the attitude of plumbers toward picket lines established by other unions. Most of the plumbers subscribed to the general union principle that a picket line is to be respected: "When people are on a picket line they are fighting for improvement in their living conditions and it isn't up to me to spoil it. I don't ask any ques-

---

[7] The initiation fee was $200.00 and the monthly dues $6.00, plus an assessment of 25 cents for incapacitated members. The dues were scheduled to be raised soon to $7.00 and the assessment to 50 cents. None of the men who suggested the level of dues as a motivation for non-unionism had a personal complaint about the amount.

tion; what union it is, who they are, what their nationality is or their religion—I don't care what their political beliefs are. They are working people fighting for a better way of life." A small minority, however, explained their unwillingness to go through a picket line in terms of union rules and the sanctions imposed for violation: "We're not allowed to. They would get after us quick and our card would be taken away. We'd be taken before the Board and then . . . bang! [What would the Board do?] I don't know, but they don't let them off easy." Others asserted that they would cross a picket line only under certain conditions, as when the union officers ordered them to do so. Though the building trades generally respect each other's picket lines, in a particular case a local union or its officers might decide that pickets were to be disregarded. Building tradesmen usually accept without question the instructions of their officers in such cases.

Aspirations of Plumbers

Considering the advantages of the trade and the length of the apprenticeship, it is not surprising that all the plumbers expected to remain in their occupation permanently. Many stressed the intrinsic satisfactions that their work afforded and their preference for it over other occupations, even the highly respected professions; others emphasized their fitness for the work or its attractions in comparison with other types of available employment: "I like plumbing and that's that. Nothing else comes up to my standards. What could a guy do like me? Go into a factory and punch a clock and take orders? We are free and go to work on the job and no boss is there. If you want to quit early or take a few minutes more for lunch, nobody says anything; you aren't controlled by a clock like in the factory. Another thing is that I'm used to giving orders and being my boss. I often run the job and give orders to other plumbers. The only time the boss interferes with you is when you want to ask something special or to order materials."

Whether the plumber remains a journeyman all his life or becomes a master and opens a business of his own is a matter that he can decide, within limits, for himself. Though there are some large employers in the industry, the typical unit is a jobbing shop or neighborhood repair business, for which only a moderate amount of capital is required. Because of the regular employment and high earnings, it is not too difficult for many plumbers to accumulate the capital necessary to open a business or become a partner in an established one, though many journeymen shrink from the responsibility that running a business entails or doubt that they possess the business skill necessary for success. The goal, however, is a realizable one for the plumber, and not the improbable dream that it is for most factory workers.

Half the men stated that at one time or another they had thought of entering business for themselves. Most of them had discarded the idea because of the lack of financial resources, the risks and headaches involved, or the difficulty of finding a suitable partner. A few had made the effort and had failed, and were back in the ranks of journeymen. The older men who were still journeymen expected to remain in that status, and the city employees did not wish to give up the security of their pensions. Most of the men under middle age, however, talked of opening a business of their own in order to achieve greater independence or higher income.

The plumbers' union maintained a staff of full-time business agents, at salaries above the level earned by journeymen, to police the widespread building activities and settle difficulties that arose. Business agents, like other officers, were elected by the membership. Despite the relatively high pay, prestige, and clean work, most of the plumbers did not want the position. They felt that the work made severe demands; it was a responsible job requiring intelligence, skill, and the ability to handle troublesome situations. More than that, it required the business agent to be forever quarreling with somebody. As one said, the job "is mostly trouble. Then you have too many people to please. If you help one, you might be hurting another and you might make enemies. The business agent doesn't get a call unless it's trouble." Several summed up their attitude with variations of "I don't want their money or their troubles."

A substantial minority, however, said that they would welcome an opportunity to become business agents. A characteristic response was that of a middle-aged plumber, a veteran of twenty-seven years: "I think it would be a nice job. I would still be in the plumbing line and it's a nice salary and a nice car [furnished by the union]. You put in a lot of hours; get to go to different conventions and it's a clean job. Don't have to put your legs in dirty overalls everyday. But we can't all be chiefs—some have to be Indians."

Of the groups we studied, the plumbers alone were generally willing to have their sons follow in their occupation. "Every plumber's ambition," said one, "is to have his own business, and there's nothing he wants more than to have his son in business with him as a partner." This attitude reflects the fact that they were the highest skilled and best-paid group studied, a group that had achieved the relatively high income, economic security, and prestige of craftsmen desired by many of the less-skilled workers for their sons. The plumbers placed the same value on education that others did, but they saw education as a desirable cultural goal, not as a means of escape from their own occupation. It is interesting to note that the plumbers, who could afford to prepare their sons for a profession, seldom listed that as a goal, while many lower-paid workers, who would find the expense of a professional education much harder to bear, placed great emphasis upon it. Those plumbers who did not particularly wish their sons to enter their own occupation usually wanted them to learn another of the skilled trades.

Disappearance of the Union

Plumbers found it hard to conceive of their trade without a union, a number of them suggesting that a new union would have to be formed immediately. The disappearance of their union, in the eyes of the plumbers, would result in an influx of unskilled workers, the loss of part of their jurisdiction to other skilled groups, deterioration in working conditions, cutthroat competition, lower wages, the loss of the code and working rules, and even injury to the health of the public. All of these would add up to the collapse of the standards of the trade upon which their income and status depended. Yet this hypothetical threat was viewed as coming only to a minor degree, and indirectly, from the employers, who were seen as victims along with the journeymen of a larger situation beyond their control.

Many of the plumbers emphasized the influx of less-skilled workers, with the resulting oversupply of labor and lowering of wages. "Without the local union," one member said, "you'd have to work for nothing like a slave." "You would have more plumbers than red dogs," said a veteran of forty years, and a young plumber pointed to the effect on the code as well: "For one thing, the code would be broken. Every Tom, Dick, and Harry would get a pipe wrench and do plumbing. I imagine wages and working conditions would be affected because there would be a lot of handymen competing together and a lot of plumbers would lose out." Evidently a fair percentage of the plumber's work can be done by less-skilled men; otherwise the plumbers would not fear their competition so greatly.

A master plumber, much more secure than journeymen because of his independent business, expressed the reluctance of the owner of a small shop to see the union disappear: "In the small way I operate, it probably wouldn't make any difference. Again, it might. There would be less trouble arising with Local —— in there on bargaining rather than having individuals bargain for themselves. The way it is now, you know what your competitors are paying for labor, too. The union stabilizes the industry and that is good for everyone."

The plumber's union is an effective collective bargaining agency, which has protected him by increasing the amount of work and reducing the number of men eligible to do it; and the loyalty he gives it is understandable in view of the benefits he has received and the dangers from which it protects him. Yet the union serves other purposes as well. It insures social contacts with fellow craftsmen who also have a lifetime commitment to the trade, and it also keeps him informed of trends and conditions in a highly unstable segment of industry. For these reasons the union occupies a more central place in the plumber's life than is likely to be the case with most other groups of workers. Yet the economic function of the union remains central; without the union the plumbers would fear not merely a lower income but a collapse of the trade standards upon which their security depends.

4

STEEL WORKERS
Militant Unionism

The southwestern coast line of Lake Michigan offers an impressive, even an imposing, sight to the visitor. For almost fifty miles the area along the lake front harbors a complex of blast furnaces, oil refineries, factories, and railroad and shipping facilities that few areas in the world can match. A good share of the industrial muscle of the United States is concentrated in a narrow arc along the curving shore. Though Chicago dominates this industrial empire, it goes by a variety of corporate names. Gary, Hammond, East Chicago, and Whiting are all thriving Indiana industrial towns whose borders merge with each other and with those of its big sister city across the Illinois boundary line. Except for the signs, there is no way of knowing that the crossing of a busy street carries one from one corporate entity to another.

Steel dominates this manufacturing empire, providing the basic product upon which an industrial civilization so heavily depends. Steel is here because abundant, high quality ore from the iron ranges of Michigan, Minnesota, and Canada can be floated at low cost on the Great Lakes to any point where coal and other materials necessary for steelmaking may also be brought economically, and from which the finished product may be supplied quickly and cheaply to the industries dependent upon it. The Gary-Chicago lake front, close to the heart of the industrial Midwest, meets all these requirements. "Chicagoland," as its newspapers love to call this sprawling midwestern commercial and industrial aggregation, would be an important center without steel; with steel, it is one of the leading metropolitan areas of the world.

The Community Setting

The steelmill with which we are concerned is located in a busy in-dustrial town where it is the largest employer. More than fifty other concerns operate plants in the city, most of them having some relation to steel, with oil and chemicals the next most important industries. Expanding employment opportunities attracted large numbers of European immigrants to the city in the period before World War I, and Negroes and Mexicans have come since then as a result of both the 1919 steel strike and restrictions on immigration. Almost one-fourth of the population was foreign-born in 1940, the Poles constituting the largest single national group, with smaller numbers in decreasing order from Hungary, Mexico, Yugoslavia, Czechoslovakia, Rumania, Lithuania, Italy, Greece, and twenty-six other countries. Almost one-fifth of the population consists of foreign-born Poles or children of Polish immigrants; not quite as many have native-born parents.

The town's booming industries, which provide employment to almost one hundred thousand workers, draw their labor force widely from Chicago and many other smaller towns in the area, for the city proper has a population under sixty thousand. Since the city is surrounded on all sides by other cities and the lake, it cannot increase its corporate area. What little vacant land remains within the city limits is virtually all owned by industry and kept in reserve for plant expansion. As a result, perhaps half the workers in the steelmill live outside the corporate limits. Since most living quarters in the city are undesirable, the better-paid workers and higher management officials tend to live elsewhere. All of this contributes to a very noticeable lack of community spirit. Over and over again residents tell visitors that their city is one of the most backward places in the entire country.

This is a very different situation from the usual one where people live and work within the same corporate boundaries and where a union may claim without serious challenge to represent the community interests of a group of people who earn their living as industrial employees. What meaning can the term "community" have in such a situation other than the purely legal one of persons residing within fixed and arbitrary geographical boundaries? On the one hand this truncated community, without an upper class of residents and with a limited middle-class population, provides an unusual opportunity for working-class influence; on the other hand the nonresident character of most of the union leadership and the presence within the union of large numbers of workers with community ties elsewhere lessens the union's interest in local community affairs and reduces its effectiveness when it tries to exert influence.

One way to conceive of such a community, which is hardly one in the usual sociological sense, is as a forum within which competing power groups strive for the loyalty of their members and for the ability to control strategic points where vital decisions are made. The chief power groups in the community include the local industries, which operate through the chamber of commerce for which the single banker in town is the spokesman; the Democratic political machine, whose control has not been seriously challenged for some years; the Catholic church; and the unions, which contribute needed votes on election day and receive their reward in the form of friendly police action during strikes and picketing. The gambling syndicate, which contributes heavily to the political machine as well as to churches and charities in an effort to insure its own uninterrupted operation, has otherwise shown no interest in community needs and problems.[1] Many union members are identified with one or more of these power groups. In collective bargaining and related matters their loyalty may be given wholeheartedly to the union; which leadership they follow in other matters depends largely on their degree of involvement in union affairs.

Union members listed as the individuals or groups who ran the community or comprised its "big shots," in order of frequency, the mayor, other city officials, the banker, the syndicate, the chamber of commerce, and the steel company or its former plant manager. The local union, as the largest organized labor group in a highly unionized town, is potentially the most powerful group, but, interestingly enough, not a single worker mentioned the union or any of its leaders as being among the "big shots" in the community. Asked who was looked up to in the community, union members listed the same individuals or groups, with the addition of the clergy or the Catholic church. Three out of 107 who answered the question also mentioned the union or its officers, two of the three being themselves union leaders.

The Company and Labor-Management Relations

The company, which began its operations in the early years of this century, has steadily expanded until today its annual rated capacity is about four million tons, and its annual production about 4 per cent of

[1] For an appraisal of the syndicate's political influence in the community see E. W. Kenworthy, "This Town Lost the Election," *Survey Graphic,* XXXI (December, 1942), 581–84. Since the field work was conducted, the syndicate is reported to have left the community, although gambling still flourishes on a more decentralized basis.

the country's steel output. It operates blast and open-hearth furnaces, blooming mills, rolling mills, bar and sheetmills, and coke ovens. It owns its own iron ore mine, coal mine, limestone quarry, fluorspar mine, and steamship line. In its expansion program it has acquired a steel-warehousing organization, along with concerns producing fireproof building materials, sheet-metal products, and steel drums and pails.

The company is a progressive and efficient one, led by an able group of executives and enjoying a high earning rate. Its excellent location, modern equipment, and efficient management make it one of the low-cost steel producers in the country. Always in an advantageous competitive position, the company has enjoyed high levels of production and profits as a result of the sustained demand for steel during World War II and the postwar boom. The company has about eighteen thousand employees, of whom more than fourteen thousand are in the bargaining unit. Like the bulk of the steel industry, it has tended to follow the wage pattern set by the United States Steel Corporation.

The first attempt to organize a union among company employees was undertaken in 1918 by the Amalgamated Association of Iron, Steel and Tin Workers, as part of the campaign that led to the steel strike of 1919.[2] The strike was defeated in the company's plant, as in the rest of the industry, and for the following three or four years an Employee Representation Council existed under company sponsorship. There was no further employee organization of any sort in the plant until after the passage of the National Industrial Recovery Act of 1933, when the company again sponsored an employee representation plan. In 1934 the Amalgamated Association of Iron, Steel and Tin Workers made another effort at organization and threatened a strike unless it received recognition. The company, however, made open preparations to defeat a strike, such as by routing railroad dining and sleeping cars into the plant area, and the union ceased its organizing efforts.

The tempo of events speeded up with the establishment by the Committee for Industrial Organization of its Steel Workers Organizing Committee, which sent organizers in the fall of 1936 to work among

[2] For an analysis of the background of the strike see Commission of Inquiry, Interchurch World Movement, *Report on the Steel Strike of 1919* (New York: Harcourt, Brace & Howe, 1920); see also William Z. Foster, *The Great Steel Strike and Its Lessons* (New York: B. W. Huebsch, Inc., 1920). For an earlier study of working conditions and unionism in the industry see John A. Fitch, *The Steel Workers* (New York: Charities Publication Committee, 1911).

company employees. The SWOC increased the intensity of its campaign following its recognition in March, 1937, by the Carnegie-Illinois Steel Corporation, the biggest operating subsidiary of the United States Steel Corporation. A few weeks later the decision of the United States Supreme Court upholding the constitutionality of the National Labor Relations Act sounded the death knell of the employee representation plan, and the company then sought to stimulate the formation of an "independent" union which could compete with the SWOC organizing drive.

Refusal by this and other steel companies to recognize the SWOC led to the bitter "Little Steel" strike of 1937. While National Labor Relations Board hearings on charges of company unfair labor practices were in progress, a strike settlement was negotiated by the governor of the state which provided, along with other terms, that the company would bargain with the union on behalf of its members. While the union-management differences underwent prolonged litigation before the NLRB and in the courts, the company dealt with the union concerning plant problems and grievances, though it refused to sign a collective bargaining agreement. Nevertheless the local union successfully adjusted a number of grievances and obtained many other concessions by negotiating with departmental supervisors and by engaging in militant activities such as sit-down strikes, wildcats, and slowdowns. In the meantime the independent union was captured by SWOC members, who promptly declared it dissolved.

The war emergency gave the union an opportunity, through the machinery of the National War Labor Board, to stablize its position in the plant. In 1942, obeying a WLB order, the company signed its first agreement with the union—an agreement including, among other provisions, wage increases, a maintenance-of-membership clause, and the checkoff of union dues. In August, 1945, a few days prior to V-J Day, the local union conducted a plant-wide work stoppage to compel the reinstatement of its president, who had been discharged for taking an unauthorized vacation. In 1946 the local participated in the nationwide steel strike, and in the following year it shut the plant down again in a disagreement with the company over contract terms. The local took the lead in the industry in insisting that retirement and pension plan provisions were bargainable, opposing the company successfully in grievance procedures, before the NLRB, and in the courts.

At the time the field work was conducted the membership maintenance plan was still in effect in the plant, as generally throughout the industry, combined with the checkoff of union dues. In the fall of 1950, shortly after the interviewing had gotten under way, the bargaining unit of production and maintenance workers authorized the union, in a vote conducted by the NLRB, to seek a union-shop clause, at a time when such union security votes were being conducted generally throughout the industry. The plant under study returned one of the highest votes in favor of authorizing the union shop, 76 per cent of the eligibles voting in favor and only 8 per cent against, with the remainder not voting. The 1952 contract provided for maintenance of membership, together with an escape clause at the expiration of the contract for existing members, and for a modified union shop for new employees, who were required to join the union at the time of employment but who had the right to elect not to become members between fifteen and thirty days after starting work. In 1956 this was changed to provide for a union shop without modification for new workers, combined with membership maintenance for old employees.

Company bargaining with the local union is carried on within the framework of the pattern set by "Big Steel" with the United Steelworkers of America.[3] The company has no difficulty meeting the competitive wage pattern and sees no reason to exceed it except in very minor respects. Like the other smaller steel companies in the country, it holds back in its wage bargaining until the United States Steel Corporation has established the basic rates. The company's bargaining relationship with the union has been of the antagonistic, arm's-length variety, although recently there has been some effort, not altogether successful, to replace suspicion and hostility with a more co-operative spirit.

The Local Union

At the time the field work was conducted the local had almost fourteen thousand dues-paying members. It maintained this large member-

[3] For a review of collective bargaining history and practices in the steel industry see Robert R. R. Brooks, *As Steel Goes...: Unionism in a Basic Industry* (New Haven: Yale University Press, 1940), and the chapter by Frederick H. Harbison in *How Collective Bargaining Works* (New York: Twentieth Century Fund, 1942), pp. 508–70. On postwar collective bargaining developments see Albert Rees, "Postwar Wage Determination in the Basic Steel Industry," *American Economic Review*, XLI (June, 1951), 389–404, and Frank T. DeVyver, "Collective Bargaining in Steel," in *Labor in Postwar America*, ed. Colston E. Warne *et al.* (Brooklyn, N.Y.: Remsen Press, 1949), pp. 387–98.

ship partly because of its prestige among the workers and partly as a result of its militancy in relation both to the company and to non-unionists. The new worker or the older employee who did not wish to join the union found himself subjected to a variety of pressures, ranging from derogatory comments from fellow workers to the dues picket line periodically mounted by the local union.

The dues picket line was a device, used between 1941 and 1948, by which the union posted pickets from time to time over a three-day period at all gates of the mill during shift changes, requiring each worker desiring to enter the mill to show his union membership card. Non-members had to join the union during these dues inspections, climb the fence surrounding the plant to get to work, wait until the picket line dispersed, or return home and lose three days' work. After 1948 the company was able to end dues picketing promptly by threatening to invoke the appropriate sections of the Taft-Hartley Act. Since the modified union-shop agreement was entered into there has been no need for a dues picket line, except perhaps with regard to the three hundred to four hundred old employees who are within the bargaining unit but who are not required by the contract to join the union.

The local union's record of militancy is borne out not only by its use of the dues picket line but also by its long history of aggressive job actions. During the period before it obtained a written contract, and occasionally since then, the union has brought pressure on the company through departmental strikes of the walkout or sit-down variety, or through slowdowns. In the postwar period the slowdown was the weapon most frequently employed, becaused of the difficulty of discovering and penalizing those responsible, and because departmental supervisors, concerned with their production records, were likely to make the necessary concessions. There have been no slowdowns in the plant since early in 1953.

In earlier years, when the company permitted its lower-level supervisors to make their own decisions on grievances, the union was able to use concessions won in one department as precedents to obtain similar concessions elsewhere in the mill. The company put an end to the use of this "whipsaw" tactic by organizing an industrial relations department whose members participate in grievance meetings and study the possible impact on other departments before permitting a settlement favorable to the union. This in turn has led some supervisors on occasion to settle disputed issues orally with the grievance committeeman in his department, without involving members of the industrial relations staff.

The local has a record of independence in its relations with the United Steelworkers of American that matches its militancy in its dealings with the company. In a union in which controls from the national office have traditionally been strong, the local is conspicuous in its opposition to the policies of the national officers.[4] The international representative assigned to service the local—and, incidentally, to help guide and control it—has always had one of the more difficult administrative assignments. The local has given so little co-operation to certain international representatives that the national union has been forced to transfer them.

The local has generally regarded the national officers, along with the particular international representatives assigned to it, as too inclined to compromise, and has preferred to control its own relations with the company whenever possible. In turn, the influence of the international representatives, and therefore of the national union, has usually been exerted on the side of the more moderate faction in local union elections.

The factional alignment in the local was based partly on personalities and partly on a right-left split, on the difference between those who advocated a more cautious and conciliatory policy as against those who demanded more militancy in dealing with the employer. The latter group tended to attract those who were more liberal in their political orientation—those who wanted to go farther than the New Deal or who were attracted to any of the leftist but non-communist political tendencies.[5] The right-wing group consisted mostly of pure-and-simple trade unionists who tended to support the policies of the national officers of the United Steelworkers. Factional organization did not reflect a difference in skill or departmental rivalry. Despite their general ideological differences, the factions were shifting groups, coalescing around popular and ambitious figures who jockeyed

[4] In the 1957 election for president of the United Steelworkers the members of the local voted overwhelmingly for Donald C. Rarick, who headed a protest movement against an increase of union dues, over the incumbent, David J. McDonald.

[5] A few years earlier, several Communists had been active in the political life of the local, but had ceased activity following adoption by the United Steelworkers in 1948 of a constitutional provision making Communists ineligible for nomination or election to any office or even to membership on a committee.

for position and combined forces in different ways in each election as rival slates took form.

Following an election held every other year, the factions tended to be quiescent, permitting the victorious officers to run the local with only a moderate amount of strife. About six months before the next election, however, factional alignments formed again, with the leaders of each group meeting informally to agree upon major candidates and prepare for their more formal caucus meetings. At these meetings, in turn, slates of candidates were worked out, care being taken that the various departments were represented by candidates with wide popular appeal, and that large minority groups such as Negroes and Mexicans were also represented. The position of vice-president of the local is one which traditionally has been held by a Negro. Sometimes dissident slates appeared, made up primarily of minority groups or organized by an independent candidate for president or another leading office.

The Workers and Their Jobs

The workers in the bargaining unit reflect the heterogeneity of the labor force in the surrounding industrial area. Most are white and native-born, though largely of recent immigrant stock; there are many of European birth, substantial minorities of Negroes and Mexicans, and a small but growing number of Puerto Ricans. For the most part semiskilled or unskilled workers, their formal education on the average had ended with the second year of high school. The fathers of half of them had been industrial workers of various degrees of skill; many of the remainder had a rural background, though the fathers of a few had been small businessmen. Two-thirds of the workers were Roman Catholics, reflecting the heavy immigration in the past generation from the largely Catholic countries of central and southern Europe. The Protestants were found chiefly among the skilled workers of northern European descent or among the Negroes. Scattered through the work force, mostly at the higher-skilled levels, were a small number of Jewish workers. Especially in the case of Mexicans and Negroes, but also for many of the whites, the steelmill provided greater earnings[6]

[6] At the time the field work was conducted, the base rate per hour ranged from $1.31 to $2.84 for the 35 job classes in the plant. In addition there was a premium rate of 4 cents an hour on the afternoon shift and 6 cents on the night shift. Incentive rates existed throughout the plant wherever practicable. The 1954 contract raised the hourly base rates from $1.57 for job class 1 to $3.27 for job class 35.

and higher living standards than they or their fathers had ever experienced.

The skilled men in the plant (who included the union leaders and active union members) generally liked their work, which tended to be easier physically, more interesting, better paid, and less subject to close supervision than the jobs assigned other workers. Although most of the less-skilled employees also liked their work or were satisfied with it, a substantial minority had reservations about their jobs, often because of the monotony, hard work, dirt, danger, or the character of the supervision.

Most of the steel workers had a high regard for the company, many of them asserting that it was the best place they knew of to work. Characteristic of such responses was that of a thirty-six-year-old worker who had been with the company for five years: "Treated me very well from the start. Best place I've been so far. As long as you work, they don't bother you. They try to make you feel that you're doing your job right." Some pointed to good working conditions or stressed the fair treatment they had received; still others emphasized the steady employment, the good wages, or the safety program. A number of the workers could think of nothing they disliked. A middle-aged straightener operator commented: "They are easy to get along with. Make a mistake and there isn't too much hell over it." Several distinguished between the company and its foremen, as did an Italian-born roll-turner, a veteran of thirty years: "The company has always been pretty fair with me; it wasn't the company's fault but the fore-man's fault when I was mistreated." There was widespread agreement that "men get a break there."

Some of the workers, particularly the active unionists, gave the union a lot of credit for making the company a desirable one for which to work. Typical of these was a roll-line operator in the plate-mill who had worked fifteen years in the plant: "As long as you're holding a stick over them it's OK. If there was no union, none of us would like anything about the company. If there wasn't any union, we'd go back to the days in 1935 and it would be hell. . . . The men aren't fired anymore like they used to be because of the union." Large numbers of the workers, while expressing no enthusiasm for the company, found no fault with it, on the ground that it was "no better or worse than any other steel company," or that "anywhere you go you've got to work." A middle-aged keeper on a blast furnace, asked whether he disliked anything about the company, commented philosophically that, "Like my wife, there was something I didn't like about her. Always room for improvement."

Some of the employees could think of nothing about the company that they liked. "Just a job, that's about all," was the usual reaction of these men. Others complained about the treatment of workers, asserting that "they try to put something over on you," or that "you've got to fight for your rights." Other sources of dissatisfaction included working conditions, supervision, the safety program, shift work and scheduling, and lack of company co-operation with the union. An active member complained that: "Top management has forced the local union to strike for every gain. Things they fully intended to give us, that we asked for, we have to strike for. That's my main gripe. Every time they concede anything to the union you have to strike for it."

Among minority groups there was some complaint that Negroes and Mexicans were discriminated against by being given for the most part the worst jobs and being denied fair promotion opportunities. Many of their white fellow workers agreed that this criticism was justified, sometimes adding that the discrimination was due to the prejudices of lower-level supervisors rather than company policy. The company, for its part, asserted that its policy was to hire and promote on merit, without regard to race, religion, or national origin. It was our observation that practices with regard to the hiring and promotion of Negroes and Mexicans varied from department to department, depending on the attitude of the supervisor and of the union grievanceman. Certain departments, usually at high levels of skill, remained "lily-white" because the supervisor believed that Negroes and Mexicans lacked the necessary aptitude or training, or because he thought that his men would not want to share locker rooms with members of minority groups. Where the union grievanceman shared this attitude, no Negroes or Mexicans were employed, or, if employed, they were kept in less desirable jobs. A union grievance committeeman who objected to discrimination of this sort, however, could force the company supervisor to promote with due regard to seniority and ability, as provided in the contract.

It was an interesting fact that discrimination could exist in many departments, readily apparent to anyone who cared to look, despite strong pronouncements against discrimination by both the company and union. The company, interested primarily in production, did not go out of its way to discipline competent supervisors for prejudice against minorities; and union officials, though campaigning for office on platforms opposing discrimination, were anxious for support from "lily-white" departments and did not wish to court trouble with fellow unionists there.[7]

Joining the Union[8]

Effective unionism had begun in the plant only a dozen years before the study was begun, and a written contract with a union security clause had been in effect for only seven years. It was still possible for workers to be employed in the bargaining unit without being union members, and about 5 per cent were non-members at the time. Joining the union was a decision that each member had had to make.

Interviews were held with 114 members, of whom 28 were leaders, 24 active members, and the remaining 62 inactive members.[9] The great majority in each of the three groups—86 per cent of the leaders, 83 per cent of the actives, and 61 per cent of the rank-and-file inactives joined with some degree of conviction or sympathy. This large group listed family background, prior work experiences, or experience while in the company's employ as responsible for their pro-union orientation at the time of joining. Smaller numbers joined under the informal pressure of their fellow workers or as a result of dues inspection lines; some who joined under such circumstances were favorably disposed toward the union, while others were indifferent or opposed to it.

Among those who gave family background as an explanation for joining were several whose fathers had been members of the Industrial Workers of the World, the United Mine Workers, or other labor organizations and who held strong pro-union convictions. One of the leaders, son of a union miner, stated, "I attended union meetings with

[7] This situation has changed since the field work was conducted. The 1954 contract contains a stronger clause providing that there should be no discrimination against any employee because of race, color, religious belief, or national origin.

[8] For a fuller treatment of this subject see the authors' article, "Why Workers Join Unions," *Annals of the American Academy of Political and Social Science*, CCLXXIV (March, 1951), 75–84.

[9] Active members were defined as those who had attended between four and seven union meetings in the past year, and inactive members as those who had attended none.

my father before I was ever inside a church." Another remembered when he was a small boy attending socialist meetings with his father. An inactive member said, "My dad was a great union man and that's where I got it—if it wasn't union, it wasn't no good." Another inactive, who followed his father into the company's employ, had already seen the benefits that his father received through the union, and joined for that reason. One of the few women members had also come from a mining family whose head was strongly pro-union: "I've heard about unions off and on since I can remember. My father was blackballed in the Alabama mines for his union activity and that's why we came up here. He thinks that John L. Lewis can do no wrong, is the greatest man in the country. Well, I didn't hesitate about signing. I guess I was one of the first in the department." With one of the leaders it was family poverty that had made him pro-union at an early age: "I was union-minded long before I came here. . . . Family background is one of constant struggle during the depression. Even as a kid you hate the bosses when you know there is plenty, yet the family hasn't a thing."

With others it was prior work or union experience that had made them union sympathizers before they entered the company's employ. Many of these had been members of other unions, and several, even among the inactives, had been union officers earlier. "I always belonged to the union every place I worked," and "I'm a union man from way back," were typical responses. One of the Mexicans in the inactive group who had belonged to a union in his native country said, "I see that any people without organization are worthless." Others with earlier union experience, however, had been wholly unconvinced by it and did not join the steel union until they became interested for other reasons or were forced to join. Still, the existence of a core of workers with pro-union sympathies helps explain the rapid success of the organizing drives in the 1930's.

Thirty-nine per cent of the leaders, 21 per cent of the actives, and 15 per cent of the rank-and-file inactives stated that they were made sympathetic to unionism by experiences at the plant. With some workers it was a single episode; with others it was the general treatment they received. Examples of the former were men who were discharged for offenses they considered minor or who felt that they were improperly charged with misdeeds of one sort or another. Several complained that under non-union conditions they were "pushed around" too much. One inactive member explained in broken English, "Somebody told me it was good and foreman not holler at you, so I joined." A leader said he expected to stay with the company "because they did so much harm to me between 1933 and 1939 that it will take thirty years more for me to repay them."

Once the union was established in the plant, its machinery provided an incentive for employees with grievances to join in an effort to get adjustments. Two inactives had joined under such circumstances. "I was getting less days than I should have and different pay rates," one said; "a fellow said that I should get into the union and let them take care of it and I did." Another, who had language difficulty, said, "When I had case, I joined."

A number of the workers, including two who later became leaders in the organization, joined as a result of pro-union talk in the plant or organizing speeches. Their responses indicated only a very mild pro-union orientation at the time of joining. One of the leaders said: "I heard the fellows talk about it in the mill. They were all saying that you can't get any place by yourself, but you have to get the guys together and then maybe you can do something." One of the inactives was influenced by President Roosevelt as well as by his fellow employees: "In the campaign in 1936–37, the workers got together and wanted to organize and then, too, President Roosevelt told us to organize the working class. So we did." This reaction, which was fairly common in the 1930's, illustrates the extent to which the appeal of unionism depends upon a generally favorable social and political climate.

Another active unionist reacted primarily in terms of the personality of the grievance committeeman or "griever" in his department: "When the union was coming up, the first grievance committeeman we had came to me and asked me to join, but I didn't want to. This griever was an old rum-head who used to come to work drunk, and so I thought what the hell kind of union is this. But the next election we had he was beaten and the new griever that got the job was a good man and I joined when he asked me."

Not all who entered the union did so willingly, however. A number joined with doubts, with indifference, or even despite their opposition, as a result of various pressures. Sometimes their doubts related to unionism in general, sometimes to the particular union operating in the plant. Fully a fourth of the inactive members had joined without caring one way or the other. In most cases the workers asserted that their attitudes had changed as a result of union experience, almost always in a direction more favorable to the union. Several of those who joined without conviction later became enthusiastic members and were elected to positions of leadership.

A number reported that they joined because others were doing so. As one who later became a leader said: "I didn't know anything about the union. Another fellow persuaded me. I suppose I joined in order to jump in line with the majority to say I was a union member. It didn't mean much to me at that time." Another volunteered to join just three weeks after he started work, when his fellow workers talked about the union one day. "I always figured that if you're working with a bunch of men and they're all union members, you should be, too," he said.

An unusual case was that of a foreign-born worker who became a member because he had been allowed to use the union hall without charge: "I had a boy to be baptized and needed a hall. A man give me hall free and then ask me to join. I figure I get hall free so I give him a dollar. At that time, I no figure there be a union there. Afterwards, I know I would have to join but I in already."

A few members joined the union, despite their opposition, because of the informal pressures in their work group. One of the inactives did not want to argue with fellow workers who were already members. Another who was and still is opposed to unionism yielded to avoid constant pressure: "It was like compulsory—you had to. They approached you, kept after you, hounded you. To get them off my neck, I joined. In my opinion there shouldn't be a union. If I had a plant, I would never have a union because I would treat the men right and pay them right. That's the only reason you have unions." Occasionally there was reference to a fear of violence, as on the part of one worker who personally had wanted to join, but who added: "It's just about a must—whether you want to sign or not, it's a good idea unless you want to get your car turned over or your head conked in."

A few had joined when barred from the mill by a dues inspection line. Some of these, however, were not opposed to becoming members, but had merely delayed signing a card. One man who had had a low opinion of the union because it was made up of "radicals stirring up a lot of trouble" joined during one of the dues inspections at the suggestion of his foreman: "One of the foremen convinced me to join because everybody else was joining. A couple of times I climbed over the fence to get into the mill. The foreman said that instead of holding men out of the plant, we might as well join and get our production going." It is interesting to note that, by the time the study was conducted, this man had become one of the leaders of the union.

These responses show that the reasons for joining a union depend upon concrete circumstances and do not fit neatly into any preconceived motivational scheme. Such factors as prior union sympathy, informal group pressure, and militant union tactics of the dues-inspection-line type are of crucial importance.

Reactions to Non-Members

Members were asked why the 5 per cent of non-members refused to join. The chief reasons given emphasized the fear of antagonizing the company, the desire to get benefits without paying dues, dislike of unions in general, and the feeling that the local did nothing for the workers. The leaders overwhelmingly stressed the desire for promotion or fear of the employer, reflecting, perhaps, their unwillingness to consider factors involving criticism of their performance as union officials. "Some are company stooges who think they can get ahead by not joining the union" was a characteristic remark.

There was general agreement that "free riding"—the willingness to accept union benefits without helping to pay the cost—was an important reason for not joining. Except for representation in case of a grievance, all workers enjoyed the same benefits whether or not they were union members. As one inactive member said: "Some just figure two dollars a month to use for something else; others say they get the same benefits and why should they pay dues."

Another reason, more often suggested by the rank-and-file members, was that some of those who did not join the union were simply ignorant of the benefits to be gained. This, they thought, was particularly true of the younger ones who had entered the industry when the union was already established. One of the inactive members, an immigrant who still spoke in broken English, felt that the failure to join was due to a combination of ignorance of union achievements and a desire to save union dues: "Some of them don't know what union do for us before. . . . Some kick for pay two dollars and spend ten dollars in saloon. Company call him to pay Red Cross or Community Fund, he pay—but every month he cry like baby when two dollars are taken off."

Also widespread was the belief that non-members had a general dislike of unionism because of their family background or the anti-unionism of the daily press or school system. One such explanation referred to "the environment they've been under all the time, the propaganda they hear about the union." A leader felt that this had been particularly true of veterans: "The GI's were the hardest fellows for a long time, not the ones who worked in the mills before they went into the service but the new ones. The papers and the company did a job on them and they fell for it."

Some thought that use of the dues inspection line as an organizing technique turned people against the union, since many resented "being pushed around and pressured." An active member who emphasized this reason stated: "A lot of guys see what they do at the gates and they won't join for hell. If you tell a man he has to do something, it turns you against it. It turned me against them and I was already a member. I don't like to see that kind of stuff." One of the leaders argued, however, that dues inspections were popular with the union members: "The average guy in the mill likes the dues inspection line because during the last session they kept asking, 'did you get the so-and-so? He isn't any better than we are—get [him].'"

Union Achievements

The achievements of the union in the plant have to be considered against the background of industry practices regarding wages and related matters. Like other steel establishments, the company has always maintained a level of direct wages and other benefits comparable to those of the pattern-setter in the industry. It did so during its non-union and company union periods, and it has continued to do so in its bargaining with the United Steelworkers. Despite its favorable profit position, it refuses to exceed the industry standard except in minor respects, and the union, even if it wanted to, lacks the economic power to compel the company to increase its labor costs significantly above those of its competitors. For these reasons the accomplishments of the local have been in the areas of working conditions, job security, and treatment by foremen rather than in that of wages.

A typical view of the local's accomplishments was expressed by a tinmill worker with fifteen years of service: "They've done a lot of things: safety, clean locker rooms, bus service inside the plant, canteens—I can't think of all the major items. Working conditions in the cold strip and tinmill are better than in any other place. I don't know, but the boys told me that conditions were rough before the union. I understand that if the foreman didn't like the color of your hair, he wouldn't promote you, or could even get rid of you if he wanted to. Now that's all eliminated." One of his fellow workers graphically described the improvement in working conditions: "Before, 130 men drank out of one water bucket. There was no locker room, no place to put our lunches. All that has been eliminated. Now we have lockers, shower rooms, and we don't have to get the bosses drunk on pay day to keep our jobs. That's a thing of the past."

Most of the rank-and-file members asserted that workers had been badly treated by supervisors before the union was organized; they agreed almost unanimously that treatment was good now because of the existence of the union. Part of the result was greater job security: the arbitrary power of foremen to discharge workers had been curbed, with the result that the men were no longer "afraid for their jobs." Equally important were the personal relations with supervisors. Union members declared that foremen now treated them with respect, gave their instructions in a civil fashion, avoided threats and cursing, and listened when a worker wished to say something to them. Behind this changed attitude lay the company's realization that, from a long-range view of productivity and profits, it was more important to have a satisfied work force than one driven by fear; and also the knowledge that a worker who felt mistreated would likely report the fact to union officers, who might take the issue to higher company officials.

Members of minority groups were among those who valued highly the greater respect shown by supervisors since the union was organized. One of the Mexican leaders of the union, who asserted that improved working conditions had been won for all "regardless of race, creed, or color," added: "I have been able to be respected by supervision. They have had to come up to me and respect me, which is a wonderful thing, since I'm a Mexican. In the old days they would say, 'Hey you!' Now they ask you to help civilly." A worker who felt that treatment by foremen had improved "one hundred per cent" stressed name-calling by foremen as one of the evils that had been eliminated: "They don't come around any more and call you a God-damn Hunky or a God-damn Polack like they used to. In 1935 the foreman would come up and tell you to do something, and if you hesitated, he'd fire you on the spot. No more. Pay day would come around and if you didn't give the boss a couple of cigars, off you went. You were treated like an animal—never knew where or when you'd work."

A number of the workers, including both whites and members of minority groups, also credited the union with reducing the amount of discrimination in the mill by opening up new jobs for Negroes and Mexicans and giving them more security and greater opportunities for promotion. "If it wasn't for the local," a Negro sheetmill operator asserted, "the colored guys would still get fired and whites would get hired." One of the Mexican workers, while convinced that the union protected Mexicans from arbitrary dismissal, was critical of union representatives in some departments for permitting discrimination regarding promotion: "They can't fire a Mexican like they used to. The union protects them. . . . We have seniority now, but I've seen departments where Mexican men have high seniority but the representative of the union doesn't do anything for them. They don't get the same chances for promotion." Others criticized the union for not moving more energetically to "crack lily-white departments."

Some of the workers, while appreciative of the gains achieved by the union, were critical of one or another phase of its operations. Much of the dissatisfaction centered around the grievance procedure, either because of its slowness or because of the lack of interest or aggressiveness of the particular grievance committeeman. A rank-and-file member complained that his griever often said that he was too busy to handle a complaint; as a result, he added, "we don't have a union . . . all we're doing is paying dues." Other members objected to the checkoff, the periodic dues inspections, or the centralized control over strikes. Some of the skilled workers complained that the union had done relatively little for craftsmen while obtaining substantial improvements for the less-skilled workers, and among the Mexicans there were objections because the union had not had the contract translated into Spanish.

Many of the union members, including actives, inactives, and leaders, took the union's wage achievements at face value, giving it credit for whatever pay increases it negotiated. "If it wasn't for the union," a millwright with a long background of union experience said, "the men would be practically slaves as far as wages are concerned." Only a few

81

of the better-informed workers recognized that the local had relatively little influence on the wage level.

Union leaders' accounts of the achievements of the union are subject to bias, since they are in effect appraising their own accomplishments; even the newly elected leaders are estimating the achievements of an institution which they now head and represent to the management and the public. The authors also studied opinion within the management hierarchy, however, and found that the management group as a whole credited the union with important contributions to the well-being of the workers, the company, or both.[10] The union was given credit by various officials for raising wages, for reducing inequities, for improving working conditions, for establishing a grievance procedure, and for improving the safety program. It was also credited with getting the company to improve sanitation, provide more adequate locker facilities, improve the lunchrooms, and institute transportation facilities within the plant area. It is significant that all areas in which the union claimed credit for achievements were mentioned by management officials.

The representatives of management overwhelmingly agreed that supervisors have been less arbitrary in their treatment of employees since the union was organized. They listed fairer scheduling of work assignments, more respect shown the employees, the establishment of a grievance procedure, the reduction of discrimination, and the elimination of many bad managerial practices among the improvements due to the presence of the union. Several officials emphasized that men could no longer be bullied as in the old non-union days and that the union had effected very desirable changes in the manner of treating employees. In the words of a general foreman: "I came in those days when a foreman was king and the superintendent was God. The foreman would come out to the gate when they were hiring, and there would be a bunch of men out there looking for jobs, and the foreman would say 'I'll pick this fellow or this fellow or that one,' and then you had to stay on the right side of the foreman, no matter how good or bad you were. The foreman could order the men around like a bunch of cattle. But not any more. They had to keep on the good side of the foreman by giving them some kind of contribution on pay day. But

[10] For a fuller treatment of this subject see the authors' article "Management Views the Local Union," *Journal of Business*, XXVI (April, 1953), 91–102.

now they're getting to understand that a worker is a man, too. I was a foreman in those days and I know how it was."

On the negative side of the ledger some members of management believed that the union was responsible for forcing the company to retain lazy and incompetent workers, for restricting production, and for reducing through the seniority system the incentive for workers to be ambitious and seek advancement.

Strikes and Slowdowns

Most of the union leaders, a somewhat smaller percentage of the active membership, and a small number of the inactives considered strikes to be always justified. A typical statement was that "the only weapon the working man has is the strike." Some emphasized the cost of striking as an indication that workers would never shut down a plant unless there were serious grievances. As an active member put it: "To get the guys on strike you've got to have issues. It's a hell of a job to get the men to shut it down and it's got to be over the boiling point before the guys will do it." A similar idea was expressed by one of the officers of the local: "Men don't strike unless they have good reason for it. They know that when they strike, they lose money and that hurts. But that doesn't stop them. There's always a good reason." Several of the officers and active members asserted that strikes were never lost regardless of the immediate outcome, because management would remember and respect labor's show of strength.

Among the inactive members the prevailing opinion was that strikes were sometimes justified and sometimes not. A similar view was held by a substantial number of the leaders and active rank-and-file members. Some drew a distinction between important issues such as higher wages or better working conditions, which affected everyone and for which they were willing to strike, and less significant matters affecting only a few. Others argued that a strike should be called only as a last resort, as when management refused to make a reasonable compromise, and many emphasized the losses that both they and the company suffered during a strike. There were a small number of inactive members, finally, who asserted that strikes were unnecessary, usually on the ground that differences between union and management could always be settled by negotiation or arbitration.

Workers were also questioned about their attitude toward picketing, a strike activity that arouses emotional overtones among convinced unionists. Many of them engage in picketing because they consider it their duty, just as soldiers have a duty to fight, and old-timers swap picket-line stories the way war veterans retell their exploits. A "good union man," who has internalized the standards of behavior expected of unionists, would never think of crossing a picket line, except in an unusual case specifically authorized by his union. To workers less involved emotionally, picketing may simply be an unwelcome assignment to be avoided if possible. Because the picket line is so crucial in the life of a union, often serving as a measure of its strength and influencing its bargaining effectiveness, workers' attitudes about picket-line duty or crossing a picket line are very revealing of their attitude toward the union.

Since the company had made no attempt since the 1930's to operate during a strike, picketing had come to be largely symbolic. Nevertheless, union leaders and active members, along with a minority of the inactives, felt an obligation to picket regularly whether or not they were specifically assigned to duty. Often they took pride in the number of times they had picketed or in their exploits on the picket line.

Most of the rank-and-file members, however, were content to picket as little as possible, coming only when specifically called by the union. Often, it was evident, they responded to group pressure with little feeling of involvement. Several picketed rather than incur a fine that they said was levied against those who failed to serve their turn. During a recent strike the union committee had refused to certify to the welfare authorities as needing relief anyone who failed to picket, and one worker actually stated that he picketed in order to be eligible for relief. A number had not picketed during this strike because they were not called, because they disapproved of the way picketing was being conducted, or because picketing was "a waste of time" since the company was making no effort to operate and they knew that no workers would get into the plant.

Less dramatic than the strike, but requiring an even greater degree of group co-operation, is the slowdown, a form of on-the-job activity in which workers, while appearing to be engaged in their usual routines, deliberately limit their output in order to exert pressure upon management. The slowdown calls for a high degree of solidarity and careful organization, since it requires the co-operation of all, or almost all, workers in the unit concerned if it is to prove successful. It may be carried on with or without formal union sanction; indeed, because it so often constitutes a violation of the contract as well as of company regulations, union leaders may go to great pains to avoid official responsibility, whatever their share in its organization or leadership may be. The slowdown is hard to identify, since workers appear to be performing their jobs in the usual manner. The employer is apt to assert that a slowdown is in progress whenever he fails, for reasons that he cannot otherwise explain, to get the anticipated volume of production, whereas from the workers' point of view they may simply not be responding to an incentive rate too low to provoke any effort beyond the minimum necessary to hold the job.

The mill has experienced a number of slowdowns; because these were concentrated in certain departments, however, most workers had never participated in any. While a majority supported the tactic as justifiable in special situations, there were strong objections on the part of a substantial minority, usually on the grounds that it violated the grievance procedure or that a strike should have been called instead. The lower pay earned by piece workers during a slowdown also operated as a deterrent to some. Most workers who had engaged in slowdowns participated freely, though instances were reported of social pressure against those who refused to co-operate.

Most slowdowns in the mill have been caused by dissatisfaction with the incentive rate: workers have felt that the additional sums to be earned by increased production were not worth the effort required. One slowdown in effect when the interviewing was conducted arose from an increase in the base rate in a department without an adjustment in the incentive rate: "Now, practically, no incentive exists. So now they figure that they might as well take their time. Instead of patching things up they do a thorough job. Go for parts and spend time on the way. Actually we don't declare it a slowdown. We just say there's no incentive, so why hurry."

Another group of slowdowns occurred over the issue of the volume of work expected, as when the company required higher production or demanded the same output from a smaller crew or a group operating with less equipment. Still others originated in efforts to force action in a dispute without waiting for settlement by means of the slower grievance procedure; other issues that gave rise to slowdowns included alleged violations of the seniority provisions of the contract and company efforts to discipline workers. In another case the workers slowed down in protest against the unco-operative attitude of a newly appointed foreman: "They promoted a man who didn't know beans and he wouldn't play ball with the boys, so they slowed the job down and wouldn't do a thing till he told them to do it. Things were getting bad until the company got wise and put the guy straight."

In most instances where slowdowns occurred the affected workers participated freely, since all of them smarted under the same grievance. There were occasions, however, where one or more workers were unwilling to participate at first. The pressures used on such an individual were, perhaps with rare exceptions, of the social variety; fellow workers argued with him and, if he persisted in his opposition, called him names or ostracized him: "We put pressure on the men who don't co-operate voluntarily, by ostracism. Nobody will talk to him—we give him the silent cure. Nobody tells him anything, although he's free to come to group meetings. We apply the same pressure to anybody we catch fraternizing with him." Usually the need to be part of a group and to have friendly relations with his co-workers persuaded the reluctant employee to go along with the others.

A union officer told of an unwilling worker in his department who was forced to co-operate: "I told him to get in line or we'll take action against him and he got in line," he said. What that worker understood by "action" is open to conjecture, though not one rank-and-file member reported any instance of actual violence or threats of violence against workers refusing to participate in a slowdown; in the higher ranks of management, however, it was widely believed that such forms of pressure were used.

Aspirations of Steel Workers

The steel workers, despite their various criticisms, were on the whole favorably disposed toward their company and, with few exceptions, expected to remain there permanently. Many of middle age and beyond who planned to stay pointed to their age or to their investment in the pension and retirement system. A fifty-six-year-old car bracer, for example, said that he expected to remain "until age sixty-five, and then get my pension. At my age, I can't leave and go to another place." Others, like a thirty-nine-year-old helper in the open hearth with seventeen years of service, did not intend to leave because he had "lots of seniority and [made] better than four hundred dollars a month and that's good dough." A tinmill worker in his mid-forties also expected to continue: "As far as I can see, unless I go into some kind of business. As far as different factories are concerned, it's too late to build up seniority anywhere else."

A note of defeatism was apparent in many of the responses; a number of the workers planned to stay until retirement not because of positive advantages the company offered but because they saw no alternative. "You have to work somewhere" was a typical response, and one said he would remain with the company "unless some miracle comes up." An Armenian-born worker in a shipping department was another who gave the impression of being trapped in the company's employ. "I'm forty-nine," he said in broken English; "where do I go? Go no place. I think so, if I no die."

Only a relatively small group did not anticipate permanent employment at the mill. Most of these hoped to buy farms or open up small businesses, such as a neighborhood grocery, an automobile repair shop, or an electrical contracting business. Most fortunate was the union leader who already owned a farm and could look forward to returning to it when his children's schooling had been completed: "I have a farm. My children are growing up and I'm getting to the point where I don't have to look up to this company for a living. What I expect to do is give my children a good education so they won't have to come into a God-damn mill and work, and I think I'm succeeding. After my responsibilities are over, I'll go back to my farm." Those who hoped to go into business for themselves had far less chance to achieve their goal—a fact of which they were usually conscious—and yet they found relief from the frustrations of factory life by planning for or dreaming of the day when they would manage an enterprise of their own. A few others, who disliked the health hazards of steelmill employment, the difficulty of the work, or the changing shifts, had no dreams of leaving the ranks of wage-earners, but hoped, nevertheless, to find more agreeable jobs in other industries.

Only a small minority had any expectation of being promoted to a supervisory position. Large numbers felt that the company preferred men better educated than themselves, some thinking it inevitable that educational background should be stressed, while others resented the bringing in of college men to be trained as supervisors. It was widely believed, especially among the active unionists, that favoritism was the most important factor in promotion to foreman, with ability of far less consequence. On the other hand the company had offered supervisory posts to several union officers, evidently influenced by their demonstrated leadership and the need for supervisors who could get along with the union. Rank-and-file members, while rating favoritism or "connections" high, thought that ability and educational background were much more important considerations for promotion.

Negroes and Mexicans together comprised about a third of the production force in the mill; none of the Negroes and only one of the Mexicans believed that he could ever become a foreman. Negroes asserted that "they don't promote colored," whereas the Mexicans usually ascribed their lack of opportunity to poor education or lack of command of the English language. One of the Negroes argued that discrimination prevented workers of his race from holding the positions from which foremen were selected. "Most foremen," he asserted, "come out of the heater sequence and there are no colored workers in the heater sequence. A couple of years ago two colored men were put on a heater-helper's job, but the foreman made it so tough on them that they couldn't continue. He put more work on them than on any white workers."

Some workers of eastern European birth or descent believed that foremen were never chosen from among their nationality groups, and that ability was far less important than national origin. A first helper on an open hearth, for example, a native-born worker of Polish descent, remarked: "I'm a Hunky and a Hunky has no chance. Your name has to be Smith or Reilly or something like that. For the foreman's job, ability don't mean a thing. If ability counted, half the foremen would be taken off because they have no ability."

Many workers considered the foreman's job unattractive, often because of the changes in personal relationships that would result. Asked whether he would like to be a foreman, one answered, "No, I want to keep what friends I have." Another, more doubtful, offered this explanation: "Well, I don't know, sometimes 'yes' and sometimes 'no.' As far as a steady job and security, 'yes,' but you create a lot of enemies. It seems that everybody who is made a supervisor does a good job for a while and then bang, he becomes a bastard. I guess they are afraid of their jobs and they have to push the boys." Others disliked the foreman's position on the grounds that he had too much responsibility, he received insufficient support from higher management, he was caught between management and the union, he could not possibly satisfy everybody, or he did not receive enough compensation for all his "grief."

Generally the steel workers hoped for better things for their children than they themselves had enjoyed. They wanted their sons to be better educated so they could "get somewhere"—an admission that most of them had failed in their own eyes to do that. They showed great trust in education as a means of obtaining more interesting work, greater economic security, or increased prestige. The recognized professions, such as medicine, law, engineering, and teaching, were mentioned frequently, along with white-collar jobs and skilled industrial work. The well-paid, highly skilled men could afford to educate their sons for white-collar employment; the less-skilled generally hoped that their sons would qualify for skilled industrial jobs. Most wanted their sons to stay out of the steelmill, though some were willing to have them enter the company's employ provided they first received enough education to qualify for the better jobs. A smaller number saw no objection to having their sons work for the company; in a few cases this had already happened and the fathers were quite satisfied with the results.

Disappearance of the Union

Almost all the workers asserted that the disappearance of their local would matter to them. They were most concerned about a return to arbitrary and oppressive acts by supervisors; many believed that jobs would be insecure, that favoritism rather than seniority would determine promotions, that pressure on workers would increase, and that they would be pushed around. There was only occasional mention of reduced wages.

Most of the rank-and-file union members feared a reversion to the unlimited power of the foremen. "We would go back to the old whipping days," said a middle-aged crane operator; "in the old days, the foremen would swear at you in any language they were in the mood for." A millwright thought that the disappearance of the union "would be like stepping back two thousand years; go back to common slavery." A foreign-born motor inspector expressed a similar idea: "Oh, boy, we gotta be slave again. I don't want union to disappear. Might as well go to jail, that's all. Used to be, if foreman want to fire, he do it. Not anymore. I think the majority the same way." "If you made one little mistake you would be out, if they wanted you out," another worker declared.

A small minority, however, said that the loss of the union would not disturb them personally because they were good workers, because the company was benevolent, or because the union had done nothing for them in the past. These few sometimes argued that the strongest union supporters were poor workers or "goldbricks" who couldn't keep their jobs without union protection. Some of the staunch unionists, on the other hand, were apt to identify workers who would be glad to see the union go as "stooges" or as friends of foremen who could then be promoted without regard to seniority. Others suggested that those with no experience in the mill under non-union conditions, such as the younger workers or men newly arrived from the rural South, would be those least concerned about the union's disappearance.

These steel workers as a group, it is evident, think highly of their company as an employer, and highly of their union as an agency to insure fair treatment. Their appreciation for the achievements of their union in the past, and their reliance on it for benefits and security in the future, are far greater than the low level of formal participation in local affairs would lead one to expect. Unionism is no hothouse development here; it is a tough growth that has taken root and thrived in an unfriendly environment and that is prepared, if necessary, to battle storms in an effort to survive.

5

METAL WORKERS
Factionalism and Conflict

The casual visitor to the Chicago metropolitan area cannot help but notice the steelmills and oil refineries near the bend of the lake, the stockyards a few miles southwest of the Loop, or the network of railroads clustering in the city. What he is less likely to notice are the industrial plants that ring Chicago, many of them located well beyond the city's limits. The presence of steel and other raw materials, excellent transportation facilities, and a large and skilled labor force, together with its location near wealthy cities and prosperous farms in the heartland of America, have combined to make Chicago one of the country's leading manufacturing centers.

The Plant and Its Two Operating Companies

The plant with whose workers we are concerned in this chapter, and the local union into which they are organized, have gone through two distinct phases. The plant was one of the large ones built by the United States government during the defense boom of 1941 as part of the effort to transform the country into an "arsenal of democracy." From 1941 until the end of the war the plant turned out aircraft engines for bombers, providing peak employment for about ten thousand workers.

By late 1941 the employees had organized into a local of the United Automobile Workers of the CIO, which in the following spring won sole bargaining rights for production employees. Subsequently the local obtained a union security clause providing for maintenance of membership, combined with an escape provision of which very few workers took advantage. The local followed the leadership of Walter Reuther in the bitter and incessant factional conflicts that preceded his rise to the union presidency. In its relations with management the local was militant, just as management was tough. Several cases that arose within the plant raised issues of nationwide significance, and went to the National War Labor Board for final settlement.

At the 1943 and 1944 conventions of the UAW the delegates from the local sought to abrogate the wartime no-strike pledge, and its officers urged the membership, in the nationwide referendum conducted by the UAW after the 1944 convention, to vote against continuing the pledge. In the spring of 1945 the local, incensed by the upgrading of workers without regard to seniority and by management's failure to settle the issue, took a strike vote, but the company bargained swiftly and the strike was averted. Before the issue was resolved Nazi Germany collapsed, and production was cut back sharply.

In September, 1945, following the surrender of Japan, the plant ceased operations. Two months later it was purchased from the government by a leading manufacturer of farm equipment and other products, which still owns and operates it. Early in 1946 the new owners began to hire workers, and in April of that year, with the setting up of production lines, the labor force expanded rapidly. By midsummer a UAW organizing committee, led by unionists who had been active in the plant during the war period, was again enrolling members. Some former officials of the old local were denied employment by the new management, however, on the ground that hiring them might subject the company to charges by some other union of unfair labor practices. The new UAW organization kept the number of the old local, issued a monthly paper under the same name, and in other ways maintained its continuity despite the change of ownership and of product. For a time the UAW committee was challenged by a rival group affiliated with the Farm Equipment Workers of the CIO; this rivalry was settled by an NLRB election held in November, 1946, in which the UAW was chosen the bargaining agent by an overwhelming vote.

The present owners operate a string of plants throughout the United States, in addition to facilities in foreign countries. The plant with which this chapter is concerned produces diesel engines for industrial power purposes and crawler tractors used in highway and other construction work as well as in logging operations. The company's concentration in the manufacture of heavy equipment for construction and farm use makes it peculiarly sensitive to the demands of the market; relatively minor changes in business conditions, so far as the general economy of the country is concerned, can cause major shifts in the company's level of operations.

The company, which employs well over fifty thousand workers, carries on collective bargaining relationships with more than two hundred local unions affiliated with about twenty national unions, some in the old AFL, some in the former CIO, and some independent. It has a reputation for being tough in bargaining and for holding unions at arm's length. Shortly after the field work had been concluded, however, there was some evidence that the company was trying to change its policy in the direction of a more harmonious union-management relationship. The company has been a leader in such personnel practices as apprenticeship programs, leadership training for promising employees, foreman education, and integration of minority groups into the labor force.

The Local Union

The local has always been an active and lively one, with vigorous factionalism in its internal political life and militancy in its relations with management. In both these respects it has carried on the traditions it developed during its earlier wartime period. When the local was reorganized, during the reconversion period, the constant bickering between Reuther and his factional opponents within the national UAW organization was reflected within the affairs of the local. Most of the leaders of the local were associated with the Reuther caucus, which has stood, among other things, for aggressive dealings with management and for opposition to the influence of Communists within the union. Until the local elected its own officers, however, it was governed by an administrator allied with the rival Thomas-Addes[1] caucus, then in control of the national union. The first local election, held early in 1947, produced an anti-Reuther administration. In the following year Reuther's supporters won control of the local, and they were

[1] R. J. Thomas was then president of the UAW and George F. Addes was secretary-treasurer. Though their caucus was composed primarily of conservative unionists, a small but well-organized group of Communists was influential within it. At the UAW convention held in March, 1946, Reuther was elected president by a narrow margin, though his factional opponents elected most of the other officers and a majority of the executive board. The Reuther group consolidated its control of the national union at the November, 1947, convention. For an account of the factional life of the union see Irving Howe and B. J. Widick, *The UAW and Walter Reuther* (New York: Random House, 1949).

still in control when the field work was conducted four years later.

From the regime of the administrator through the period when the field work was carried on the local's relationship with the company was a stormy one. During the earliest period, following the local's winning of exclusive bargaining rights, its relations with management were governed by an interim agreement signed in December, 1946. The agreement, however, lacked provision for the arbitration of grievances, with the result that management had the final word in every case that arose. During 1947 the local called several brief walkouts to express its dissatisfaction with the operation of the grievance procedure and to bring pressure on the company to enter its first regular contract with the union, which was signed later that year. In 1948 there was an eleven-day strike, a major issue of which was the desire of the various UAW locals in the company's plants to obtain a master agreement; this the company successfully resisted, though it did agree to a number of uniform contract provisions and granted a substantial wage increase. The following year the contract was renewed without a struggle, but in 1950 a strike that lasted seventy-seven days was called in another effort to obtain a master contract, as well as to win a union shop[2] and safeguard the piece-rate structure.

The strike ended with a master contract negotiated for a five-year period, following the precedent that the UAW had just established in the automobile industry. The union security clause of the contract, while not compelling old employees to join the union, required new workers to join upon the completion of their three-month probationary period. At the end of a year they had the privilege of withdrawing from the union, though their failure to do so at that time bound them to remain members for the duration of the contract. Workers who were union members when the contract was signed were similarly required to maintain their membership. This union security clause, which replaced a maintenance-of-dues type of provision, was the one in effect when the interviews were conducted. The local then had approximately thirty-four hundred members, representing over 99 per cent of those in the bargaining unit.[3] The contract gave the union the right to strike

[2] The union was authorized to seek a union shop by a vote of the employees conducted in 1949 under NLRB auspices; 95 per cent of those in the bargaining unit voted in this election, with 89 per cent voting in favor of the union shop.

[3] The bargaining unit included all production and maintenance workers, except for a handful of skilled workers represented by AFL craft unions. It excluded supervisors and salaried employees.

during the five-year period if a dispute over production standards could not be resolved otherwise; and in 1952, shortly after the interviews had been completed, another prolonged strike occurred over such an issue.

From time to time the local has engaged in a kind of guerilla warfare against the company. Among other tactics, it has flooded the grievance machinery, deliberately walked out of grievance meetings, organized employees against working overtime, held back production to the minimum guaranteed rate, and called "quickie" walkouts. The local's militancy, directed against a fairly profitable company, has helped to bring piece rates and working conditions to very high levels, equal to the best in the industry. The militancy of the union may be partly explained by the company's complicated system of piece and time rates, which has been the cause of constant disagreement in its application to specific jobs.

The local is a leading member of the council of UAW locals representing the workers in various plants of the company and meeting periodically to co-ordinate collective bargaining demands. At the time the field work was conducted there was still a division within the company's chain of plants between those in the UAW and those represented by the Farm Equipment Workers, which was expelled by the CIO in 1949 on charges of Communist domination and which subsequently merged with another similarly expelled union, the United Electrical Workers. The result of this division, according to the UAW, was to weaken labor's bargaining position by permitting the company to play off one union against the other. Since then the last FE-UE local has come over to the UAW.

The internal life of the local has been characterized by factional struggles for control. During the war period the factional alignment reflected the split in the nationl UAW, with the Reuther adherents—Socialists and other non-communist radicals together with non-politicals who supported aggressive union action—in one caucus, and a combination of more conservative unionists and a small number of Communists in the rival grouping. Socialists, though few in number, have played an important role as leaders in the Reuther caucus, which has been in control during most of the local's history. It has always had opposition, either concentrated in a single faction or divided into two groups; since personalities and issues have undergone numerous changes, these factions are difficult to characterize except for their steady opposition to the incumbents. Despite internal conflicts, the local has always presented a solid front in its dealings with management.

As a result of factional slates, along with independent candidacies, virtually every office is contested at the regular yearly elections, affording the membership ample opportunity to rid itself of unpopular personalities and policies. The substantial vote in elections—usually 70 to 85 per cent of the membership—is undoubtedly due in large part to the regular contests that organized factionalism makes possible. Only candidates indorsed by a caucus have ever been elected to a local-wide office, though from time to time a caucus has supported a candidate from outside its membership.

The officers of the local, together with two members elected at large, comprise the executive board, which is responsible for internal local policy. More important than the executive board, however, is the shop committee, which negotiates the collective bargaining agreement and processes the grievances that arise under it; this body consists of seven committeemen, each of whom is elected from a "zone"— a major department or a cluster of nearby departments. The workers in each department on each shift, in addition, elect a departmental steward who functions as their union representative and who participates in the first step of the grievance procedure as a kind of assistant to the zone committeeman. The shop committee selects its own chairman, who, under the agreement, devotes full time to his union duties; the agreement provides, in addition, that the company pay the committeemen for all the time taken from their production jobs to investigate and process grievances.

The local has had a number of leaders of considerable ability, some of whom have become international representatives or have been appointed to other positions on the UAW staff. Though most large locals in the region have changed from annual to biennial elections, as permitted by the UAW constitution, the local's leaders have retained yearly elections in the belief that a more frequent vote fosters greater responsiveness on the part of the officers to the membership.

The Workers and Their Jobs

The metal workers were a fairly heterogeneous group in terms of race, religion, and national origin, as one would expect to find on the outskirts of the Chicago metropolitan area. Of the forty-nine rank-and-file unionists interviewed, twelve were Negro and one was of Japanese descent. One or both parents of more than half the workers had been born abroad, mostly in eastern Europe or in Italy, and four were themselves of foreign birth. The Protestants slightly outnumbered the Catholics; there were no Jews in the rank-and-file sample, though there were some in the leadership group. Most were semiskilled workers, with smaller groups, about equal in number, either highly skilled or unskilled. They averaged thirty-six years of age and had gone, on the average, as far as the second year of high school. Most of their fathers had been skilled or semiskilled workers or farmers; smaller numbers had been clerical employees or unskilled workers, and two had been small businessmen. The workers had averaged four years of employment with the company, which had been operating the plant about six years.

As factory jobs go, those in this plant were relatively desirable. For the most part the work was clean and not very heavy, and the plant lacked the unpleasant conditions characteristic of some other industries. The pay was fairly attractive, ranging from a minimum of $1.21 an hour for labor grade 1 to a maximum of $2.07 for labor grade 14. In addition there was an annual improvement factor of four cents an hour under the five-year contract, besides a cost-of-living allowance. All production jobs were on piece rates, which permitted earnings averaging about one-fourth above the occupational rate, and which often allowed pieceworkers to earn more than higher-skilled workers paid on an hourly basis. The high pay and good working conditions had attracted a rather youthful work force, including a number of high-school graduates and an occasional employee with some college training. They were in no sense a marginal labor group, such as tends to gravitate to the less desirable types of employment.

Generally the men liked their jobs; this was particularly true of the more highly skilled. As a fifty-year-old plumber with six years of company service remarked: "It's a varied job, it's not like being a machine operator. It's not monotonous—do one thing one day and something else another day. . . . It prevails throughout the skilled trades that men like their work." Those who found their work appealing pointed to its interest, the stimulation it afforded, and the opportunities it provided for different experiences and for learning. Even less-skilled jobs were satisfying to many workers; a machine operator, for example, liked his work "because I have a decent job. My job pays and I understand my job. It's always a pleasure to work on a job that you understand." Freedom from close supervision and the opportunity to exercise initiative were also highly valued. A thirty-six-year-old machine inspector who earned $1.82 an hour said of his job: "I like it very much. I just transferred from another department. I like the freedom of this new job, you're on your own. It's only seldom that the boss talks to you. You go to him if you have problems. Otherwise they leave you alone."

Those who disliked their jobs, primarily the less-skilled workers, complained most frequently of piecework and monotony.[4] Typical of the complaints about piecework was that by a machine operator in his mid-thirties who earned an average of two dollars an hour: "I could think of a lot of other jobs I would prefer. If you are young it's all right to work on piecework . . . but when you get older, you want some straight daywork. I would like to see piecework eliminated, myself. The only appealing thing is that the earnings are decent." Several older workers also protested about the strain of piecework, but felt themselves no longer able to obtain more satisfactory employment elsewhere. Dissatisfaction was very high among Negroes, who generally lacked the white workers' hope for advancement.

The workers had a predominantly favorable attitude toward the company, despite frequent qualifications or an underlying note of criticism. No such qualification was apparent in the judgment of a setup man, however, who said: "In my opinion I've never worked for a company that treats their employees better." Others were pleased with the foremen's attitude, as was a thirty-nine-year-old lathe operator with three years' experience: "It's a nice company to work for; the foremen don't push you, and let you do your work at your own pace." Many compared the company favorably with previous employers. A Negro storekeeper, with two and a half years' service, gave the union part of the credit: "The company is pretty good to work for; they are pretty fair considering other companies that I've worked for. It seems to be pretty liberal so far as racial conditions are concerned. I suppose the union has a lot to do with bringing out that policy. I just like to work there." A number believed the union was primarily

---

[4] Compare the general dislike for their jobs of workers in a General Motors automobile assembly plant: Charles R. Walker and Robert H. Guest, *The Man on the Assembly Line* (Cambridge, Mass.: Harvard University Press, 1952).

responsible for the decent wage standards and desirable working conditions. In the words of a twenty-nine-year-old Negro drill operator:
"The company is OK because the union is in there. You can see the
things they do against the working men. If it wasn't for the union you
would be working for nothing. No telling what might happen if you
didn't have a union in there." An ambitious worker felt that the union's
emphasis on seniority was holding him back, yet was afraid that in
its absence favoritism rather than merit would be the deciding factor
in promotions.

Though very few workers definitely disliked the company, large
numbers criticized various policies or practices. Many disapproved
of piece rates or the entire piece-rate system, and there were complaints that wages were too low, that one couldn't advance fast enough,
that the company expected too much work, and that particular supervisors were unpleasant. A few saw the company as no better or worse
than other large employers; their usual attitude was: "All big corporations are the same; you have to fight for what you get, you have to
fight to hold it."

The overwhelming majority were favorably disposed toward their
foremen, with comments ranging from enthusiastic responses such as
"he is a wonderful guy" to statements like "he's all right" or "we get
along." Many praised their foremen for not pressuring them too much,
for allowing them freedom of decision, for being concerned about them
as well as about the company, for being fair among workers, for ap-
preciating a job well done, and for being friendly or good-natured.
Some attributed the foremen's good behavior to their own competence
or satisfactory performance, as by saying, "I do my work," while a
smaller number pointed to the pressure of the union as a cause. As
one put it, "The foremen treat us good because the union rep is on the
job and sees that we are treated right." A relatively small minority
criticized their foremen for being slave drivers, for being afraid for
their own jobs, for never praising the men under them, or for favoring
some men over others.

Joining the Union

For the great bulk of the workers, joining the union had been a
voluntary act, at least in the sense that there was no legal compulsion
to become members. The overwhelming majority had joined willingly,

with some degree of conviction that the union was a valuable institution deserving their support. About one in five had joined with some hesitation, either because of loyalty to a rival union or because of general reservations about unionism. While the modified union-shop clause had brought new employees into the union automatically, only rarely had it forced them into the organization against their will.

Most of the workers came to the plant already convinced of the virtues of unionism. Seventy per cent had worked in non-union shops at one time or another, and a slightly larger number, 75 per cent, had been union members in other employment. Whereas the non-union experience, with few exceptions, had been unfavorable, almost all had been satisfied with their union membership. As a result, the great majority joined the union at the plant, not because of anything the company had done or failed to do, but because of the conviction growing out of their earlier experience that, with a union, a worker enjoyed better conditions and fairer treatment, and was better able to adjust any difficulty that arose.

Of those who had worked under non-union conditions, only a very small number had no complaints about the treatment they had received. Most were sharply critical, with a decidedly emotional tinge to their responses. They emphasized unreasonable discipline and bad treatment by their foremen, including arbitrary dismissals, favoritism, "slave-driving," "being pushed around," and inability to talk back or complain. Objections were also voiced, though somewhat less frequently, to low wages, unsanitary conditions, and disregard of safety.

Workers with previous union experience were usually ready to join the union operating in the plant. A middle-aged Negro welder who had formerly been a steward in a steel plant sought out a union official shortly after beginning his present job: "I joined a month after I started work. I was the one who approached the committeeman; I told him I wanted to join. I felt it was a good thing to join the union— I wouldn't work in a plant unless there's a union." This welder, it is interesting to note, hoped to leave the ranks within the next five or six years in order to enter the real-estate business.

The fact that a worker had been a union member did not always mean that he would join another union willingly when he changed employment, however. There were several whose earlier union membership had proved disappointing. One such worker, a layout inspector, had belonged to an AFL union without ever seeing any union activity in his shop; nevertheless he was happy to join the union at the plant after reading about the UAW and becoming convinced that it was an effective organization.

A few of the workers had been conditioned in favor of unionism by their family background. An inspector, for example, was influenced by his father's union experience: "I was told about unions before I knew what work was about. He got union wages. He needed 'em to support six kids. I guess when you come from a big family you get the idea that when you're bound together you got strength. When there's six kids, you kind of get in favor of unions because you learn to work together."

There were also a few who had become dissatisfied with their treatment in the short interval between the company's acquisition of the plant and the organization of the local union. "Fellows were being pushed around," one said, being hired for as little as possible, cheated on their time, and not given the top rate when it was due them.

Still others waited for some tangible benefit before joining the union. A drill-press operator, for example, delayed joining until he saw that the union was trying to improve the poor lighting in his workroom.

Several workers reported pressure from their work group. A toolroom employee, for example, told how he happened to join: "Well, it made it easier if you belonged to it. It wasn't compulsory, but it was just the idea of going along with the fellows because you're treated better. . . . After I was hired out there, the department steward came over and told us the toolroom was mostly a hundred per cent and that it would be a good idea to make it a hundred per cent. Most of the other fellows were in, so I joined." The fact that pressure of this sort is mentioned does not mean that the worker necessarily joins the union unwillingly; this employee is a case in point, for he had worked previously in non-union shops and had resented the way "they expect you to keep hitting the ball and keep after you for production." He favored unions as a protection against unreasonable discipline and arbitrary discharge, and had joined the UAW willingly.

There was even one worker who wanted to be subjected to pressure before he joined, as a test of union strength: "I've always been a union member and had a transfer card . . . when I came out here. I told the fellows that I would like to stay out for a month and see how the union was and how they put pressure on a man. They really put pressure on. I joined because I like a strong union—the kind that puts pressure on the men to get them in and goes out to help the men when they get into trouble."

An employee who had been a union member while working for a railroad and who was moderately favorable toward unionism described the treatment given to non-members: "You pretty near had to join—you're not forced, but they're pretty rough on you if you don't . . . like calling you a scab and playing tricks on you. Some of the guys are pretty dirty, but not everyone is like that. We got some guys there who don't belong and they get along OK." Though none of the workers said that he was forced into the union by ostracism, there was reference to such treatment. A young tool grinder, for example, said that, while he favored unionism, he didn't believe in "that stuff about a guy who don't belong to the union—don't talk to him." A union steward remarked: "There's quite a few ways you can get [a non-member] to join. We use just the logical ways—the guys rib him or give him the cold shoulder. Eventually he comes in. A guy don't like to work with a lot of guys who give him the cold shoulder."

Several workers had joined the union under the modified union-shop clause in effect in recent years. Some of these said that they would have joined anyway because of the protection they received, though there was one who admitted that otherwise he would not have become a member. Joining the union "didn't bother me any," he said, "but I felt I could get along without it, because those who didn't join get the same thing." Very few admitted, as did this worker, that they delayed joining because they could receive most of the benefits without paying monthly dues, though union members were quick to assign this as a leading motivation of non-unionists.

Others who were forced to join by the contract clause had reservations about unions at the time, but most of them changed their attitude as a result of experience with the UAW local in the plant. A thirty-eight-year-old inspector, for example, had resented being forced into the union; he had always been opposed to unions, he said, adding that "now I don't see why, because I can certainly see a lot of things they're doing today." Only in isolated cases was resentment still apparent.

Union Achievements

Since the plant was a new one, there was no opportunity to contrast earlier non-union conditions with those existing at the time of the field work. By the time the plant was acquired unionism had been strongly established in the area, other plants of the company throughout the country had been organized, and the company's policies had been adjusted to the necessity of operating with a unionized labor force. It was not surprising, therefore, to find a generally restrained note in the estimate made by members of the union's achievements,[5] though there was general agreement that these achievements had been considerable. Most of the emphasis was on higher wages and improved working conditions, though there was also mention of job security, better treatment by supervisors, the grievance procedure, job-posting, and, in very rare cases, better relations with management. There were also several workers who were somewhat skeptical of the union's claimed achievements, or who felt that these had been purchased at too high a price.

An over-all estimate of the union's accomplishments came from a middle-aged utility man, inactive in the union, who had worked five years with the company: "They've done a lot of good out there and we've gone a long way. Through the union we got a good working wage, a cost-of-living increase. . . . When I started at 89 cents an hour the union wasn't recognized; now I'm making at least $1.95 an hour. . . . I think working conditions and everything would be lousy if we didn't have the union out there. I believe [the company] would rule with an iron hand, they would have speed-ups and piecework prices would be much lower. . . . Now all conditions are as good as any place in the area, and even better than in many places. . . . They have an awful lot of grievances, and their purpose is to improve working conditions. They got a lot of colored people—the union stands for no racial or religious discrimination—there's a lot of Negroes who are getting to work themselves up in the plant to better themselves." A Negro welder who served as a union steward also included fairer treatment for minorities among union achievements. The local union, he said, had "accomplished protection of the men in layoffs, increased our wages by automatic raises according to the cost of living and general raises, and also, in our chain, brought all workers to a uniform earning rate, increased our vacation time. . . . They have made a great step toward breaking down discriminatory practices in hiring and firing

---

[5] Eight per cent of the rank-and-file workers appraised the union enthusiastically; 59 per cent were positive but restrained in their judgments; 25 per cent were critical but appreciative; and 8 per cent were sharply critical.

and other places where racial and religious discrimination might have been practiced."

There was widespread agreement that the union had raised the level of wages. "We've been getting an increase quite often," an assembly line worker remarked; ". . . if it wasn't for the union we'd be down to half of what we get now." A number referred favorably to the escalator clause providing for automatic pay changes to match increases in the cost of living. Yet there was an occasional worker who viewed the escalator clause as a fraud and a defeat, a device "handed down from management and accepted by the union." Others gave little credit to the local for wage gains, on the ground that the company followed wage patterns set elsewhere.

A machine operator who served as a union steward believed that the union, besides giving the worker a sense of freedom, had helped achieve security and justice, and that these were more important than wages: "We got a spirit of freedom and independence in the mind of the worker—and it's wonderful to see—as a result of the union and having had fifteen years of good times, where a man didn't have to worry about his job. It isn't strictly union because even with a good union, if you're in danger of losing your job without any seniority, you'd have fear in your heart. . . . Working conditions, wages, paid holidays, vacations, pension plans, liberal health and welfare plans, a real strong grievance procedure, so a man has a greater sense of security and freedom—that he'll get justice—those things are more important than wages, because if a man comes to work and is hounded by his foreman, he won't like to come to work; but it's different when he works in a good union shop without the foreman hounding him." Responses of this sort, indicating a knowledge of a variety of union achievements, a concern for the welfare of workers as a group, and an interest in intangibles like the sense of freedom, were rare among the inactive union members.

There was general agreement that the union had played an important role in improving the treatment of workers by foremen. "Now a foreman can't push one man around without having to take on all the men," one worker remarked, and another added that "abusive tactics" by foremen were no longer possible. Some emphasized the control over foremen resulting from the presence of the union steward and the existence of grievance machinery. A middle-aged machine operator who acted as a union steward stressed the end of promotions by favoritism and of "apple-polishing": "As far as promotions are concerned, prior to the union, the foreman would pick out whoever he wanted and would pick his pets. Now he has to go according to seniority. If the union went out we would have to go back to apple-polishing, mowing lawns, painting houses for the family of the foreman."

Several workers stressed the increased job security, sometimes even asserting that it had become difficult to fire a worker: "The boss, nowadays, couldn't fire a man if he wanted to; he'd have to have something on him—real good. In fact, he'd have to have it on three or four times. Before the union was there, if a foreman didn't like a guy, or saw a better man and wanted to hire him to the job, he could just fire the first guy; now he can't." A middle-aged inspector who had worked previously in non-union shops was rather surprised to hear how the men talked to their foreman at the plant: "The men realize they've got a say-so through the union, and management knows that. It gives the fellows a feeling of independence. . . . At first I felt the men had an extreme view about the bosses; you almost felt that the men tell the bosses what to do, instead of the other way around. Then I realized that they just enjoyed talking back. They did as ordered, in reason, but they could argue back—they feel that they have protection. It's a more healthy feeling, that one of having protection."

A number greatly appreciated the system of posting job openings, an innovation obtained by the union in the most recent contract. Previously there were complaints that only those who worked in the office or had connections there knew of job openings, with resulting favoritism. Under the recently negotiated contract, however, openings had to be posted at the departmental window. Workers had twenty-four hours to bid for the job, and the applicant with the highest seniority was given a trial period to see whether he could do the work satisfactorily.

Several workers were critical of the union in some respects, while recognizing achievements in certain other areas. Among these was a middle-aged worker in the toolroom who said that the union had "a lot of good points and some points I'm not in favor of." Among the former he listed job security, protection from "riding" by the foreman, and pay increases. Concerning the matters he disliked, he said: "Lots of fellows are holding jobs which they aren't qualified to hold. Lots of these fellows hold seniority, and consequently buck people with less seniority. I know some who can't read a scale, let alone a micrometer. . . . The guys take advantage of the fact that the company can't come out and fire them and they lay down on the job. I've always felt that if you're satisfied with the wages you're getting, you should give them an honest day's work." Quite similar in his general orientation was a young lathe operator, eager to become a supervisor, who thought the union had raised wages and improved working conditions. He was critical of the union, however, for having undermined discipline to the point where workers failed to do their jobs properly without fear of discharge: "They [the union] uphold certain cases that they shouldn't. Well, like this—we've got a man in the shop, he isn't worth beans, yet the boss can't fire him. I've seen guys sleeping in the washroom, and the boss can't fire them. . . . Another thing on the same line—on racial discrimination it's come to the place, if the boss even looks at a colored man, he hollers 'discrimination.' . . . Some of them take advantage of their color." Other criticisms were that there were too many strikes, that union dues were too high, that the union made exaggerated statements about the company, or that the leaders controlled union decisions or looked out too much for themselves.

Strikes and Slowdowns

Because of the frequency with which the union has called strikes during the relatively short period the company has owned the plant, all but the newest employees have had strike experience. Even though picketing has been largely symbolic, with no effort by the company to operate the plant during strikes, three-fourths of the workers had served on the picket line. The married men in particular were very conscious of the wages lost during strikes. They saw the strike as a weapon of last resort, and tended to justify strikes in defensive rather than offensive terms. Strikes, they said, should be called when the company was unreasonable, when it failed to accede to the union's just demands, or when it permitted wages to lag behind the cost of living or the level paid in comparable plants.

Generally the workers felt that strikes had accomplished a great deal. They usually listed higher wages and improved working conditions as the greatest achievements, with smaller numbers pointing also to the escalator clause, paid vacations, pensions and the welfare fund, seniority, and job posting. A few credited the strike with all their gains. As one said: "I think that strikes have accomplished practically everything we've got. It's our only weapon. The only time we ever went out on strike it was as a last resort. It's the only argument they understand. If you keep on working they'll talk till doomsday." An occasional worker felt that strikes, besides winning better contracts, increased union strength, though rank-and-file members rarely mentioned an institutional factor of this sort. At the other extreme a handful believed that strikes accomplished nothing because it took so long to make up lost wages.

Though decisions to strike were made by majority vote at local meetings, there was an undercover of resentment among a minority against such decisions. One who thought that strikes were foolish complained that most workers failed to attend the meetings, and that a few hot-headed members voted for the strikes. A few others blamed the officers of the local, sometimes asserting that ordinary workers like themselves, though opposed to strikes, were powerless when the union leaders decided to call one.

Workers usually considered it their duty to picket during strikes, and some pointed out, in addition, that their job interests were involved. A large minority, however, showed little or no sense of emotional involvement; they picketed because they were called, because they "received a card," or, in rarer cases, because they had nothing else to do or wanted to "see the other boys." A few who had never picketed did not think their failure to participate mattered in the least, pointing out that the company made no efforts to operate during strikes.

An unusual case was that of a worker who was opposed to strikes under any circumstances, but who feared violence or ostracism at the hands of his fellows if he violated their picket line: "I don't care to go on strike. I have to. If I walked in the plant, they probably would beat me up. If I got in maybe they would boycott you later on like they did with one guy who was in the plant during the strike. Nobody talked to him after the strike and he had to quit the plant."

Slowdowns[6] have likewise been resorted to from time to time, particularly when the workers were strongly dissatisfied with the established piece rates. Almost a fourth of the workers disapproved of the slowdown, however, usually on the grounds that the grievance procedure was available, that a slowdown was too risky, that it would reduce their earnings too much, or that a strike should be called instead. Occasionally a worker objected on principle because he liked to feel

[6] For a fuller treatment of this subject see the authors' article, "The Slowdown as a Union Tactic," *Journal of Political Economy*, LXV (April, 1957), 126–34.

that he was doing a conscientious job. Others disliked slowdowns so long as they remained pieceworkers but had no objections to participating if they were paid by the day. Some workers asserted that, if they thought their rate too low, they would slow down their machines, produce what they considered a fair day's work, or simply meet the quota with no attempt to exceed it.

A number testified to the ease with which they could slow down production. "If a job could take me fifteen minutes," said one, "it would be no trick to spread it out to four or five hours." Another described the techniques used in one of the slowdowns: "In one case the line got tied up—guys seemed to stumble over each other, parts were in short supply, guys gimmick up the machines—make shear pins go on the drive shaft, air vents get plugged up where they don't draw air, and a lot of other things which causes equipment to break down. The only limits are the ingenuity of the workers, and I haven't seen any limits to that. . . . I was called upon to check the blower once, and found a roll of toilet paper in it and a lot of other crap and garbage. We searched another time for hours to see why a conveyor was stopped and couldn't detect it."

One of the employees described the successful use of the slowdown to force the company to restore a rate that had been cut: "Just work and don't accomplish much—they can't say a word to you as long as you are working. Say you and I are working together, and we decide we'll do so much and make the work stretch. If they want 700 pieces give them 300 pieces, but always have your hand on something. It would never work unless the men stick together. They were making radiators, for example, and we were supposed to put out 700 radiators, and the men decided to give them 300 to 350 radiators, and the men stuck it out for three weeks. The bosses asked them to give them a few more radiators, and they said, 'We're working.' They boosted the rate to what it was, and they went to 700 radiators again. They were busy putting out the 300 radiators, even with six or seven foremen around them. The only way you can pull a slowdown is for the men to stick together and not let the bosses intimidate you."

Another worker described a slowdown in which he and some others were then engaged: "They retimed my job and changed the price on it, and I don't like it. . . . I've never made out on it since they've retimed it. I used to turn in 32 pieces the way the job used to be, but since they retimed it, the first day I only turned in 13, the next day 14, the next day 15, and now I'm up to 16 and I'll stay just about there. . . . After I turned out 16 a couple of days they came down and retimed the job." Asked about the men on the other shifts doing the same work, he replied: "Well, they usually co-operate—in fact, they've got to. If I turn out 16, and the other guys go on turning out 32, my ass would really be in a sling. There's one guy on the night shift—the first night after the job was retimed he turned in 32 pieces as usual, and I got him in the washroom, and I told him, 'Look, bud, you're going to have a dental bill if you don't cut out this ——; after all, I'm not taking this risk for nothing. Our line's a pilot line, and if we get retimed and get new rates, then all the rest of the lines that do similar work are going to get retimed and get a better rate; and no one guy is going to louse it up.' . . . So the next day he turned in 16, and the next day he turned in 12, and then I had to see him again and tell him not to be a damned fool. They know he can do more than 12, so now he's turning in 16 just like I am."

Disappearance of the Union

Almost all the workers expected disastrous consequences in the event the union disappeared.[7] They feared a deterioration of wage standards and of working conditions, a lack of security and freedom, a return to the arbitrary power of the foreman, and the loss of seniority protection and its replacement by favoritism. They were afraid that workers would be treated like machines, that conditions would be "miserable," and that the company, unchecked by any other force, would do whatever it pleased. Insecurity and anxiety were evident in the rather widespread view of the company as a potentially threatening power, prepared to sacrifice the welfare of its employees in the interests of greater production and higher profit.

A middle-aged assembly line worker who was inactive in the union gave a graphic description of the conditions that would exist were the union to disappear: "We would get a cut in wages and bad working conditions right away. They'd throw the book at me and everybody else. They could throw you out of the shop, if they didn't want you. If

---

[7] Forty-five out of forty-nine rank-and-file members were apprehensive about the consequences to them of the union's disappearance; three feared for other workers, though not for themselves, and only one saw no unfortunate results for anyone. Just under half anticipated lower wages, and almost as many were afraid of the uncontrolled power of the company.

you looked cross-eyed at the boss, you'd be out. With the union in there, you don't have to go on your knees for anybody, to no boss—don't have to be afraid of the boss. In fact, the boss respects you if you stick up for your rights. Without a union, you wouldn't have any chance to do that." A union steward, a young mechanic who had never worked in a non-union shop, equated the loss of the union with a return to slavery and depression. Others said that the plant would be like a prison or a return to the old sweatshop days.

A number of workers were concerned with the arbitrary power that foremen could exercise in the union's absence, with the lack of security, the "pushing," and the favoritism that could exist. As a thirty-one-year-old machine operator put it: "Conditions would be awful, there could be a lot of preference, overtime would be pushed to the favorites, foremen would ride you. . . . The foremen could really push you around for nothing without the union." An assembler who had worked seventeen years for the company, four of them at this plant, said: "I'd get the feeling that we're bringing the days back of bringing presents and cigars to the foremen; favoritism would operate. We'd work harder and get less money—it'd be a hell of a condition to work under."

Aspirations of Metal Workers

Despite their fear of the company's power in the absence of a union, most workers were favorably disposed toward their employer and expected to remain at the plant permanently. Those with a few years of service stressed the protection against layoffs provided by the seniority system; those who were getting older were doubtful of employment opportunities elsewhere and feared losing their pension rights; and many, particularly those with little or moderate skill, did not believe they could better themselves by changing employment. In comparison with other jobs they had known or thought they might be able to get, they found the level of pay, the working conditions, and the treatment by supervisors very satisfactory. Many responded with some variation of: "this job is as good as I could get anywhere."[8] Occasionally a worker mentioned union protection as one of the factors that made permanent employment with the company attractive.

[8] Compare the findings in Ely Chinoy, *Automobile Workers and the American Dream* (Garden City, N.Y.: Doubleday & Co., 1955), and in Robert H. Guest, "Work Careers and Aspirations of Automobile Workers," *American Sociological Review*, XIX (April, 1954), 155–63.

The older workers, especially, found their dreams of an independent business fading; for some of them, staying with the company was a matter of regret, a necessity due to the lack of an acceptable alternative. Some of the younger men were more hopeful that some day they would be able to enter business for themselves.

Despite the protection afforded by the union and the generally high estimate of the company, it was interesting to observe the number of responses in which a note of apprehension appeared. Again and again, workers referred to the fear of being fired or spoke of their plans provided "nothing happened." In part the sources of these fears were the company or one's immediate supervisors; to some degree they were impersonal forces imbedded in the economy—undefined but very real forces that had caused major layoffs or plant shutdowns in the past and might well do so again. Even highly skilled men were not entirely exempt from these fears, which were strongest among the semiskilled and unskilled.

Only about one worker in four felt that he had much chance for promotion to a supervisory position. Many did not have the educational background they thought the company preferred, others thought themselves lacking in ability or personality, and Negroes generally believed their race to be an insuperable handicap. A number said they did not want to become foremen, either because they lacked the necessary qualifications or because they found the job unattractive. Only a small minority both believed that they had a chance for promotion and actually aspired to it.

Many workers viewed the foreman's position critically or with ambivalence. A middle-aged machine operator was one of those who felt that, on the whole, he was better off as a production worker: "I don't know—the way those guys are going, they got grief, too. I feel right now I'm better off to work my eight hours—punch in, punch out, and go home." In the judgment of a welder, the foreman was under too much pressure, between higher management on one side and the union representatives on the other: "I don't think I would like to be under those pressures and restrictions that they are under. Especially since I don't expect to stay there until I'm sixty-four. It's like being in the army—the orders are passed down from the top to the foremen, and they are always on the spot. Many times the foreman is expected to do things, and the union representative jumps on him; many times he's in the middle, between the union representative, and the officials; he gets pushed around."

Others rejected the position because of its limited pay and little authority, or because of the threat to established and satisfying relationships with fellow workers. The responses suggest that economic as well as psychological factors are important to most workers, who wish to feel secure in both senses. It is also likely that many, originally ambitious, have reacted to their failure to be promoted by lowering their level of aspiration. Some might be trying to bolster up their self-respect and status in the eyes of others by saying they do not desire a position they think will never be offered them. If the position were really offered, they might accept it eagerly.

Those who would have liked to become foremen were attracted by the higher pay, the greater economic security, and the prestige accompanying the position. Since the workers were at various levels of skill and pay, some but not all would have increased their income substantially by becoming foremen. Yet other motivations were involved. A setup man, for example, described his reactions to the job in these terms: "Yes, I'd like it. . . . I feel if I got to be foreman I'd be accomplishing something. Uncle Sam gave me the equivalent of one year of a college education as an engineer when I was in the army and I'd like to put that knowledge to use. It isn't just money. I'd like to do something besides be a button pusher."

Although the workers generally liked their company and their jobs, more than half did not want their sons to follow them into the plant. These usually hoped that their sons could get more education than they themselves had received, and become doctors, lawyers, or engineers. A typical response was that of a pieceworker: "I'd like to have my boy get an education so he wouldn't have to beat his brains out on piecework. Whenever I get four hundred dollars in the bank, I seem to get laid off. Seems like the company knows how much I have in the bank. I would like him to be a draftsman, or a building engineer—some profession of that kind." Occasionally a worker objected to the people one had to associate with in an industrial plant, and hoped that education would enable his son to mingle with more desirable individuals. Others, less ambitious or more realistic than those desiring professional careers for their sons, merely wished that they could enter skilled trades rather than do semiskilled piecework. While some were entirely willing to have their sons enter the company's employ, others added a qualification—"provided they get something better."

The great bulk of these metal workers, it is clear, have a high regard both for their company and for their union. If they are dissatisfied with their lot in life it is more their own lack of education and training rather than any specific policies of their employer that they hold responsible. They credit their union with having raised wages, improved working conditions, provided job security, and improved their treatment by the supervisory staff; and they value it for the protection it offers for the future. There has been some evidence of late that management was seeking to foster a more friendly relationship with the union; it remains to be seen whether this will be achieved and, if so, what the effect will be upon the rank-and-file members' attitudes toward the company and union.

6

KNITTING MILL WORKERS

The Impact of an Organizing Strike[1]

Half a century ago portions of northern Wisconsin were a lumberman's paradise. Enterprising businessmen sent crews of loggers into the seemingly endless forests to satisfy a growing nation's need for wood and wood products. Sawmills mushroomed along the banks of the rivers to process the logs that poured out in a never-ending stream. Vigorous men were needed to do the heavy work, to match their muscles and stamina against the might of the forest and the rigor of the climate. Merchants followed the lumber industry, providing supplies for the logging companies and the woodsmen.

Little is left of the lumber industry in that area today except for an occasional sawmill. The lumber companies have long since exhausted the profitable stands of timber and moved on to the virgin forests of the West. The rough and hardy loggers have given way to farmers and factory workers; and the towns that grew up to service the lumbermen now act as distribution centers for the farmers of the area, besides housing a number of manufacturing enterprises.

The Community and the Miller Family

The community with which we are concerned has a population of about fourteen thousand, fewer than it had fifty years earlier in the booming days of the lumber trade. Of the twenty-eight sawmills that once lined the river, only one is left. The town now houses some thirty-five manufacturing establishments, many of them making paper, boxes, or other wood products and obtaining most of their lumber from farther north. There are also other enterprises—a chemical plant, a glove fac-

[1] This chapter is based in part on an article by the authors, "The Union Organizer and His Tactics: A Case Study," *American Journal of Sociology*, LIX (September, 1953), 113–22.

tory, a plant making aluminum pistons, and a knitting mill. Dairies and a fishing fleet provide additional employment. Some of the families that acquired their wealth in the lumber trade have remained in town, their mansions still to be seen overlooking the river. Later migration to the United States has added Poles and others of central or southern European origin to the original Yankee and French-Canadian settlers and to the Scandinavians, Germans, and Irish who were attracted when lumber dominated the area. Residents of Scandinavian or German descent are the predominant groups today.

The leading family in town, the Millers,[2] traces its history there back to the lumber era around the turn of the century. The brothers who laid the foundations of the family's success operated a small retail store, bringing supplies by horse and wagon to the lumber camps in the backwoods. In a few years they were serving a broad section of the industry through northeastern Wisconsin and the upper peninsula of Michigan. As their fortune grew they developed a wholesale produce business, built a very large department store, acquired substantial real-estate holdings, and obtained an interest in two local banks. For the past forty years the family has also operated the knitting mill whose employees are the subject of this chapter. For more than a generation the Millers have been the dominant family in the community, enjoying great prestige as a result of their business success, their support of the Catholic church, and their general patriarchal position. Their influence is felt not only in economic affairs but also in the political, social, and religious life of the community.

The Employer and the Work Force

The mill produces an expensive line of women's knitted dresses and men's and women's sweaters, which are sold through showrooms maintained in Chicago and New York City. At the seasonal peak the plant has approximately 180 employees, all but about 15 of whom are women. The small group of men are mostly highly skilled knitters; the women, less-skilled for the most part, are sewing-machine operators, cutters, pressers, sorters, inspectors, and the like.

The company has provided reasonably steady employment in a competitive industry subject to seasonal fluctuations and frequent style

[2] This name is fictitious, as are the others used in this chapter, but no essential fact has been altered.

changes. The average worker in the mill was forty-one years old when the study was made and had been with the company for nine years. Almost all were native-born, though the parents of most had come from Europe—usually from Germany or Sweden—or from French Canada. More than half the employees were Catholic, the remainder being Protestant except for one Jewish worker. Since there was no other knitting mill in town, the men could change their employment only at the price of leaving the community or dropping to the ranks of less-skilled workers in another industry. Only one of the men was intending to look for a better job.

The women, similarly, had little opportunity for other employment. Few other jobs were available in town and those that were, as in the glove factory, required somewhat different skills. Nor were they free to leave the community, since most of them were married and were secondary wage-earners in their families. Except for the younger women who hoped to leave to raise a family, or for some of the older ones who expected to quit when their children were self-supporting, they planned to stay with the company permanently. They were conscious of the fact that few alternative jobs were available, and that their future work plans depended more on their husbands' experiences and opportunities than on their own. The women generally liked their work and were attached to their jobs and to their employer.

Before the strike, relations between John Miller, the head of the company, and his employees were extremely close. He had hunted and fished with many of them, and others had been guests on his boat. The employees had enjoyed his annual Christmas parties and had looked forward to the yearly bonuses based on length of employment and the company's profits. Before the union was organized the employer regarded his workers as loyal and friendly: "We were just one big happy family before this thing started. I called 95 per cent of the employees by their first name—they were people I knew all my life."

The workers, in turn, generally respected and in some cases admired their employer. It was indicative of their informal, friendly relationship that most of them called him by his given name. Several reported that they had gone directly to him with problems and had obtained satisfaction. Some had grown up with him in the same small town, and all found him to be a well-mannered person with a pleasant way of dealing with people. In the words of one union member: "John was always very nice. I thought he is a friendly person. . . . He seemed to treat everybody nice and he always had a friendly 'hello.'" The comment of another member illustrates the long-standing ties which bound some employees to the owners of the mill: "My sister has been working at the Millers' store for fifty-seven years. . . . I can say this much about the Millers—you can't find better people in time of need. When my father died, the undertaker told us that the bill had been paid for and we found out later that the Millers had paid for it. They gave me the living room set you're sitting on when I got married. My family knew the Millers years ago. I always heard nice things about them."

Despite the fact that the field work was conducted shortly after the close of a bitter strike, many workers emphasized their former or still existing personal relations with the employer, their loyalty to the firm, and their admiration for a leading family in the community that had given them employment. All this reflected a completely different relationship between employees and employer than is usually found in an urban environment. Workers here did not struggle with abstract concepts, such as "the company," but based their reactions on personal experiences with its head.

Unionism in the Town and the 1947 Organizing Effort

Only in very recent years has organized labor become a force in the community. During and after the war, unions, which had been largely confined to the building trades and several other crafts organized by the AFL, spread beyond the skilled trades to include several of the factories in this and a neighboring community. The knitting mill employees, however, lagged behind this general trend—a reflection both of the weak economic position of a force composed largely of semi-skilled women and of the powerful position of the Miller family. The knitting mill continued to be a major non-union stronghold until the fall of 1950, when it was organized by the International Ladies' Garment Workers' Union[3] of the AFL.

Nevertheless, the women in the mill had not been untouched by the spread of unions during the war. The fact that many of their husbands and fathers had been swept into the ranks of organized labor helped to

[3] For the history, problems, and achievements of the ILGWU see Benjamin Stolberg, *Tailor's Progress: The Story of a Famous Union and the Men Who Made It* (New York: Doubleday, Doran & Co., 1944). Unionism in the entire group of garment industries is treated in Joel Seidman, *The Needle Trades* (New York: Farrar & Rinehart, 1942).

arouse their own interest in the possibilities of organizing. The leaders of the AFL central labor body in the town, anxious to unionize the mill because of its drag upon wage rates in the community, tried to capitalize on this interest. Learning that some of the employees wanted to organize, the AFL officers informed the ILGWU. Following this lead, the chief organizer in the area for the ILGWU, Frank Rosen, assigned a member of his staff to the mill. She found that, while a number of the workers were dissatisfied with wages and working conditions and were interested in forming a union, none wanted her interest to become known, not even to fellow employees. There was widespread fear that those who participated openly in a union campaign would lose their jobs and fail to find satisfactory employment elsewhere in the community. Two weeks of effort by the organizer produced only about twenty-five signed cards. The entire burden, moreover, rested on the organizer herself, since none of the workers was willing to play an active role or assume leadership inside the mill. At just this point the Taft-Hartley Act was passed, convincing Frank that the campaign was doomed to failure at that time.

The 1950 Organizing Drive[4]

Three years later a few of the workers again told officials of the central labor body about their dissatisfaction with conditions in the mill and their desire to unionize, and again this information was forwarded to the area officials of the ILGWU. Frank assigned another staff member, Helen Anderson, to survey the situation. As Frank put it: "If you send an organizer out and she comes out with the information that the people don't want a union, that their wage scale is good, that their treatment in the shop, their working conditions are good, and that they don't want any part of a union, then the organizer doesn't stay there very long." Helen's preliminary survey convinced her that the plant could be organized. Dissatisfaction was widespread, and she found employees who were willing to aid actively in the campaign.

[4] Among the better treatments of organizing in the literature are the chapters in Jack Barbash, *The Practice of Unionism* (New York: Harper & Bros., 1956), pp. 1–44, and in Robert R. R. Brooks, *When Labor Organizes* (New Haven: Yale University Press, 1937), pp. 1–27. See also Educational Department, International Ladies' Garment Workers' Union, *Handbook of Trade Union Methods* (1937), and the description of an organizing effort and a subsequent strike in Eli Ginzberg, *The Labor Leader: An Exploratory Study* (New York: Macmillan Co., 1948), pp. 83–170.

When Helen returned to the town several weeks later to begin work in earnest, she placed emphasis on secrecy, personal contacts, an approach tailored to the dissatisfactions of each prospective member, and the involvement in the campaign of a number of workers inside the mill. Some employees, afraid of reprisals by the company, were willing to sign union cards only after being assured that their names would be kept secret—a pledge the organizer scrupulously kept.

Most of the early organizing work was concentrated into two long weekends during which Helen contacted workers individually. Helen had no set approach. Instead she encouraged her prospects to air their grievances, and then emphasized the value of a union for solving their specific problems. She also formed an "inside" organizing committee that was representative of the various departments in the plant. Each committee member contacted workers in her department and arranged departmental meetings with Helen in her hotel room.

Helen was well fitted, both by background and by personality, to work with the women in the plant. She had grown up in a small community not far away where she had worked in a garment shop for fifteen years before joining the union's organizing staff. She made friends easily, moreover, and inspired confidence in her ability to handle any situation. She was much less successful with the men, who preferred to deal with a male representative who understood the problems of the skilled knitters. The men joined the union when Frank[5] visited the town; because of their skill, and also their sex, they constituted a key group in the union organization.

News of union activity spread rapidly through the plant, and by the end of the second week of active organizing Helen had obtained signed cards from 72 of the 180 workers. Each worker had to decide whether or not to join the union under very difficult circumstances.

[5] It is interesting to note that Frank, the chief union organizer, was Jewish, as were several of the higher union officials who later addressed strike meetings. Only one worker in the mill and very few other persons in the community were Jewish. This religious difference did not become an issue in the strike, though in other small towns it has been used to create antagonism toward the organizer. Sometimes, though not in this case, foreign birth, New York City residence, and socialist inclinations of the needle trades unions have been additional elements in fostering prejudice against the union. In many small-town organizing situations in the garment industries, however, the employer has himself been Jewish, often foreign-born as well, and only recently arrived from New York City or another metropolitan center of the industry. In some such communities "the Jew" and "the employer" have become synonymous in the language of some of the employees, who must then reorganize their thinking if a Jewish union organizer comes to work among them.

There was real fear that those who joined might lose their jobs or that, if the union were established, the plant would close down or move away. Besides those who became members during the initial organizing period there were many who signed up during the strike that followed, when the decision to join was complicated by all the emotions aroused by the strike. Eleven of the thirteen union leaders and three-fourths of the rank-and-file members reported that they joined with some degree of conviction; the remainder joined in order to be with the group.

Sources of Dissatisfaction

The dissatisfactions that led employees to join the union, at this time or later, were varied in nature; some resulted from the general wage level or the lack of opportunity for certain groups of pieceworkers to earn satisfactory incomes; others related to bad treatment by supervisors, favoritism, lack of job security, or the fact that there was no satisfactory way to adjust complaints.

Many complained about the relatively low pay, although comparison was more difficult than in a larger center where a number of factories make similar products. Nevertheless, some comparison was possible, as the response of one of the young women indicates: "Well, I guess it was on account of wages. They had gotten worse, and piece rates, as well as minimum, were too low. All of us had girl friends who worked in other factories, and my gosh, sometimes when we compared our pay checks we were almost afraid to show ours."

Most of the women employees, virtually all of whom were pieceworkers, earned only about 65 cents an hour until the minimum wage required by the Fair Labor Standards Act was raised to 75 cents in January, 1950. The company then increased the minimum pay without changing the piece-rate structure. The effect was to reduce the incentive to produce and to make those of higher skill resentful, since their customary margin of earnings over the less-skilled was now diminished. There was also an arbitrary aspect about determining piece rates that irritated the workers. As one said, "Piece rates were bad and unequal—they were getting different rates for practically the same style."

Equally widespread was dissatisfaction with the treatment by the supervisory staff, especially the floorladies and the foremen. Workers found fault with supervisors for screaming at them, calling them names, being mean and crabby, playing favorites, and behaving in an arbitrary fashion. Many complained that their floorlady yelled at them, spoke to them in a "snotty" or sarcastic fashion, and often made the girls cry. "She was always mean and crabby," said a machine operator who had worked nine years in the plant. "Everything one did was wrong; even if it wasn't your fault you got blamed for it." One of the male workers who became a union leader said that one of the supervisors "swore and cursed and called me a 'damn Polack.' I guess he just didn't know any better; he is ignorant. And also he is John Miller's cousin and so he thinks he can do it. When he knows you are dependent on your wages he thinks he can do it."

A number asserted that they were "pushed around" or treated unfairly, that work was badly distributed, that machines were reassigned in arbitrary fashion, or that layoffs were made without regard to seniority. There were complaints that some floorladies divided the work so that a few favorites consistently earned more than other workers at the same level of skill. There was even some suspicion that playing favorites was a deliberate tactic to keep the workers divided and unorganized: "There was a lot of partiality, that was another reason why the union didn't come in earlier. They just pampered some of the workers so that they wouldn't ask for a union."

Dissatisfactions were intensified by the feeling, shared by a majority of the union members, that there was no way to settle complaints. "They wouldn't listen to you before," said one of the union leaders. "They'd say like they said so many times, 'If you don't like it, you know what you can do—there's the door.'" A knitter who later became one of the union officials told of an incident, long before the organizing drive, that started him thinking about a union: "One day a couple of years ago, we were asked to work on Labor Day at straight earning—no overtime—and we had a bad day. It seemed like things went wrong all day and we didn't even make our guarantee of $1.20. We made $1.14 that day. We were mad at the company not paying us for the holiday already and this added to it. So the six of us went to see [the plant superintendent]. We went in together. We knew that once before a group of girls in the looping department had a gripe and went to see him in a group and they were all let out. But we went anyway. He didn't do anything for us for the Labor Day pay. I was doing most of the talking and he said he wouldn't pay us our minimum because he said we weren't working hard enough. I told him that his desk was only a few feet away from my machine and he was there all except for about an hour the whole day and was watching how hard I was working, and he knew that that statement was a lie. He burned me up with that stuff. Then he said to me, 'If you don't like it, there's the door.' In my mind, that's where the union started for me."

There were a scattering of employees who had had union experience elsewhere, besides a substantial number of women whose husbands were union members. The officers, with only one exception, consisted of workers who had previously been union members on other jobs, or who had been encouraged to join the union by members of their families. The rank-and-file members who were strongly in favor of the union were also influenced by pro-union husbands or other family members. On the other hand, most of the lukewarm members—those who dropped out and rejoined or who did not join at all until after the strike started—had not been subject to such influences.

Particularly among the lukewarm members, but also among the more convinced unionists, an important motivation for joining was to be with the group. Workers without personal convictions or strong family influences were most likely to be affected by the actions of their fellow workers. One of the married women, for example, "stayed neutral" for a while: "I just didn't figure that my job was worth bothering my head about. . . . I didn't even care whether or not they had a union—I didn't figure I would be working much longer. . . . When the strike started I joined to be united with the girls." A hand sewer who had worked twenty-five years for the company described how the women in her department had acted as a group in withdrawing and rejoining: "I didn't join right away. I joined after the strike was on. When it started out I was in favor of it, as far as the union is concerned, but my department couldn't make up its mind, and we decided to stick together. . . . When they first organized we signed up, but then the whole bunch in the department withdrew and so did I. . . . I remember that the petition went around and that we just signed because all the others had signed before us. . . . I wouldn't work during the strike, and I knew the best thing was to join again; most of my girls signed at the same time. . . . You never quite know what's right and what's wrong, and if you got a bunch together you just like to do what they are doing."

The Employer's Counteroffensive

With 40 per cent of the employees in the union, the organizers decided to bring the campaign into the open. The union members had gained strength and confidence from each other, and the organization had grown past the point where the discharge of one or two leaders could stop it. Leaflets were distributed at the plant announcing the time and place of the first meeting, and the organizers were overjoyed to find more than a hundred workers, a majority of the employees, in attendance.

Until the first open meeting was held the employer took little or no notice of the organizing drive. The large turnout, however, convinced him that it was necessary to take vigorous action. His first move was to mail a letter to each employee asserting that wages and conditions at the plant were good, that a union could produce no benefits, and that the organizers were professional labor promoters interested primarily in the collection of dues. The workers were reminded that they enjoyed the legal right to refuse to join the union, and they were warned that union membership would subject them to the "commands" of union officials who would force them to engage in "picketing and similar outside union activities." The company also held a meeting of all employees during work hours, at which officials stated their opposition to unionization, asserting that unions, by their excessive demands, often forced employers out of business. Several days later supervisors circulated petitions of withdrawal from the union, to which twenty-five signatures were obtained.

Meanwhile the union had asked for recognition by the company on the basis of its membership, and, when this was refused, filed a petition for an election with the NLRB. The company argued against an election on the ground that signatures on the cards were not valid. Following hearings, the Board ordered an election, which resulted in a 57 per cent vote for the union. The company contested the election, arguing that a union leaflet quoting a Catholic clergyman on unionization constituted illegal pressure, and that the leaflet had been distributed near the polls in violation of NLRB rules. After several months the Board ruled in favor of the union, whereupon the company asked the Board to reconsider; this was refused, and the union was finally certified, almost six months after the election had been held.

In the interval the company raised the minimum hourly rate from 75 to 90 cents, while raising piece rates only slightly. Like the earlier increase, this had the effect of further reducing the incentive to work hard. Many workers, however, readily associated the increase with the pressure from the union. Before the first negotiating session the company head called another meeting of his employees at which he again stated that unions often forced companies to close down or move away, and suggested that the workers write to the union office withdrawing their membership; following the meeting sixteen did so.

The union's basic contract demands included a union shop, wage increases, a seniority system, union participation in the setting of piece rates, a grievance procedure, improved vacation and holiday benefits, and company-paid health insurance. For three months negotiations dragged on without progress on any but minor issues. Since the union offered to arbitrate all issues including the leading one of union security, the company's refusal to arbitrate weakened its position both with its employees and the community at large. It appeared to the union organizers that the company was stalling in the hope that the union would break up. Yet Frank was unwilling to call a strike, except as a last resort, because of the strong feeling of identification with their employer that still persisted among the new union members. Nor did he think it wise to make a direct attack on Miller, for fear that some members might take his side. Though the workers would have to shift their loyalty to the union if the latter were to be successful, there was danger of alienating prospective members if John Miller were openly denounced at that time.

As negotiations wore on, however, increasing loyalty to the union developed. Some of the workers became disillusioned with their employer as a result of his actions during the prolonged and fruitless negotiations. "I used to have a lot of respect for him," one member of the negotiating committee said; "I turned against him when I watched him during negotiations . . . for me he showed his real face then." Typical of those influenced by the in-plant leaders who participated in the negotiations was an operator who said: "I never thought that our big boss could be so dirty. I always liked him. I thought he was a nice man. But after Louise told us how he acted in meetings during negotiations, I couldn't think much of him any more. All the money he gave to lawyers he could have given to the workers. I felt that before the strike; the strike didn't change my feelings too much. I was already mad." Precisely because the workers had so much respect and loyalty for their employer before organizing, reactions tended to be the more extreme when their expectations of his behavior failed to materialize.

A final effort to reach some agreement was made at a two-day bargaining session, at the end of which the parties found themselves almost at the same point where negotiations had started. The union representatives were willing to accept any reasonable compromise that would permit the union to live. As Frank put it: "We didn't want to call a strike. . . . We got some minor concessions, but nothing major that would permit the union to remain in existence. We knew that without any wage increases, the granting of a couple of paid holidays or some other very minor adjustments would be considered a defeat by the people in the shop for all their time and effort. . . . We knew that there were so many people that were not in the union that before a year was up there would be no vestige of a union left." The only recourse was to strike, and the union leaders quickly called a meeting, attended by about 115 workers, at which a standing vote to strike carried with 10 to 15 not voting and none voting against.

The Strike

The strike,[6] which lasted sixteen weeks, was an exceptionally hard fought one, involving a number of unusual features. The first day was crucial, since the workers, new to unionism and to strikes, did not know what was expected of them and waited for the union organizers to assign them to picket posts, organize a kitchen to provide meals, and make the many other necessary preparations. Meanwhile about thirty workers entered the shop and many others, who had come prepared to work, watched from across the street. Some who attempted to enter the plant were persuaded by the pickets to abandon the effort

[6] For studies of the strike as a weapon see E. T. Hiller, *The Strike: A Study in Collective Action* (Chicago: University of Chicago Press, 1928); Arthur Kornhauser, Robert Dubin, and Arthur M. Ross (eds.), *Industrial Conflict* (New York: McGraw-Hill Book Co., 1954); and George W. Hartmann and Theodore Newcomb (eds.), *Industrial Conflict; A Psychological Interpretation* (New York: Cordon Co., 1939). There have also been a number of studies of particular strikes. See, for example, W. Lloyd Warner and J. O. Low, *The Social System of the Modern Factory. The Strike: A Social Analysis* (New Haven: Yale University Press, 1947); Alvin W. Gouldner, *Wildcat Strike* (Yellow Springs, Ohio: Antioch Press, 1954); and Tom Tippett, *When Southern Labor Stirs* (New York: Jonathan Cape & Harrison Smith, 1931).

or found their entry blocked by force. The mayor and chief of police, aided by about a dozen policemen, formed a wedge to take a group through the picket line, but withdrew when the pickets pushed and kicked back.

The appearance of a group of non-strikers unified the strikers and made their behavior, until then relatively unorganized, co-operative and determined. The vigorous efforts to prevent non-strikers from entering involved workers who until then had been hesitant and un-decided, and drew them into the ranks of the strikers. The size and spirit of the striking group, the determination of the pickets, and the abuse to which non-strikers were subjected all had an influence on the undecided members of the work force.

On the second day of the strike the parties agreed, at a meeting called by the city attorney, on a code of conduct that would prohibit pickets from entering the plant, blocking the entrances, using threats or vile language, or assaulting or molesting employees entering or leav-ing the premises. Despite this agreement pickets continued to obstruct non-strikers and even tried to upset one of their cars. Several days later the company sought and obtained an injunction limiting the number of pickets and regulating their conduct. Meanwhile the county sheriff and several of his deputies had joined the city police force on duty at the plant.

Gradually the strike settled down into an endurance contest. Un-able to keep non-strikers out of the mill, the strikers tried to make their lives miserable, not only when they had to pass the pickets but also during their day's work and their off-hours in their neighborhoods. The pickets sang parodies of popular tunes that made fun of the super-visors, hung them in effigy from lampposts, and wore costumes cari-caturing them. A large circular saw, pounded incessantly with auto-mobile axles, created a terrific din. Since it was summer and the plant windows were kept open, pickets focused mirrors to catch the sun's rays and reflect them on workers at their machines. As a counter-measure windows were closed and covered with brown paper.

The pickets then developed another harassing device. Taking ad-vantage of the fact that the doors of the loading dock had to be opened frequently, they burned a mixture of tar and tar paper in large drums, using a draft to direct the thick, odorous smoke into the plant when-ever the doors were opened. In addition, pressure was brought on non-strikers through relatives who were members of other unions.

The knitting mill strikers received substantial help from the other unionized groups in the area. In part this took the form of volunteer picketing by members of other unions, though the company was probably hurt more by the refusal of members of the Teamsters' Union to bring deliveries through the picket line. Even more impressive, from the point of view of the community at large, was the organization of a United Labor Committee made up of AFL and CIO unions in the area which sponsored mass meetings and otherwise sought to mobilize community support behind the strikers. The aid received from other unions increased the strikers' sense of power, besides providing evidence that they were fighting for a reputable cause. Helped both by this support and, materially, by the strike benefits provided by the ILGWU, union morale remained high; parties, dances, and picket line stunts also helped to sustain morale.

The publicity caused by the knitting mill strike brought the Millers' department store to the attention of the Retail Clerks' Union, which sought to organize it and posted pickets when recognition was refused. Store patronage, which had fallen off earlier because of sympathy for the mill strikers, now dropped even more substantially. The United Labor Committee held two demonstrations, unprecedented in size for the community, on two Friday evenings when shopping was at its height, bringing the store's business virtually to a standstill.

The passage of several months, with no break in the strikers' ranks, increased the financial pressure upon the company. Production was very low, with only about thirty workers in the mill and deliveries hard to obtain. In addition, fuel was running short and local coal merchants were unwilling to supply the company for fear of incurring the displeasure of the town's unionists. The company resorted for a time to the expensive device of having coal shipped in small quantities by parcel post. The approach of a new season confronted the company with the likelihood of losing some of its customers unless it could resume production promptly, and its sales organization was likewise in danger of disintegrating. As a practical matter, therefore, it faced the danger of being forced out of business unless it settled the strike quickly.

The terms agreed upon provided for a 10 per cent wage increase for all workers, along with higher piece rates in selected departments. An equitable piece-rate system was to be determined by a representative of the ILGWU Management Engineering Department working with an industrial engineer selected by the company. A seniority system was instituted, grievance procedures agreed to, and a union shop established, subject to a vote on that issue to be conducted by the Wisconsin Employment Relations Board. The resulting vote, held after the strike had ended, was 131 for a union shop and 46 against. To keep their jobs the non-strikers had to become members of the union within ten months, and all of them did so.

Attitudes toward the Strike

Virtually all the leaders and most of the rank-and-file members saw no alternative to the strike by the time it was undertaken. Some leaders even welcomed the strike, as did one who resented being "herded . . . into a room like cattle and told that he [the employer] would shut down the shop . . . and that we would lose our jobs." "Oh, we felt good about it at the beginning," he said. "We could give it back to the company for all the misery we put in. I was for it, because I figured they could at least have talked with the union." Some of those who hesitated when the strike was first called because they doubted its effectiveness or because of close ties to the Miller family grew in enthusiasm as it progressed. Several supported it merely because most of their fellow workers did; and there were a few against the strike from the start who remained opposed to it.

The view that workers held of the strike was reflected in their attitude toward picketing. The convinced union members, especially those who saw no alternative to striking, were emotionally involved in their picketing duties from the outset, though there was some initial uncertainty due to inexperience. Others who supported the strike without much emotion simply resolved not to cross the picket line and resisted the employer's appeals for them to return to work. Those who were lukewarm about or opposed to striking usually found the language and conduct of the pickets offensive and preferred service in the union kitchen.

Many of the strikers found that picketing, far from being an unwelcome chore, was a stimulating experience; it brought fun and excitement into their lives and made them the center of attention in the community. People began to talk about them, their names were published in newspapers, and other unions supported their efforts. All the workers were greatly impressed with these developments. One of them pointed out that: "You learned a lot of people there I never knew before. You got to know what the big shots in the company were like. It was exciting. I met different cops and deputies and I know them all. We drew a crowd every night." The feeling of being the focus of attention did much to draw the members of the group even closer together and induced them at the same time to define the world in terms of "we" and "the others."

This solidarity was reinforced by many opportunities for informal gatherings and fellowship which tended to foster and maintain a sense of intimacy and sympathy. The sharing of picket line experiences contributed to the growth of group spirit and friendship. "We were all together and jolly on the picket line," one striker said; "we would dance together and we're friends now." Others also emphasized the good times they had during the strike, particularly the devices employed to annoy strikebreakers and the parties held for strikers: "We made the picket line a lot of fun. We did all sorts of things—you've heard about the noise-makers and the barrels, I am sure. We made dummies of the scabs and hung them on the poles around the factory. We actually made fun out of a grim struggle. It got so we couldn't stay away from the picket line for fear we'd miss some fun." Indeed, the meaning of "union" grew out of these experiences and was for most workers synonymous with the solidarity developed on the picket line. One worker observed: "I really don't think we had a union, not much of it anyway, before the strike. We became one with the strike, and we got stronger throughout. Well, I mean we knew we wanted a union but it was sort of wishy-washy. If he [Miller] gave a speech we believed him, and then we turned around again and believed the union. Then during the strike we really saw that the company was fighting us and what they really were like."

The attempts of non-strikers to enter the mill played an important part in welding the strikers into a cohesive and determined group. Because of the generally high regard for their employer that had prevailed he did not easily become a symbol of oppression. The non-strikers now appeared as the tangible threat, the visible enemy; they demanded continuous attention and alertness, and furnished an out-group upon whom resentment could be focused. Their presence influenced some of the undecided workers to join the union; it became more difficult, if not impossible, to remain neutral in the struggle, for those who remained outside the union were suspected of siding with the non-strikers.

Feelings toward the employer changed sharply. His daily efforts to get non-strikers into the mill, the obtaining of a court order against mass picketing, the protection of non-strikers by the city police and the county sheriff, and the other attempts to break the strike built up and sustained resentment. One striker characteristically remarked: "To see him meeting those scabs, barring all windows, letting them through the back door, and also calling for the police force to come down and do something with us—all that changed my feelings quite a bit." Another worker expressed her feelings as follows: "We thought that John had some feeling for his workers, and then you saw that all he was thinking about was his God Almighty Dollar. . . . The machines got more consideration than we did." As the strike was prolonged it became defined by many participants as a protest against a family that had controlled the community for much too long; they saw themselves not merely engaged in a strike against the owner of the knitting mill but crusading against a powerful and antisocial family for the benefit of the entire community.

Fence-Sitters and Non-Members

A fourth of the union membership—32 of the 127 who were members when the field work was conducted[7]—were labeled "fence-sitters" by the more convinced unionists. The fence-sitters included two groups: those who had joined the union prior to the strike only to withdraw and join again; and those who waited until the late stages of the organizing drive or until the strike was in progress before joining. The fence-sitters therefore, illustrated the conflicts, confusion, and fears which preoccupied many individuals both before and after their decision to join the union. Because of their middle position, they also suggested the problems faced by the non-strikers who ultimately sided with the employer.

As a group, the fence-sitters differed from the strikers in several important respects. They were older, had been with the company

[7] Though the plant had about 180 employees at seasonal peaks, only 158 were employed at the time of the field work. Ninety-five of these were convinced unionists, as we have used that phrase, 32 were fence-sitters, and 31 were non-strikers; none of the latter had yet joined the union.

longer,[8] and they included several handicapped persons. Many were afraid they would be unable to obtain satisfactory employment elsewhere if they lost their jobs as a result of union activities. More of them were primary wage-earners than was the case with the convinced unionists. Younger members of the group had close relatives who went through the picket line or who were employed in the Millers' store. Still others were relatives or close friends of supervisors in the mill. In addition they had little or no prior knowledge of unions, and no close relatives or friends who were union members trying to affect their decision. These factors, conflicting with the influences attracting workers to the union, produced indecision and confusion. As one fence-sitter stated: "Well, you know there was an awful lot of confusion. You just didn't know what to think. First you hear the union and then Mr. Miller would come and tell you something else. You really didn't know what to do. I wanted to do what the rest of the other girls did."

This indecision left some workers unusually dependent upon their associates. In a department lacking the leadership of a determined union member the example of a single individual strongly opposed to the union was often enough to persuade the undecided to give up their membership. In the case of those who joined the union and then dropped out the most frequent explanation was: "I dropped out because all the other girls next to me dropped out, too." For the individual fence-sitter the group cohesion and spirit of the strikers offered more security than did the group of non-strikers, daily exposed as they were to abuse and violence. As the strike continued many of the doubtful became convinced that the union would win and that their jobs would not be endangered if they antagonized their employer.

The fence-sitters were never fully integrated into the group of strikers. They preferred work in the strike kitchen to picket duty, and the strike leaders chose to assign them there for fear they would not be sufficiently militant on the picket line. Though the fence-sitters cared for the pickets, shared their experience indirectly, played games and joined in parties, and in all these ways were drawn closer to the entire group, their lack of direct involvement in picketing prevented the growth of a group spirit comparable to that enjoyed by the active pickets.

[8] The fence-sitters averaged forty-seven years of age and nineteen years in the company's employ. The strikers, by way of contrast, averaged forty years of age and eight years' with the company.

Partly due to their original indecision and ambivalence, and partly as a result of their different status and strike experience, the attitudes of the fence-sitters on a number of key issues were at sharp variance with those of the strikers. The fence-sitters were far less critical of their employer from the start, and their opinions of him did not change substantially during the strike. "I knew it was hard for him," one pointed out; "I sympathized with him in a way. He is really a man who wants to do things the right way. He didn't want people to come in and take over his business. I felt sorry for him." Those who criticized their employer's behavior usually added a qualification such as: "I know that Mr. Miller is broad-minded and he'll come around." Criticism of the Miller family's power in the community was also at a minimum. The group had little fear of reprisal from the employer, and the least expectations of future benefits from the union.

The fence-sitters also differed sharply from the strikers in their estimate of the non-strikers. The strikers, and especially their leaders, tended to lay blame for the strike squarely upon the employer; while they criticized the non-strikers severely, they saw them primarily as pawns caught in an unfortunate situation. The fence-sitters, however, primarily blamed the non-strikers rather than the employer for dragging out the conflict; at the same time they sympathized with the non-strikers and condemned the name-calling and other abuses to which they were subjected. Following the strike, accordingly, the fence-sitters were more willing to forget the past and to welcome the non-strikers into the union.

Accurate data could not be obtained about the thirty-one non-strikers because of their reluctance to be interviewed. Yet the evidence indicates that as a group they were even older in years and longer with the company than the fence-sitters, and that they included a number who might have experienced great difficulty, because of age or physical handicap, in obtaining other employment.[9] Some of the younger ones were relatives or close friends of members of the supervisory staff. A large number were primary wage-earners lacking other sources of income. At least one had been displeased with his union experience in a previous place of employment.

In most cases, moreover, the non-strikers worked in relative isolation

[9] These older, long-service employees, forced to join the union following the strike, found themselves protected by the union's emphasis on seniority. As a result the very factor that led them to work during the strike transformed them within a year or two into enthusiastic union members.

from active unionists. More than half of them were concentrated in two departments, eleven in end-pulling and six in yarn-winding, where not one worker joined the union during the organizing period or the strike. Several others, like the truck driver and the mechanic who serviced the knitting machines, were the only ones performing that kind of work and were therefore less exposed to group pressure than other employees.

All of this suggests that those who are least likely to join a union belong to several recognizable types: they are workers who cannot afford to risk losing their jobs because of their marginality in the labor force; they are bound to the employer by friendship or antagonistic toward unions as a result of some unpleasant experience; or, because of the uniqueness of their jobs or the absence of active unionists in their immediate work group, they are little exposed to union influence.

Union Achievements

The knitting mill workers were interviewed just after the strike had been concluded and while the union was in the process of negotiating its first agreement. Although no changes in wages had yet been made, most workers felt that they were already treated better by the floor-ladies, that work was now distributed fairly, that layoffs were handled according to seniority, that they were more secure in their jobs, and that their situation had improved in other ways. In appraising the achievements of the new union the leaders emphasized increased security, protection, and better working conditions; some of the rank-and-file workers, in addition, pointed to the improved relationships within the work group. Several also stressed the fact that complaints could now be voiced. The fence-sitters, who had had few complaints prior to the strike, were less convinced that conditions had improved.

Virtually all the union leaders believed that the workers were treated better by the supervisory staff as a result of the formation of the local. As one of the union officers, a middle-aged woman with twenty-seven years of company experience, put it: "It's much better now. They treat the majority of the employees as human beings now. They always used to have the attitude that if you don't like your job you can go somewhere else; they would lay them off, say nasty things, and often made the girls cry. I mean the floorladies and the supervisors, not John Miller. Now they treat the girls nicer, they try to please them.

It's because of the union—they are kind of afraid of the job, they think they might lose it if they don't treat the girls right. They also know the girls don't take too much anymore." Other leaders asserted that the floorlady "doesn't scream at us any more," that there was less favoritism, that supervisors were nicer, and that workers were no longer afraid to talk back. Some of them reported, however, that their friendly relations with supervisors had been destroyed since they had become union officers.

One of the rank-and-file unionists, a woman in her mid-thirties, also emphasized the better treatment they now enjoyed: "It's a wonderful feeling to have a union in the shop. You were their slave before and had to do everything they said. Now they respect you as a human being and not as a dog. That's a good feeling." Others said that they no longer had "to worry about being pushed around so much," that the floorladies "haven't been quite so unreasonable," and that "now you can sit at the machine and not worry about the boss coming up and shouting." Several reported that supervisors now made an effort to be pleasant. One said that her floorlady now "smiles once in a while; a smile goes a long way, don't you think?" Another said, similarly, that her floorlady "used to yell before, but now she goes out of her way to be nice." A woman nine years with the company was sure that the union had affected the way her floorlady talked to her: "It has had some effect—you bet it has. There have been several instances where the other girls have heard her talk to me in a gruff way and they've told the steward about it and that made her more polite and pleasant."

Some employees pointed to greater fairness and a sense of security as achievements of the union. Work was now distributed without favoritism, they said, and layoffs were also handled fairly. An officer of the union described the improvements as follows: "I feel . . . a lot safer when I walk into the mill. You know they can't fire us for any little thing we do. Now we can go to [the floorlady] and ask her to tell us how to do a little thing when we don't know how to do it. Before that we wouldn't ask her that—we would have to ask another girl, and if she showed you wrong it was your fault. It has done good so far, we have security now. They can't lay us off according to their wishes, they can't lay off the older people. And now you can go to the highest boss and talk to him, and he has to listen; before that we couldn't."

A number of rank-and-file members placed great emphasis on the feeling of belonging that came with union membership, and on the improved relationships within the work force. Several asserted that the plant now had "a much more pleasant atmosphere . . . we are all friendly now," or that the employees were "like one big happy family now." A middle-aged woman who had been active during the strike said that "It's hard to put it in words, but you just feel that you belong; that's the main thing."

Hopes for the Future

Most of the knitting mill employees were very conscious of the fact that few other opportunities for employment were open to them where they lived. Not surprisingly, then, the great majority planned to stay with the company permanently, except for those women who expected to quit in order to raise a family or who looked forward to leaving when their children were grown. Where the women were uncertain about the future, their husbands' job opportunities and experiences rather than their own were primarily responsible. Those who planned to remain emphasized their fondness for their work and their attachment to it. There were few opportunities for advancement in the mill, a fact that was generally understood and accepted. Most of the women felt they had no chance to become a forelady and also said they did not want the job because of the responsibility and trouble it entailed.

Despite their newness to unionism, their strike experience had given them some conception of the qualities a union leader should have. Paid jobs on the staff of the national union were out of the question for them, needless to say; only the unpaid positions in their small local union were available. Most workers, however, said they would not run for union office, either because they lacked the time or were not suitable for such a post. Many of the women said that they would decline because they were "just not a leader," "too bashful," "not built that way," too old, or unwilling to assume the responsibility. Those attracted to the position asserted most frequently that "it would be a nice thing to do," or that "it is nice to help other people." There were certainly no indications that either great prestige or hopes for advancement were attached to the job.

Less than half the workers wanted their children to follow them into the mill, despite the scarcity of other employment, especially for their daughters, in the community. Like urban factory workers, they hoped that their children would get "something better." Yet their aspirations were scaled down to reality; generally the women wished that their children, on the basis of more education than they themselves had received, could qualify for white-collar rather than factory employment.

Disappearance of the Union

Most of the workers, because of their part in the recent strike, feared reprisal in the event their union should disappear. Both among the union leaders and the rank-and-file members there was widespread belief that the head of the company would get rid of them at the first opportunity, or make life so miserable that they would quit. A typical response was that of an active unionist: "They would fire us all—if we wouldn't quit, that is. . . . We would get all the junk to do, I guess. . . . I would quit before they'd fire me. It would be hell on earth." Many pointed out that "they've seen me on the picket line" as justification for their fears. The fence-sitters lacked such fears on the whole, though even some of them were apprehensive that their jobs might be endangered. There was also a general belief among fence-sitters as well as convinced unionists that the recent gains would be lost if the union ceased to exist; seniority would no longer govern in layoffs, favoritism would return, and wages would be reduced.

It seems reasonably clear that, except for the presence of professional organizers, the plant would not have been organized when it was. Yet the organizers could not have succeeded had there not been a condition of unrest, a widespread feeling of dissatisfaction. The professional organizer does not create this condition; he probes for it, brings it to the surface, emphasizes it, and tries to place the responsibility for it upon the employer so as to convince the worker that his grievances can be removed by unionizing. The organizer seeks to transform discontent into a collective condition and to channel it through the formation of a union. He serves as much more than a catalytic agent, however, for he has experience and the economic and political resources of a national organization, and he determines tactics and objectives until the local group is able to help direct its own affairs.

Even in a crisis such as this no sharp line can be drawn between workers' loyalty to their employer and to the union. A degree of overlap almost inevitably exists. Accordingly, one of the prime objectives of the organizer is to polarize the loyalty of the workers. This requires the creation of an in-group feeling that embraces union members both inside the plant and elsewhere and excludes the employer and his supervisory force. As against this the employer may try to promote a group solidarity that will include everyone associated with the company from the owners to the unskilled workers, with all other persons, especially the union organizers, considered outsiders. The struggle is carried on within the consciousness of the individual worker as he responds to these conflicting pressures and decides on his own course of action.

Perhaps the most significant aspect of the strike was the growth of this strong feeling of solidarity and group identification on the part of the strikers. This solidarity was fundamental to the morale which the group developed during the strike; it was reflected in the persistent and determined behavior of the strikers, in their expectations of future benefits under union conditions, and in their feeling that they were engaged in a vital mission for the benefit of the community as a whole. The shift in identification from the employer to the union was not easily achieved by all the strikers, some of whom developed in milder form the ambivalence so characteristic of the fence-sitters. Nevertheless, group consciousness did develop and grow stronger while the strike lasted, welding the strikers into a unified and cohesive group engaged in a common effort to which they attached great importance. To a group that has undergone such an experience their union will have a meaning that later members will never quite be able to share.

7

TELEPHONE WORKERS
White-Collar Unionism

When one thinks of the American labor movement, one thinks primarily of manual workers—of factory workers, miners, building tradesmen, transportation workers—of men and women who wear work
clothes, punch time clocks, and get paid by the hour or by the piece.
These are workers whose formal education is usually limited, whose
chances of promotion are restricted, and whose conditions of work tend
to encourage solidarity; their habits of life and neighborhood associations permit the rough language and militant behavior associated with
the strike, the picket line, and the union hall.

Unions are also found, of course, among white-collar workers, the
fastest growing segment of the labor force.[1] Some white-collar groups
employed by manufacturing concerns are organized into the same unions that represent the production workers. Others are found in a variety of white-collar unions, whose jurisdiction ranges from office or
clerical work through the ranks of salesmen to a variety of professional
groups such as journalists, actors, or musicians. Over such a wide range
of occupations at varying levels of skill, pay, and prestige, the differ-

---

[1] A University of Chicago research group estimates that the proportion of white-
collar workers in the civilian labor force rose from 5.7 per cent in 1870 to 15 per cent
in 1910 and to 27 per cent in 1950; and that 16 per cent of these workers were
unionized in 1950, as compared with approximately 45 per cent of manual workers.
See Benjamin Solomon, "The Growth of the White-Collar Work Force," *Journal of
Business*, XXVII (October, 1954), 268, 271; and Robert K. Burns, "The White
Collar Worker in the American Economy," *Office Management Series No. 127* (New
York: American Management Association, 1950), pp. 22, 36. See also Benjamin
Solomon, "Dimensions of Union Growth, 1900–1950," *Industrial and Labor Rela-
tions Review*, IX (July, 1956), 544–61, which deals particularly with the white-
collar portion of the labor force. For a recent study of the experiences and the psy-
chology of various groups of white-collar workers see C. Wright Mills, *White Collar:
The American Middle Classes* (New York: Oxford University Press, 1951). See also
George Strauss, "White-Collar Unions are Different!" *Harvard Business Review*,
XXXII (September–October, 1954), 73–82.

ences are bound to be great as each union seeks to solve the distinctive problems of its particular occupation or industry.

Yet as a group white-collar employees differ from manual workers in education, manner of speech, habits of dress, and style of life, just as they differ in the work they do and the conditions under which their duties are performed; and all these differences, in turn, affect their willingness to unionize and their attitude toward their work, their employer, and their union. Among the white-collar unions one of the largest is the Communications Workers of America with about a quarter of a million members, almost all of them employed by the various units of the Bell System.

The Industry and the Bell System

There is no parallel in American industry, perhaps none in the entire world, to the Bell System. By its nature telephone service is a monopoly in any area; by a combination of patent rights, licensing arrangements, and aggressive and astute management the Bell System had been built up by 1953, when we studied a local of its employees, to the point of servicing over 41,000,000 telephones, four-fifths of all those in the United States. It had assets of $12 billion, annual operating revenues exceeding $4 billion, and 700,000 employees. The several thousand independent telephone companies in the country serviced small towns, with rare exceptions, and the 60,000 rural co-operatives completing the industry were usually very small. The parent company of the Bell System, the American Telephone and Telegraph Company, had 1,265,000 stockholders, the largest of whom owned less than one-half of 1 per cent of the stock. About 200,000 shareholders were themselves employees of the Bell System.[2]

This giant system originated with the telephone patent obtained by Alexander Graham Bell in 1876. As the popularity of the instrument became evident, a variety of operating companies were formed, each of which received exclusive rights to use Bell patents in its territory in return for the controlling interest in the company's stock. The expiration of the patents, as a result, did not affect the Bell System's network

[2] Most of the figures in this paragraph are taken from the American Telephone and Telegraph Company's *1953 Annual Report*. The largest stockholder is a leading firm of stockbrokers. By 1956 the number of telephones had increased to over 49,000,000, operating revenues to almost $6 billion, the number of employees to 786,000, and the number of share-owners to almost 1,500,000.

of operating companies covering the country. AT & T has a remarkable record of paying regular annual dividends of $9.00 on its stock, even during depression years when the payment had to be made out of surplus. Telephone rates are subject to government regulation, intrastate charges being determined by state regulatory commissions and interstate rates by the Federal Communications Commission.

AT & T, at the top of the Bell System, co-ordinates policy and provides a variety of services for the operating companies, besides directly owning and operating the long-lines division for interstate long distance calls. Under AT & T are twenty-one operating companies which together cover the United States, each providing telephone service within its area. Telephone equipment is manufactured and installed for all these companies by the Western Electric Company, an almost wholly owned subsidiary of AT & T. Research for the Bell System is the function of Bell Telephone Laboratories, the stock of which is held equally by AT & T and Western Electric. Other subsidiaries are engaged in specialized activities such as the manufacture of teletypewriters. Through their control of the stock of the operating companies and their power to appoint and promote administrative officials, the officers of AT & T co-ordinate policy and procedures on a wide range of questions including industrial relations, so that the entire Bell System operates with a high degree of uniformity.[3]

The Nature of Telephone Work

Each of the operating companies is divided into four departments: (1) traffic, with by far the largest number of employees, which completes telephone calls; (2) commercial, which arranges for service to subscribers; (3) accounting, which keeps the company's books and records; and (4) plant, which maintains telephone equipment in addition to hooking up and maintaining radio and television equipment. There are also staff units to handle such specialized functions as personnel, legal, and engineering matters. Virtually all traffic and accounting employees and the great bulk of commercial employees are women, whereas the equipment technicians in the plant department are all male.

[3] For an account of the Bell System's structure and methods of operation see Committee on Labor and Public Welfare, U.S. Senate, *Labor-Management Relations in the Bell Telephone System* (Report No. 139, 82d Congress, 1st session, 1951), especially pp. 5–14.

The traffic department in a typical exchange consists of a long row of switchboards; in front of each sits an operator wearing the headphone that is the distinctive mark of her calling. As the lights of her panel flash she completes calls and writes out tickets according to company rules. The work requires discipline and is performed under conditions of close supervision unusual for white-collar employment. The operator cannot normally leave her switchboard without being replaced, nor can she converse with fellow workers; the possibility of missing a signal demands close attention to the panel before her. Behind the operators there is a thinner row of service assistants, one to perhaps each nine to twelve operators, who train new girls and give help whenever necessary.

If the work of the operator is clean and of the white-collar variety, the supervision is as close and the discipline as exacting as one can find on a factory assembly line. The hours, indeed, are likely to be less desirable than those in a factory, because the switchboards must be manned around the clock every day of the year, necessitating nightwork, Sunday and holiday work, and split shifts. The operator enjoys few of the usual status symbols of the white-collar worker—a desk, nearness to higher management officials, absence of close supervision, nine-to-five hours, or freedom to leave her work and move around the office.[4] If any groups of white-collar workers begin to develop attitudes similar to those of industrial workers, the telephone operators have reason to be among them.

The service assistant, though a step upward from the operator, is not considered a supervisory employee. Above the service assistants are the chief operator and her assistants, who are genuinely supervisory employees outside the bargaining unit. The chief operators of several exchanges are responsible, in turn, to the district manager of traffic; he co-ordinates his activities with the corresponding district managers of the commercial, accounting, and plant departments, and all of them report to their superiors at the level of the division, a subdivision of the operating company.

There are also some clerical jobs in the traffic department; these are considered more desirable than operators' work because of the greater freedom and the chance to work at a desk instead of a switchboard.

[4] For a description of the jobs, working conditions, and pay of the operators and other women employees in the industry, see Women's Bureau, U.S. Department of Labor, *The Woman Telephone Worker* (Bulletin No. 207, 1946), and also *Typical Women's Jobs in the Telephone Industry* (Bulletin No. 207-A, 1947).

The great bulk of the clerical jobs, however, are in the accounting and commercial departments where the work more nearly fits the white-collar stereotype. The accounting employees, almost all of whom are women, sort and tabulate telephone tickets, keep books, and operate a variety of office machines. The positions in the commercial department are far more interesting than in either traffic or accounting, since commercial employees deal personally with the subscribing public. While operators are usually high-school graduates, the company's service representatives in the commercial department have usually had some college training.

The plant department is composed primarily of men, usually high-school or trade-school graduates, who are trained by the company to instal and maintain the complex equipment necessary for proper telephone service. Many of these workers are employed as linemen, cablemen, or installers, or on other outside jobs that may be physically hard or dirty. Others, however, are employed in the cleaner and more pleasant work of caring for the equipment in the central office. Members of this group look and act like white-collar workers; they come to work in business suits and do their day's work wearing white shirts and neckties. Though their pay is lower than that of building tradesmen—in 1953 they had a starting rate of $45.00 weekly and were earning a top of $103 after six years—they feel superior to such groups because of their better education, their cleaner work, and the prestige associated with telephone employment; equipment technicians feel themselves part of the great middle class, far more securely than do the operators.

The telephone companies are very careful, except as a tight labor market may force them to relax standards, in their selection of employees. They appeal, especially so far as potential operators are concerned, to recent high-school graduates, often recruiting them through school authorities or through friends already in telephone service. Very few new employees expect to remain with the company permanently. They usually plan to work only until they are married—though a substantial number, as one would expect, do stay permanently or return to increase the family income when their children no longer need full-time care. The operators' force in any telephone exchange is apt to run the gamut from the bobby-soxer to the middle-aged career "telephone girl."

The company's endeavor throughout, beginning with the initial training program, is to convince employees of the friendliness of the supervisory staff and the advantages of employment in the telephone industry. Promotional literature features an attractive, well-dressed, well-groomed young woman—possessor of "the voice with the smile"—just as it tries to convince employees and the general public that "the telephone company is a *good* place to work" and that the operator plays a role in the performance of an essential public service. If operators must work under fairly rigid discipline, this is offset to some degree by attractive lounges and lunchrooms and by recreational facilities in the company buildings. The companies provide medical assistance to employees, along with limited legal and financial advice. There is a high degree of paternalism in the telephone company—or perhaps one should say "maternalism," since employees frequently refer to their employer as "Ma Bell."

As in many other service industries telephone labor costs run high, comprising approximately two-thirds of total operating costs. The Bell System's wage policy is to pay beginners at the prevailing community rates for untrained workers[5] and to advance them through a series of pay grades as they acquire experience. In 1953 the progression schedules covered six years for operators, clerks, and plant craftsmen alike. Both the wage rates[6] and the length of the progression schedules are issues upon which the unions have steadily hammered.

[5] The Communications Workers of America has a twofold disagreement with the Bell System on this point. The CWA argues (1) that the policy of fixing wages according to community rates is a poor one and sometimes impossible to carry out, and (2) that the companies fail to match prevailing standards in areas, such as the West Coast, where standards are high.

[6] The CWA and the Bell System have disagreed sharply about the level of telephone wages and their relation to wage movements in other industries. In the 1950 wage dispute the union asserted that switchboard operators averaged only $38.00 per week, and that real wages of telephone workers had declined since 1939 while other groups of workers had maintained or improved their living standards. The Illinois Bell Telephone Company, which is probably typical of the operating units of the Bell System, asserted on the contrary that its operators were averaging $49.56 weekly, and that their real wages had advanced 37 per cent since January, 1940. See the CWA pamphlet, *Background of 1950 Telephone Wage Dispute* (1950) and the pamphlet issued by Illinois Bell Telephone Company in reply, *The Telephone Company Is a Good Place To Work!* (1950). Wages in the industry may be followed in the *Monthly Labor Review*, in the *Economic Reports of the President*, and in the reports of the Federal Communications Commission. These show that average gross weekly earnings in the telephone industry exceeded the average in manufacturing industry until World War II, but fell behind then and have remained behind since. Comparability of the figures is lessened because for some periods the telephone figures included the lower ranks of supervisory employees. In the fall of 1953 experienced switchboard operators of Class A Telephone Carriers averaged $1.40 an hour, service assistants $1.72, operators in training $1.14, and non-supervisory clerical employees $1.52. See Federal Communications Commission, *Statistics of the Communications Industry in the United States for the Year Ended December 31, 1953* (1955), p. 22. Average gross weekly earnings in the telephone industry were $65.02 in 1953, compared to $54.88 in retail trade and $71.69 in manufacturing.

While the Bell System has sought to maintain wage rates in accord with comparable skills in the area, traditional relationships have also developed among the various types of telephone jobs within each operating company and among the wage structures of the associated companies. A significant change in the wage level of any one of the companies may cause repercussions in other parts of the system. A wide variety of fringe benefits, including pensions, sickness and disability payments, paid vacations, premiums for Sunday and holiday work, shift differentials, and extra payments for split schedules have become established throughout the Bell System.

Though telephone jobs are far steadier than most other types of employment because of the increasing dependence of modern society upon telephone communication, telephone workers, especially operators, are fearful of the impact of technological advance upon employment opportunities. The conversion from manually operated to dial exchanges has sharply increased the number of telephones per employee, though the rising demand for telephone service, combined with company hiring policy, has averted technological layoff or reduced the number affected to a minimum. Turnover among operators is usually fairly high—often in the neighborhood of 30 per cent a year—as one would expect in a labor force composed of women, many of whom work only until they are married or begin to raise a family. Some, however, leave for other types of work, making turnover one of management's major problems. When dial conversion is imminent in an office the company does not fill vacancies that occur or hires only temporary employees, so as to minimize the impact on the regular staff.

Unionism and Collective Bargaining

Virtually without exception, every local union of Bell System employees is an outgrowth of a company union. Prior to the first World War only small groups of telephone workers, most of them linemen or maintenance men, had unionized. Labor organization in the industry got its real start in 1919 when the Postmaster General, who had control over the industry as part of the wartime mobilization effort, ordered that workers be given the right to organize and bargain collectively; and to forestall genuine unionism the various units of the Bell System fostered employee representation plans following the departmental and divisional structure of the associated companies. All company employees were automatically members of these organizations. Though these employee representation plans, like other company unions, were under management's control and lacked independent bargaining strength, they made labor organization familiar to and respectable among telephone employees, and provided a structure of organizations ready to evolve into genuine unionism when company domination of unions was declared illegal in 1937.

Following validation by the Supreme Court of the National Labor Relations Act in 1937, all the employee representation plans blanketing the industry revised their organizations to make themselves independent of their companies. Bargaining proved difficult, however, with some 184 separate organizations, most of them weak in finances and morale, facing a powerful group of associated companies whose labor relations policies were co-ordinated by AT & T. A number of these independent unions came together in 1939 to form the National Federation of Telephone Workers, which by 1946 was composed of 46 affiliates with over 200,000 members. Though efforts were made to co-ordinate bargaining efforts, each of the affiliates of the NFTW remained an autonomous organization—a basic structural weakness compared to the companies of the Bell System.

The first great advance achieved by the NFTW came in 1946 when all of its affiliated unions sought wage increases and other gains as part of the immediate postwar labor upsurge. The threat of a strike in March of that year brought a top official of AT & T into a bargaining session with the head of the NFTW, and the resulting agreement was quickly adopted by all of the associated companies of the Bell System. A year later, in support of an identical set of bargaining demands, some 375,000 Bell System employees struck. Though this strike was important as a demonstration of growing union strength—it was also by far the largest strike of white-collar workers the United States had yet experienced—the union proved to be far weaker than the Bell System. The contracts signed by the various affiliates of the NFTW provided for pay increases ranging between two and five dollars weekly; by way of contrast the second-round settlement in steel at about the same time provided for an increase of 15 cents an hour, and the General Motors settlement called for a direct hourly wage rise of 11½ cents plus paid holidays costing 3½ cents. The strike also revealed the weakness of the NFTW's structure with its many autonomous units, and demonstrated that the telephone companies, with largely automatic equipment, could maintain essential services with the aid of supervisors and non-strikers for longer periods than union members could afford to remain without income.

Several weeks after the strike ended the NFTW transformed itself into the Communications Workers of America, which affiliated with the CIO in 1949. The CWA sought to be a national union, not a federation of autonomous local affiliates. In 1950 it took another substantial step toward making itself like other unions by establishing a two-level structure comprised of a national union and its chartered locals, in place of the former three-level structure under which locals had been chartered by a number of divisions or regional bodies, themselves the outgrowths of the formerly autonomous unions comprising the NFTW.[7] Some of the unions that had been members of the NFTW have remained independent since the CWA was formed, though they recognize that their bargaining power as independent unions is very limited.

Bargaining in the telephone industry is carried on by each of the operating companies with the union or unions representing its employees. The CWA points to the 1946 settlement in particular as evidence that bargaining policy, except for comparatively minor matters, is controlled by AT & T; representatives of management insist, on the contrary, that each operating company is free to carry on its own collective bargaining relationships, though they admit that AT & T's stock ownership, with its power to appoint and remove officials of the operating companies, allows the holding company to co-ordinate, if not direct, the labor relations policy of the operating companies to the extent that it wishes. How far it wishes to do so is in disagreement, as is the precise meaning of the power to give "active assistance, co-operation, and support" in personnel matters that AT & T reserved to itself in its agreement with each of the operating companies.

A wide variety of bargaining units is found within the Bell System. The smallest ones may be for a single department of an operating company in a particular area, and the largest ones for all non-supervisory workers within the entire jurisdiction of the operating company, covering an entire state or a group of related states. There are also three national bargaining units, one for long-lines employees of AT & T and the two others for sales and installation personnel employed by Western

[7] For the history of unionism in the industry see Jack Barbash, *Unions and Telephones: The Story of the Communications Workers of America* (New York: Harper & Bros., 1952).

Electric. In 1950 there were 112 bargaining units throughout the system, of which the CWA represented 55, AFL unions 10, independent unions 45, and CIO unions other than CWA 2. The Bell System has resisted union demands through a variety of devices including bulletins and letters to its employees, "captive audience" meetings during working hours, and newspaper advertisements stating that higher wages would mean increased telephone rates to the public.

Only in the case of the long-lines division, which it operates itself instead of through a subsidiary, does AT & T bargain directly with a labor organization. Bargaining for the long-lines unit, covering some twenty-two thousand employees throughout the country, is carried on with a nationwide unit of the CWA, to which all its thirty-two locals of long-lines employees are attached. Prior to the collective bargaining sessions, which are held annually, each of the locals sends its proposals to the CWA national office. The proposals are then sifted by a bargaining committee elected by the long-lines delegates to the CWA convention; following negotiations with the company, the locals ballot again on ratification of the contract. Strike votes are taken in the same way. Each of the locals also comprises part of one of the nine geographic districts into which the CWA is organized for administrative purposes. The long-lines bargaining contract has a maintenance-of-union-dues provision combined with a voluntary checkoff.

The majority of the Senate Commitee that studied the industry in 1950–51 concluded that bad labor-management relations, which appeared to be getting worse, existed in the Bell System and that the basic cause was the inability of labor organizations to bargain with those possessing the authority to make final decisions. The committee minority asserted, on the contrary, that labor relations were relatively good compared to many industries and that CWA officials were as responsible as the company for such difficulties as had occurred.[8]

---

[8] *Labor-Management Relations in the Bell Telephone System,* pp. 31–32, 42. For the testimony of union and management officials see *Hearings before the Subcommittee on Labor Management Relations of the Committee on Labor and Public Welfare, United States Senate, Eighty-first Congress, Second Session, on Labor Management Relations in the Bell System,* 1950. On unionism and collective bargaining in the industry see also the chapter on "Unionization of the Telephone Industry" in the forthcoming volume by Robert K. Burns and Jay Tabb on *White Collar Unionism,* a copy of which has been made available to the present authors; and also Howard W. Johnson, "Union Organization in the Telephone Industry: A Study in White Collar Unionism" (M.A. thesis, University of Chicago, 1947).

The Local Union

The local union that we studied was made up of long-lines workers —and therefore employees of AT & T rather than of an operating subsidiary—located in a large midwestern city. Their work was similar to that of employees of an operating company, however, and there is no reason to believe that as workers on long-distance calls their qualifications, experiences, or attitudes differed in any substantial respect from those of workers employed by one of the operating subsidiaries. Indeed, many of the outgoing interstate calls were handled by employees of the operating company, whereas the remaining outgoing calls, plus incoming and through-long-distance calls, were handled by the AT & T employees. There was no significant difference between the two groups in types of duties, working conditions, security, or pay.

The long-lines division had approximately 2,450 non-supervisory employees in the area who were eligible for membership in the local union. Of these just over half, or 1,285, were union members in 1953 when the field work was conducted.[9] The various types of workers within the local's jurisdiction, however, responded differently to the union's appeals. Strongest in union sentiment was the plant group, whose members, except for a group of women with clerical duties, were the male technicians who serviced the equipment. Of the 375 workers in this group, 296, almost four-fifths, were members of the union. The largest group by far, those employed in traffic, comprised 1,855 workers, of whom about 250 were clerical workers, 125 service assistants, and the remainder operators; just under half of this entire group, 918 in number, belonged to the union. There were also 175 employees in an administrative unit consisting of engineering and technical assistants and others close to management, along with clerical help doing accounting work; only 25 of the 175 administrative workers were union members. Finally, the local included a group of 46 plant employees who worked in smaller towns throughout the area, some as far as 150 miles away. Though all of this last-mentioned group belonged to the union, they were disregarded when the sample was drawn up because of the difficulty of seeing them and because their work was iden-

[9] Union officials state that local membership has since risen to about 80 per cent as a result of intensive organizing efforts and the winning of important grievance cases. The traffic and plant employees are now about equally strongly organized.

tical with that of the equipment technicians employed in the home city.[10]

The local had the usual list of officers who, together with the executive board, carried on the bulk of local business. None of the elected officers spent full time on union business; the salaries for the positions, ranging from $25.00 to $50.00 monthly, barely compensated for the extra expenses inevitably incurred in a large city. When the local had the services of a full-time official, he was an organizer appointed and paid by the national office of the CWA. Other members whose services were needed to carry on local business were paid on a lost-time basis. The local had no organized factionalism; however, friendly candidates supported each other and sometimes ran on the same slates in local elections, which tended to be dominated by personalities rather than by issues.

Each of the offices where members worked elected one or more stewards as union representatives. The stewards, in addition to signing up new members, watched to see that the contract was observed and represented workers in first-step grievances. Because of their relatively greater mobility as well as their longer experience with the company, service assistants rather than operators tended to be chosen stewards in the traffic department. Union officers asserted that perhaps seventy-five to ninety grievances arose each month, mostly over the scheduling of shifts, but also over working conditions and the distribution of overtime and other work with premium pay.

The rules of the local provided that general membership meetings be held when necessary, but at least once a year. In practice the officers had been calling local meetings on the average of about once in two months, as business warranted. Because some employees were working at any hour, meetings were held in two instalments, the same motions presented, and the votes for and against totaled. There were also occasional departmental meetings, as of traffic or plant employees, though none had been called for some time. Stewards' meetings were usually held monthly.

---

[10] The sample as drawn included, in addition to all 11 of the leadership group, 76 operators and service assistants, 43 equipment technicians, and 21 clerical workers from traffic, plant, and administration. Difficulties were encountered, however, in getting interviews with the women employees, whether they were operators or clerical workers. Field work had to be stopped when seven leaders and thirty rank-and-file members had been interviewed. For this reason there is less data, especially from among the women, than in any of the other case studies, and the results should be considered only suggestive.

The local had participated in only one strike, the nationwide one of 1947. At that time about 70 per cent of the workers in the local's jurisdiction—far more than its membership at the time—had stayed off the job, though some had drifted back to work before the strike was settled. Union members picketed regularly during the strike, calling those who crossed the picket line names but not trying to bar their entrance. They also brought pressure in various ways on those who continued working, as by having unwanted merchandise delivered to their homes or putting skunk oil in their mailboxes. Several years later, while their bargaining committee was seeking to have seniority apply to all the offices in a building rather than to a single office, union members in this as well as other long-lines locals throughout the country walked off their jobs to participate in a union meeting as a means of exerting pressure on the company.

The Workers and Their Jobs

The telephone workers, as one would expect in the case of a white-collar group, were better educated than any of the groups of manual workers studied. They had had on the average almost twelve years of schooling, and many had had some college training. They came from homes representing, on the whole, a higher social status than any of the other groups; many of their fathers had been small businessmen or white-collar workers, and others had been skilled manual workers. There were also some whose fathers had held semiskilled jobs such as streetcar conductors; to these workers, white-collar employment with the telephone company represented a gain in prestige. All the workers interviewed were native-born whites, half of whom had parents born abroad. Except for the equipment technicians, the employees were all female. On the average they were thirty-five years old, with eight years of experience with the company; half were married, half either single or widowed, and most of them were Catholic.

Very few of the workers had any idea when they were growing up that they would enter telephone employment. After they finished school, friends or relatives in telephone work had suggested such employment to them, or they had been attracted by the company's advertisements. Except for a small number of men who had had some related experience elsewhere, as in the armed services, all had received their telephone training with the company itself. Though few had any

clear conception of the duties they would perform, there were indications that switchboard work exercised an attraction, however vague,
for many women, and that the industry possessed a romantic appeal
for young men as well. One of the men thus described his entry into
telephone work: "I was young when I first went to work for them. I
was out of high school about a year working about the country on road
construction jobs and then because telephone was kind of nice in my
mind—you know how a kid is from a small town—well, telephone
seemed kind of romantic. And I saw an ad in the paper advertising for
lineman's helper, so I applied."

Many of the women had started to work with the company
when they were quite young, had left when they were married or
shortly afterward, and had returned when their children no longer
needed constant care. They were secondary wage-earners, sometimes
planning to work permanently to supplement their husbands' incomes,
sometimes expecting to work only until specific expenses had been met.

The telephone workers were overwhelmingly favorable toward their
employer. There was often enthusiastic praise for the company, expressed in superlatives such as "It's the most wonderful place in the
world; I like it." The workers were gratified to be associated with a
large and powerful corporation, without the apprehensions prevalent
among factory workers that the company's power could be a threat to
them. They likewise appreciated the pension and other benefits, plus
the fact that they were reasonably assured of steady work, even during
business recessions. Still others emphasized the ease with which they
were extended credit because they were telephone company employees.[11]

Many also felt that the company was a source of prestige in the eyes
of the public. An operator who had worked five years with the company was among those who thought that telephone workers were highly regarded: "I think the public thinks that pretty well-respected people work for the phone company. And as a general rule when you talk
to anybody and tell them that you work for the telephone company
they tell you that you have a good thing there. . . . They don't just take
you as a laborer or somebody, they attach a little bit of prestige to it;
and the people who work there, I guess, feel the same way."

A few, however, asserted that working for the telephone company

[11] Compare Nancy C. Morse, *Satisfactions in the White-Collar Job* (Ann Arbor:
Survey Research Center, University of Michigan, 1953).

151

was "just a job, like any other," and denied that the company's prestige carried over to its employees. Some of these even felt that telephone operators were looked down upon by the public; where this view was expressed, a defense of the operators was usually added very quickly: "They [the public] don't think much of the telephone operators. It's classified as factory work, isn't it? But that isn't so—we've got college-educated people working there, and former models and ex-schoolteachers. . . . Public opinion is one reason I wouldn't want my daughter to work there. It's just the operators I'm referring to; the office workers they think better of. But we've got a couple of pretty tough operators and they give us all a bad name." Along somewhat similar lines a middle-aged operator with eleven years of service remarked: "I've heard people say that all operators are bums, but that isn't true. We have some nice girls working for us. They have some education, they dress nicely, and they know how to behave well. . . . I don't feel ashamed about it [working for the telephone company]. I wouldn't feel good if I were a waitress; they have to take too much, and that kind of feeling I don't have working for the telephone company."

Most telephone employees considered themselves to be white-collar workers. This was obviously so in the case of the small groups of administrative and clerical workers, but it was likewise accepted with varying degrees of emphasis by the equipment technicians and the operators. White-collar status does not depend exclusively on job content; social outlook is also involved. The factor most often pointed to was the cleanliness of the work; many stated that "we don't get dirty like manual workers do." There was also great emphasis on the better manners and better dress than are generally found among factory workers. A twenty-two-year-old operator, for example, pointed out that: "It's not manual labor, it's more like office work. Their language is different —you don't hear bad language in our office. They dress differently, too —quite nice; I wouldn't care to wear jeans." Several responses reflected a high degree of status consciousness, as in the case of a fifty-five-year-old widow, an operator who felt very positively that she and her co-workers belonged to the white-collar category: "It is the same as any business office. In fact, I think they [operators] should be called communication secretaries because they do a great deal of secretarial work for business firms. They are all very well mannered. You always get a few that are not, but as a rule they are."

The clerical workers, on the other hand, while certain that they themselves were white-collar workers, were very doubtful about the proper classification of operators. As one clerical worker put it: "Well, operators are sort of in-between factory workers and white-collar workers. They don't quite do factory work and they don't quite have the prestige of white-collar workers. . . . Operating is very unskilled work. I think you have to have a little bit more intelligence to work in an office. And you have more responsibility." Though these were ideas that few operators would care to accept, occasionally one did meet an operator or a service assistant who shared the clerical workers' outlook. In the case of a twenty-eight-year-old service assistant who had been with the company ten years and who also served as a union steward the alleged white-collar nature of the operator's job was a sore spot: "Ha, my pet peeve. I tell you I simply can't see that they [operators] are classified as white-collar people—as much as I hate to say it myself, because it degrades my own position. But look at the work—it's just like an assembly line; I don't think they are as closely supervised at Ford. But if you say that, they all resent it—they don't want to admit it because it degrades them. It's true they are different from other workers in many respects, such as the way they dress, their behavior, I mean manners, and on the average the girls have an education and don't walk around in jeans—I'd hate that. But I still think that working conditions put them into a different class than what may be their family backgrounds. . . . Clericals? definitely, white-collar workers. They work at a desk, they have nice offices, and they have nice working conditions."

There was much concern, particularly among the women, with the social characteristics of their fellow employees. Among the advantages of telephone employment, most of the women included the fact that they liked the people they worked with, that "the people are nice." With some of the older women this appreciation was combined with criticism of some of the younger employees, as in the case of a middle-aged operator with almost two decades of service: "When I started here first they were very strict as to whom they hired. They sent investigators out to see what home the girls came from, what background they had. You could be sure that you had a nice select group of girls. Unfortunately, they are now so pressed for workers that they cannot do that any more to the same degree. I feel the difference. The kids now don't have the same sense of responsibility, the restrooms look different now, the furniture is often mishandled and some write on the walls. That never happened years ago. . . . Also, things never disappeared, now they do. Some girls 'find' things and don't give them back. They don't have the same concern for other people and they don't have the same sense of responsibility. Sometimes I wonder whether our prestige will suffer from that; but I must say that on the whole it is still a better group of people than you find in most other places."

To deal with the public, to talk to different people, to work with nice people, and to do interesting work were among the reasons most frequently mentioned for liking the job; on the other hand the disadvantages most often cited were discipline, undesirable hours, and, less frequently, pay. A forty-one-year-old operator, a widow with two years of employment, was typical in her favorable reaction to the work: "I like the work in general—it's interesting. Of course, you get all riled up with the different people and things that happen—customers and all. But it's interesting—every call is different. The work is steady and the pay I don't think is too bad. There's one thing a lot of them don't like, I know —the younger girls don't like working Saturdays and Sundays. Of course, for me, raising a family, that boosts my pay working then." Asked whether she had any dislikes, she replied after a long pause and a query as to whether our recording device was still operating: "Well, it's the supervision. Always walking up and down in back of you saying, 'don't talk to your neighbor, sit just so, pay attention to the board'— it's terrible, worse than any job that I know of. They treat you like children."

The discipline at the switchboards was stressed very frequently as one of the chief dislikes of the operators and a reason for their leaving the company. Not only did they object to their inability to talk to the operators on either side of them during hours or to leave their post for a moment to chat with friends, but they particularly resented the practice of having the chief operators or their assistants listen in to check on their performance.[12] The disruptive effect of discipline on personal relationships was stressed by an operator not yet out of her teens: "Well, it's the discipline. I'd like to do clerical work. They have a chance to be more friendly—they form in cliques, sit at their desks eating sandwiches and talking and chewing gum—it's more friendly. We can't talk—but we do, of course, but not open and friendly like they do. No one is standing over them all the time." A number of older women recognized that

[12] Service observers also plug in on calls, to check on service to the public. The work of the service observers, who are themselves in the bargaining unit, plays no part in individual disciplinary procedures.

strict discipline was necessary in their type of work, though they added frequently that "it's hard on the young girls."

Those critical of telephone employment were in a minority. As a group the telephone workers were pleased with their employer, their jobs, and their fellow workers. Many could not think of any dissatisfactions, and others who expressed criticism did so only after some probing and reflection. When they discussed aspects of their employment they disliked, they often centered their attention on relationships with the public rather than with the telephone company. Undesirable hours and marriage were listed most frequently as the reasons why workers left the company; other reasons sometimes mentioned were the severe discipline and the low pay for workers with little seniority.

Joining the Union

The act of joining the union could only be voluntary in a situation where almost half the workers were outside the organization and no legal and very limited social pressure could be brought upon nonmembers. Since most workers held a very favorable view of their employer, the most important consideration leading them to join the union was the desire to have some form of protection available in the event it should be necessary. A young equipment technician said, characteristically, that he was interested in "the assurance of a square deal—to know that somebody is fighting in your behalf. If you're on the carpet from the lower echelons of the company, then the union will take your case to the higher echelons." Implicit in this statement was the view that the company was fundamentally fair, though this might not have been true of every minor supervisor. Factory workers are far more likely to doubt the good intentions of their employers.

Some of the telephone workers had had a background of union membership in their families. One of these was a middle-aged operator whose father had long been a member of the streetcar operators' union and who had grown up accepting unionism as a desirable and necessary institution. Several workers, in addition, had acquired pro-union sympathies as a result of educational or religious influences.

Other workers, entering the company's employ without having thought particularly about unionism, became friendly to the idea as a result of their experiences. A union leader, for example, a veteran of twenty-five years, grew union-minded as he became convinced that the

155

company cared more about its machines than its employees; the lay-offs he had seen during the depression contributed to his sense of in-security, though he himself had worked steadily.

Along with the overwhelming majority, who joined the union with some degree of conviction, there were others who simply went along with the group. A woman who later became an officer knew little or nothing about unionism when she "just followed others" and became a member: "I certainly didn't know why I was a member. I just wanted to be what my neighbor was—be part of the group. . . . I can't even re-member going to any union meeting. I don't know who or what they asked me. I must just have gotten a card and signed it because others signed it too. I paid my dues from then on and forgot about it. I never had a complaint and never needed the union." Another member of the local, a seventeen-year-old operator in her first year of employment, "had no feelings either for or against" the union; the people she worked with were union members, however, and she "didn't want to be left out."

An interesting case was that of a middle-aged equipment technician who had had a year of college before entering the company's employ. Though he had learned almost nothing about unions in school, he had formed an unfavorable opinion of them from newspaper stories and cartoons and found it hard to get over this impression even while be-coming convinced that the union was a necessary institution. Asked what made him decide to join the union, he replied: "Well, I don't like castor oil, but if I think I've got to have it, I take it. I don't like unions, but right now that's the best we have to help us do our work and take care of us, so I didn't hesitate a minute. I joined right up."

Most members asserted that unwillingness to pay dues was the chief reason why employees stayed out of the union. Non-members received the same benefits, often including representation in grievance cases, especially if failure to prosecute the case might adversely affect mem-bers. Other reasons advanced to explain the failure to join were preju-dice against unions, company orientation, or fear of losing promotion opportunities or of being involved in strikes.

Union Achievements

Though the bargaining power of the telephone workers' union was limited, the members generally felt that the union's achievements had been substantial. Wages, working conditions, job security, seniority, and the opportunity to settle complaints or individual problems were the items most frequently mentioned. Despite a widespread view of the company as a benevolent employer, rank-and-file members as well as leaders gave the union credit for winning wage increases. Many workers felt that the union provided the pressure necessary to obtain needed increases in pay.

With regard to the effect of the union on their treatment by supervisors the workers were sharply divided. The most prevalent opinion among rank-and-file members was that the union had had no effect, chiefly because the supervisors had always treated them well. One member who expressed such a view was a service assistant, a veteran of twenty-two years with the company: "I don't think the union has anything at all to do with the way the supervisors treat the operators. It's company policy—they're instructed to treat the operators in a very pleasant way. They're not bosses; the company is very strict about no bossing, showing any bossy attitude toward any operator. And the company has a very fine training program which the girls go through before they become service assistants, and besides the chief operator keeps track of how their work is going." Many of the rank-and-file operators and other workers expressed similar views, and still others stated that the union might have had an effect elsewhere in the company but not in their own departments.

One young woman, however, a scheduling clerk, felt that with some people, "it goes to their head when they get promoted; the union steps in there and tones them down." Another unusual response came from a middle-aged widow, an operator for twenty-one years: "Well, they got us better working conditions. . . . The supervisors are not allowed to yell at the girls like they used to be able to do; they used to tell the girls off, but now a girl has a right to turn around and tell her, and if she is dissatisfied she can go to the union and complain about it, and the union will make an adjustment, which has been done in several cases down there." Views such as these were met with frequently among industrial workers, but only rarely among telephone employees.

Union leaders were far more positive than the rank-and-file members that the union had improved the treatment of workers. One of the officers of the local, an equipment technician employed more than two decades by the company, was among those holding this view: "You get a few die-hards in there that will never accept the union. If the union wasn't there they would be pretty tough on the men. The supervisors had to take a little more human approach to the employees in general. Today you get your own choice about hours on the basis of seniority; they can't throw you back on a dirty job and forget you. They can't keep on picking for the same men in the premium pay jobs. It has forced them to give a bit more human thought to the employees."

Criticism of the union and of its members cropped up a number of times. Thus an operator, asked what the union had accomplished, gave it credit for winning wage increases, but then added: "There's a lot of people who expect just because they're union members they can just say anything they want—have just any kind of an attitude; I know I do the best I can at all times; then if there's anything wrong then I think the union has a place in it. I'm not like some of these kids who don't do any work, and then go to the union for every little complaint. As far as I know, I haven't any complaint against the company at all." Other members criticized the union for being too aggressive toward the company—for asking for too much money, for calling strikes, and for attacking the company too often and too bitterly in its publications. A young equipment technician who had been with the company two years thought that the union made "rash promises that lean toward the absurd"; he would like to see both union and management become more "sensible" in their wage positions. A middle-aged operator who strongly favored the union because it provided a mechanism for the adjustment of grievances was opposed to the calling of strikes, and said that the union's use of the strike might lead her to drop her membership.

A clerical worker in her thirties who had been a union member for four years objected to the constant demand for raises and the "very radical attitude" of the union's paper: "I'd like to have them stop asking for raises. No matter how much they get they always want more. . . . I don't know what the other departments want, but I'm satisfied. I mean for a while. I expect that after a while things will get better, but just every year and every year always wanting more. . . . They put out a paper and they show a very radical attitude. I think that paper spoils the reputation of the union. It says the company is just horrible, just miserable. And they always print all the bad things the company does and they make it sound so much worse than it is; it's so colored, so prejudiced—as if the company is your enemy." Attitudes such as these, which reflect middle-class values combined with a high degree of identification with a paternalistic employer, are seldom encountered among industrial employees. To the extent that workers with such attitudes are found in white-collar occupations, unions hoping to organize them and hold their allegiance must learn to modify the methods developed primarily by organizations of industrial workers.

Strikes and Picketing

The reactions of the telephone workers to strikes and picketing reflected their generally high estimate of their paternalistic employer as well as their regard for middle-class standards of behavior. As a group they had a very low opinion of the accomplishments of strikes. Fewer than half thought that wages had been raised as a result of strikes, and some of these believed that the same gains could have been made without striking. Smaller numbers mentioned improved vacation plans or better working conditions, and several who felt that strikes had accomplished "quite a bit" immediately voiced doubts as to whether the gains had been worthwhile or achieved in the best possible manner. A substantial minority asserted that strikes had accomplished nothing. Several of the women emphasized the disrupting effect of strikes on personal relationships, regretting the antagonism that inevitably developed between those who struck and those who continued to work.

Those who supported strikes as necessary to win improvements generally agreed that picketing was an essential, if a distasteful, part of striking, and that a show of strength was necessary in order to achieve the union's goals. As an operator put it, "I don't like it [picketing], but I figure if I don't go nobody will go, and where are we going to get without it?" Others found picketing very distasteful; among these was a nineteen-year-old operator whose comment was equally revealing of her attitude toward the union and her understanding of picketing: "No, I wouldn't want to picket. I wouldn't want to walk up and down outside the place. I'd feel like a big jerk. I thought it was the union's job to picket—I mean the stewards and the officials." Also involved in her attitude may be the standard of behavior in public expected of a young girl on a white-collar job.

Despite their relative newness to unionism, the telephone workers shared the general view of unionists that picket lines of other unions should be respected. "It's our code," said a youthful operator; "it's the principle of unionism—stick together even if it's your union or not." The few who admitted having crossed picket lines usually tried to explain or justify their actions by pointing, say, to an unusual need for income at the time, or by stating that they felt "terrible" as a result.

Aspirations of Telephone Workers

Though the telephone workers generally lacked strong ties to their work and to their occupational group, almost all who considered themselves permanently in the labor force expected to remain with the company until retirement. They most often emphasized the possibilities for advancement in a large and complex company, the assurance of continued and regular employment, and satisfaction with their jobs. There was some regret, especially among the younger operators, that they had not chosen employment of a more glamorous nature or more in accord with middle-class values. Those who planned to leave were for the most part single women who disliked the hours or planned to get married, or married women who were needed at home or whose earnings were less necessary now that their families were grown.

Without exception, the men who were interviewed expected to remain. Indeed, they had little choice, since their training and experience as equipment technicians were so highly specialized as to afford little opportunity for alternative types of employment. With few exceptions, however, they liked their work and could think of no other employment they would prefer. The women, mostly operators at a lower level of skill, had less to lose by changing occupations and more reason to hope for certain improvements, notably in discipline and hours. Yet the great majority of the married and widowed women, and many of the single women as well, planned to stay permanently. Like the men, they saw the telephone company as a desirable employer, one that treated them fairly, assured them regular employment and economic security, and offered them opportunities for promotion. Nowhere was there the fear of layoff or of arbitrary discharge so frequently found among factory workers.

The telephone workers looked forward more confidently to promotion than any of the other groups studied. This was understandable in view of the variety of jobs available in telephone service and the company's policy of filling many of the more desirable positions by promotion from its own ranks. The equipment technicians in particular looked forward to a variety of opportunities for promotion. The operators also had good opportunities, at least up to the position of service assistant. Beyond this the prospects thinned out, however, since relatively few could expect to be made assistant chief operator or chief operator. Nevertheless vacancies, when they occurred, were filled from the next lower rank, rather than by hiring outsiders. There were, moreover, a limited number of clerical positions which operators might hope to get.

The great majority of operators believed that the company selected employees for advancement according to impartial, objective standards, including ability, performance, and length of service. Only occasionally was there a charge that favoritism was a factor. Those who felt they had no chance for promotion usually pointed to their age or their record of absences; some who thought they would be offered promotions, however, intended to decline either because they did not wish to change their working schedules or because they did not want the additional responsibility. Many of the leaders of the local believed that their union activity, far from hurting their opportunities for promotion, improved their chances of being offered supervisory positions. A successful union officer or active member, it was pointed out, demonstrated an ability to handle people, a quality important to the company in its appointment of supervisors.

While equipment technicians, with few exceptions, preferred their work to any other, most of the women specified other more desirable occupations. Those mentioned included airline hostess, receptionist, secretary, nurse, and teacher—all secure middle-class positions carrying prestige and, in some cases, glamor. Yet many of the operators were as much concerned with working conditions, as in the case of the nineteen-year-old who said: "I guess I'd like to be a secretary. You got your own desk and nobody to bother you. Nobody interrupts your work and you do the work you want to." A middle-aged operator made a somewhat similar point: "If I had it to do all over again, I would get business training and go into office work. The people are just as nice where I work now, but it would not be so nerve-wracking. We don't have too much time to make acquaintances." Many women, however, obtained satisfaction from their work or at any rate did not prefer other employment. With some it was simply lack of knowledge about other jobs: "I don't know; I've had no other jobs. It never occurred to me what I'd like."

Telephone employees do not look to the union as an avenue for advancement. Full-time union positions are very few in the Communications Workers of America, and only for the top leaders of the local was such a position even possible. For the average worker, however, it was not even attractive. Most of the women, in addition, did not care for the unpaid job of union steward, usually asserting that they lacked the time. Unlike factory workers, very few doubted their ability to fill the post satisfactorily, suggesting either that telephone workers felt more confidence in their abilities or that they attached less importance to the steward's position and did not believe that it required any special skills. In the eyes of most telephone workers, the steward's job carried little prestige. A few said that they would accept because "I like to help people"; or as a woman, already a steward, put it, "I get satisfaction if I help to present an individual or a group problem to management and help to iron it out." Only one respondent said that she would accept "because I owe it to the union."

Telephone workers were far more willing than factory workers to have their children follow them in their employment. All of them wanted their sons and daughters to have an education first, and there was some hope that they might achieve the professional status so highly valued in our society. Yet the great majority either wanted their children to work for the company or had no objection to such a possibility, again illustrating their liking for the company and the prestige they associated with telephone employment. If their children did so, however, most workers hoped that they would have better positions than they themselves had achieved. Many said that they would like their sons, but not their daughters, to work for the company, reflecting the more desirable position of the skilled equipment technician as against that of the less-skilled and more closely disciplined operator.

Telephone workers evidently have a high regard for their employer. This should not be surprising, for a company in a naturally monopolistic position, with a relatively stable demand for its services, has every reason to try hard to build a satisfied group of employees. Because rates are regulated by public bodies, reasonable costs of operation, including wages and fringe benefits along with other expenses, are offset by the amounts the company is permitted to charge. Assurance of permanent employment, relative insulation against the layoffs accompanying even minor business recessions in other industries, wages matching those available elsewhere for comparable skills—these are among the advantages associated with telephone employment.

In addition, the Bell System has made a conscious effort to be a benevolent employer; it has been concerned with a pension system, vacation and sick-leave provisions, good treatment by supervisors, attractive restrooms and lunchrooms, recreational facilities, and the like. It has provided opportunities for advancement by its policy of promotion from within the industry, and has tried to sell itself to its employees and to the general public as a progressive, if not a model, type of employer.

Yet there are important sources of employee dissatisfaction and important functions for the union to perform; otherwise the union would never have developed to its present size and strength. The wages, planned to reflect community rates for comparable skills, necessarily follow rather than create patterns. The long wage-progression schedules and the discipline are bound to produce dissatisfaction, and in any large and complex organization there is need for machinery to adjust grievances. The Bell System has increased the frustrations of its union-minded employees by its preponderance of bargaining power, its insistence that each operating company bargain separately and virtually independently, and its ability, with the aid of automatic equipment, to provide essential services during a strike long after its employees have felt the pinch of lost income.

If, as seems to be the case, telephone employees regard their company more highly and their union less highly than most manual workers, more than the particular practices of the Bell System may be involved. Part of the explanation may lie in the fact that the employees are a white-collar group with middle-class aspirations and responses. Their qualified reactions toward the key union bargaining weapons, the strike and the picket line, show clearly the influence of middle-class concepts. Yet the existence of strong unions in certain white-collar fields, as among musicians, newspaper writers, and railway clerks, shows that the handicaps facing unions in this area can be overcome.

8

LEADERSHIP
IN LOCAL UNIONS

"Just the organization itself keeps me active. With me, the organization is what would be religion to other fellows." It is an officer of the
local union of steel workers speaking, telling what keeps him active
in the union. "But what do you get out of it?" he was asked. "Ulcers,"
he replied. Then he paused and added: "I'm very well satisfied when
I see the superintendent squirm when I put him on the pan. . . . I
remember the day when I used to squirm when the foreman looked
at me. Now it's the other way around and I enjoy it." This combination
of idealism and a sense of power, mixed with resentment against past
treatment by company officials and the satisfaction of settling old
scores, provides the motivations keeping this worker active as one of
the leaders in his local union. While motivations and satisfactions
vary, needless to say, from one situation to another and from officer
to officer within the same local, this steel worker illustrates the interplay that may occur in a single case.

In each local union in this country there is a group of leaders,
made up of local officers and chairmen or members of key committees;
together these groups comprise the backbone of the labor movement.
The general public, when it thinks of labor leaders, thinks not of them
but of the president of the AFL-CIO or of the powerful national
unions, of men such as George Meany or Walter Reuther or John L.
Lewis. To the rank-and-file union member, however, the leaders who
count most are those in his local union, in his shop or department, who
carry on the routine activities and make the large number of day-to-
day decisions having a direct impact upon the workers in the shop.
Indeed, in the eyes of the average union member the local official with
whom he most frequently comes in contact may symbolize the local
union, just as the local union in turn may typify the labor movement

as a whole. It is interesting to note that, while inactive members usually speak of the union in terms of "they," leaders typically speak of it in terms of "we." The actives sometimes use the one term and sometimes the other. This expresses better than any statistical table could the increasing identification with the local as one proceeds from the inactive rank-and-file membership through the ranks of the active members to the leadership group.

In industries such as construction, printing, or the service trades, where the contract is negotiated locally, poor local leadership has a direct and obvious impact upon the union and upon its ability to represent adequately the interests of its members. Even where contracts are negotiated regionally or nationally as in coal mining, or where pattern-following exists as in steel, the need remains for a high quality of local union leadership to adapt and then police its own contract. Because the local leader is vital to the successful functioning of the labor movement, it is essential to understand him, to know his motivations and his attitudes, to see both how he resembles and differs from the rank-and-file union member.[1]

Three Levels of Local Leadership

The term "local leadership" embraces a broad band of officialdom ranging from shop stewards through grievance committeemen and executive board members to local presidents and business agents. Though these positions may shade into each other, in general three layers of officials may be distinguished in terms of the attributes, and therefore the desirability, of the various offices.

The largest layer, at the bottom, is composed of shop stewards, unpaid union representatives scattered throughout the plants, usually

---

[1] See chap. 9, "The Local-Wide Leader," in Leonard R. Sayles and George Strauss, *The Local Union: Its Place in the Industrial Plant* (New York: Harper & Bros., 1953). Sayles and Strauss distinguish two types of local leaders, administrators and social leaders (pp. 123–26). Emphasizing motivation and career opportunities rather than social characteristics, Eli Chinoy divided UAW local leaders into three types—accidental, ambitious, and ideological leaders. See his chapter, "Local Union Leadership," in Alvin W. Gouldner (ed.), *Studies in Leadership* (New York: Harper & Bros., 1950), pp. 157–73. See also Charles A. Madison, *American Labor Leaders: Personalities and Forces in the Labor Movement* (New York: Harper & Bros., 1950); C. Wright Mills, *The New Men of Power* (New York: Harcourt, Brace & Co., 1948); Eli Ginzberg, *The Labor Leader: An Exploratory Study* (New York: Macmillan Co., 1948); and the chapter on "Union Leaders" in Jack Barbash, *The Practice of Unionism* (New York: Harper & Bros., 1956), pp. 367–402.

one to each department or group of related departments. The stewards serve as the contacts between the union and the rank-and-file members; as a rule they sign up new members, see that the contract is enforced, serve as union representatives in the first step of the grievance procedure, and in general function as the agents of the union in their portion of the plant.

The position of steward is important and even burdensome if taken seriously, since any problem within the department becomes a problem for the steward. There are satisfactions to the steward in the recognition and prestige that he receives in the department, in the opportunity for occasional breaks in his work routine, in the limited authority he can exercise in relation to the foreman, and in the hope of rising to a more important union post or to a management position if he earns the respect of those with whom he deals. There may even be a slight material reward if the steward is placed, as he must be in some union contracts, at the head of the departmental seniority list. On the other hand the steward takes on everyone else's problems and worries and gives up much of his private life to an endless round of union activities.

The steward often exerted great influence in the formative period of unionism, when relations in a plant were more fluid than now and departmental walkouts or slowdowns more frequent, but with the maturing of labor relations the tendency has been for a union-shop clause to bring in new members automatically; for union-management problems to be settled at a higher level; for the union, like management, to become more bureaucratized; for the union to curtail the power of stewards and try to discipline them as authority passes to the local-wide union officers. As a result the position of steward is not very attractive. Not only are the contests for the job relatively rare, but often a local has difficulty keeping its ranks of stewards filled. In many cases no one comes forward spontaneously as a candidate for the post; any worker who shows even a mild interest in the union and very moderate leadership possibilities may find himself appointed to office or urged to become a candidate by his fellow workers or the local leaders for a post to which election may be assured.

The middle range of local leadership, in terms of authority and general desirability, is made up of unpaid officials with plant-wide or local-wide constituencies and responsibilities. Such positions include bargaining or grievance committee members, executive board members, and local officers. These offices are far more satisfying, socially and psychologically, than stewards' positions, and consequently are sought by ambitious union activists. Holders of these offices—particularly of the important ones such as local president—are key figures within the plant, known to all members of the union, treated with respect by foremen, and frequently in touch with top management. The heads of an important local may be known to the national officers of the union and to the officers of city and state central labor bodies. They may also be figures of some importance in the community, dealing with city officials, serving on community boards, and having their activities reported in the press.

Material rewards at this level, however, are not very great. The office may carry a small monthly income, usually not more than is required for the extra expenses of restaurant meals, drinks, and telephone calls that the position and its attendant contacts involve. Where time is taken from the job in the plant to carry on union activities, pay is on a lost-time basis; union work is more interesting, however, so that the change is a welcome one. In addition there are occasional all-expense trips to conventions or other union functions away from home or to the state capitol to testify before a committee or lobby for legislation. These material perquisites of office, while not very substantial, add to the pleasures and comforts of life and help to explain the desire of ambitious unionists to obtain these posts.

For all these material and psychological rewards of local office, there is a price. The officer of an important local is likely to find all his free time and energy absorbed by union duties at the expense of home, family, personal friends outside the union, and other interests. His wife may resent the time the union takes; his children may grow up strangers to him. The tension of factional struggles within the union and of conflicts with management may strain his nervous system, and irregular hours may place an added burden on his health. His record on collective bargaining improvements and grievance cases may be subject to factional attack at the next union election, and if he takes too much time on a lost-time basis he may provide an additional argument to his opponents. The only hope for union advancement, if he has attained the top unpaid office in the local, is to a paid union job; but few locals are likely to have several such positions (large ones of building tradesmen are exceptions), and most locals have none; so far as jobs as international representatives or organizers go, the number of positions is small in relation to the number of applicants.

The rewards of office, while not to be underestimated, are not great enough to warrant an all-out effort to keep them. Nor is the possibility of keeping them over a long period of time very great. This is particularly true in a moderate-sized plant where an ambitious rival can get to know a large percentage of the electorate and build up a substantial following for the next election. While the local president can win widespread support if he has a record of achievement, he is not likely to have at his disposal the jobs, honors, or other rewards upon which one builds a successful political machine. In the course of time, therefore, he is either beaten by a rival candidate or he declines to run for re-election, preferring to go home after his day's work in the plant and let someone else carry the burdens of office.

The relatively small number of full-time union officials constitute the topmost level of local union leadership. The difference between full-time and part-time union work is not in degree; the entire style of life changes. The union official now goes to an office instead of a shop; he wears clean clothes, does clean work, eats in a restaurant, drives a good car (often one purchased by the union), carries a briefcase instead of a tool kit. He is an executive, not a production worker; his occupation as union leader is a middle-class, not a working-class, one; he may now be middle-class not only in terms of appearance, dress, and working hours but in income as well, since local union officers are typically paid as much as, or more than, the most highly skilled workers that they represent. Like middle-class income, moreover, the union pay is on a salaried basis, without the interruptions caused by layoffs that plague the lives of workers in so many industries. By becoming a working-class leader, in short, the union official in an important sense may have risen out of the working class.

Here are rewards, both psychological and material, that are worth holding on to. Defeat for re-election means, not release from the burdens of office, but reverting to a much less desirable way of life. The full-time union official, therefore, is motivated to keep himself in office; he can remain in office if he can control enough favors and rewards to build an effective political organization. In the building trades—in plumbing, for example—the very situation requiring a group of full-time union officials gives them an important political asset. Because jobs are of short duration and widely scattered, business agents are needed to patrol them; by the same token the business agent is the connecting link between the union and the workers, the one person whom the workers on the widely scattered jobs are apt to see. In an industrial local, by way of contrast, an official who works full time in the union office is cut off from regular, on-the-job contacts with his constituents, thereby suffering a political disadvantage as against an ambitious rival in the plant whose job permits him to maintain contact with large numbers of workers.

In addition the business agent in industries such as the building trades is in a position to do favors for his friends. Since he hears of jobs that will be opening up, he can pass this news on in advance to those who are friendly to him, perhaps help them to get placed by a word to the contractor. He also handles complaints and grievances, of course, as these occur within his jurisdiction. These are political assets even in the best of times, and when jobs are scarce the friendship of the business agent may mean the difference between work and unemployment. The friendship of the unpaid union official in an industrial plant can hardly be as important to his constituents, since their jobs are long-term ones, obtained from the employer with little possibility for intercession by the union officer.

Business agents in the building trades and similar industries, therefore, have the incentive to perpetuate themselves in office, besides possessing powers far greater than those of the unpaid union officer in an industrial plant. As full-time officials with personal stakes in the political control of the local, they are often in a position to manipulate and dominate the local union's executive board. Where the local has a group of paid officials the tendency is for them to pool their political strength, support each other between elections, and run as a slate in the elections. The member ambitious for paid office, knowing that his chances of success as an independent candidate are slight, has the choice of running as a member of a rival coalition or of supporting the incumbents, hoping that when a vacancy occurs they will add him to their slate. Barring major unrest in the trade, the chances of victory of a rival slate are very poor. Ambitious unionists, therefore, support the incumbents, accepting small rewards in the way of an unpaid union office until something better is available. In this way the union political machine is created, with its implications for union democracy; and as a result elections for the highly desirable, full-time, well-paid union jobs are likely to be contested less frequently than those for the less rewarding offices.

Characteristics of Local Leaders

Important differences in the characteristics of the leaders can be noted as one moves from one to another of the six locals studied. Such factors as age, educational background, level of skill, personality, relationships with the company, length of time in the positions, and the degree of authority vested in the offices make for substantial variations among the leaders of the different locals. The leaders of the plumbers were well-paid, full-time representatives of a powerful union of skilled tradesmen, men of conservative social philosophy who were greatly concerned with working rules and with the protection of the trade; they dealt mostly with small employers, some of whom were themselves members of the union, in a relationship with few elements of conflict. The officers of the steel and metal workers, by way of contrast, tended to be younger and more militant, reflecting antagonistic relationships with the large and powerful corporations that employed them and, in many cases, a more radical social philosophy as well. The leaders of the telephone workers included many who had become skeptical of the widely advertised opportunities for advancement in the company and who looked upon its paternalistic practices with some cynicism. The miners' leaders, like those of the plumbers, showed a strong attachment to their occupational group; they exercised little authority in their highly centralized union, however, and hardly differed from the rank and file that they represented. The officers of the knitting mill workers, newest of the groups to unionize, were the natural leaders among their fellow workers and included those who were young and aggressive enough to assume leading roles in a conflict situation.

The leaders of these six local unions tended, on the whole, to be of the same age as the workers they represented, but to be somewhat above average both in educational attainments and in skill. The plumbers were an exception in all these respects, since the leaders were substantially older than the members, averaging fifty-six years of age as against forty-nine for the rank and file, and had on the average eight and a half years of schooling, a year less than the other members. Yet there was a special factor operating in this case, since the membership rolls had been closed during much of the long depression period, and the present group of leaders, in office when the union was again opened to new members, had been re-elected without opposition since that time. They were therefore representative of the older membership both in age and schooling, whereas the rank-and-file plumbers included both age groups. So far as skill is concerned there was, of course, no difference, since the local was composed exclusively of craftsmen.

As with the plumbers, the leaders of the telephone workers were substantially older than their general membership and were most sharply distinguished by their far greater length of employment (an average of twenty-six years of service compared to under nine for the rank and file). The telephone workers, it must be remembered, included a majority of female operators, many of them quite young, with a high rate of turnover; a much smaller group of female clerical workers; and a relatively small group of male equipment technicians, who tended to stay with the company until retirement age. The union leaders were chosen disproportionately from among the male technicians, showing the combined effect of several factors—sex, higher level of skill, greater age, and longer service with the company. The women leaders came largely from among those who expected to remain relatively permanently in the company's employ and who had experienced some degree of disillusionment with its widely advertised personnel policies—both of these constituting factors that would tend to make for greater age and length of service with the company. In education there was no difference between leaders and rank and file, both groups having had on the average three and a half years of high school.

In the cases of factory workers wholly different considerations appeared to be present. There the leaders were somewhat more highly skilled, and with somewhat better educational background (an average of three years of high school for the steel, metal, and knitting mill leaders, as against one to two years for the rank and file). This does not mean that workers prefer to be represented by officers with superior education, but merely that those who are more highly skilled and better educated tend to be the informal leaders of the work group and are therefore likely to be elected to union office. A substantially better education, however, may create a gulf between a worker and his fellows, or lead to suspicion on their part that he hopes to use union office as a bridge to a management position.

Under factory conditions it is an advantage to a union officer, as well as a political asset to an aspirant, to have an opportunity to talk to a large number of fellow workers in the course of the day's work.

The man whose job gives him mobility within the plant, or brings other workers to him, is more likely than others to become a union leader. As an inspector who held union office in the metal plant observed, "I was able to get around the shop; it was good for campaigning." The leaders of the steel and metal workers tended also to be drawn from among those workers who were more aggressive, more dissatisfied with plant conditions, and politically conscious to a higher degree than their fellow employees—indicating that, especially under conditions of labor-management strife, workers of this type may find in union leadership an outlet for their interests and energies, just as they may prove more appealing to the membership.

While the leaders of the metal workers' union did not differ in age from their members, the leaders of the knitting mill union were somewhat younger on the average than their constituents (39 years compared to 42.4); this may have reflected the higher degree of militancy and aggressiveness—qualities more associated with youth—called for in an organizing situation characterized by open conflict. It might be expected that, as company and union succeeded in working out a more amicable relationship, the leaders selected would tend to be somewhat older and less aggressive, outstanding for maturity and balanced judgment rather than for militancy. The steel union leaders were slightly older than their constituents (an average of 42 years as against 39.5). The leaders of the miners were of the same age as their general membership and tended to have slightly more formal schooling (almost 10 years on the average as against 8.5).

How Leaders Became Active

A variety of factors operated to make the union leaders active in their organizations and to elevate them into positions of responsibility. In a great many cases they were singled out as potential leaders by the powers in the local or by a higher union official and either appointed to office or persuaded to run for some elected position. In other cases, emerging as the natural leaders of their work groups, they accepted responsibility at the urging of their fellow workers, sometimes after they had taken the lead in protesting the action or inaction of an incompetent union official in the face of poor working conditions or arbitrary behavior by supervisors. In still other cases they were persuaded by aspiring union politicians to accept a nomination in order to lend their popularity to the ticket or to help balance a slate in terms of skills, departments, shifts, or ethnic groups. In a few instances workers became active in the union after they had failed to receive desired or expected promotions, or because they hoped to obtain personal power, recognition, or financial gain from union office. However they happened to emerge as leaders, there was something that made them conspicuously promising for union office: their natural leadership potential, their experience or family background, their dissatisfaction with working conditions in the plant, or their point of view on general social issues.

In the case of the knitting mill workers the problem was to find, in a shop with fewer than two hundred employees, the most competent group of workers who were willing to assume the responsibilities of office. In some cases it was the union organizer, in other cases groups of fellow workers, who suggested to particular members of the young union that they be candidates for office. Many of those who became officers were motivated by their resentment against poor working conditions or arbitrary actions of supervisors. Particularly in newly organized unions, but also in many other locals too small to provide pay or much prestige to its leaders, there is often a shortage of spontaneous candidacies for many of the lesser offices; the result is that almost any member who shows an interest in union work and a willingness to devote time and energy to it may be proposed for one of the positions.

In the steel local,[2] also, there were instances of workers who did not seek office, but had it urged upon them by a group of fellow workers— here, by those dissatisfied with the performance of an incumbent: "When I came here in '45, we had a griever that drank a lot and was never around when you needed him. He was always off the job drunk somewhere. We couldn't get anything done, and conditions were piling up. The guys in the department asked me if I would take the job and I told them 'Yes.' So they elected me." It should be recognized that the stratum of leadership or potential leadership available in the steel plant is very thin. This may be due partly to barriers of language or education, partly to the fact that a steelmill will probably attract proportionately fewer energetic and able persons than more desirable places of employment. Not all workers with leadership ability, obvi-

[2] For a fuller treatment of the leadership group of this local see the authors' article, "Leadership in a Local Union," *American Journal of Sociology*, LVI (November, 1950), 229–37.

ously, are interested in union activity, whether because of lack of conviction, conflicting interests, or family responsibilities. Whatever the reason, the number of competent persons available for union office in this local is very limited considering the size of the membership; consequently, a worker with the ability to lead who shows an interest in the union may rise quickly to a position of influence. In this local, as in others, he may find that the lower union offices seek him, so to speak, rather than the reverse. For the more important local offices, however, which involve much more power and prestige, spirited contests are the rule.

Dissatisfaction with treatment by the company was another factor that led officers to first take an active part in union affairs. One of the steel union leaders traced his activity to a denial of promotions he thought were due after he had participated in the 1937 strike. In another case a worker was discharged for what he considered a very minor offense, and thereupon decided to become active in the union then being organized. Treatment by the foreman was another of the reasons assigned: "I was always the kind of a guy who didn't want anyone to jump down my throat all the time. Before the union came in, they [the foremen] did that in the mill." Sometimes a belief that a foreman was discriminating against members of minority groups led the latter to become active in the union. A Jewish worker reported: "I had a foreman who was discriminating, had a prejudice against my religion. He refused to recognize my seniority, and I wanted to be part of the union to settle it; and I succeeded."

Another group of leaders, particularly in the steel workers', metal workers', and coal miners' locals, pointed to prior work experience or family background[3] to explain their union activity. An officer of the metal workers became convinced, as a result of an experience with another company, that corporations could not be trusted. The father of

[3] In the cases of the metal workers and the plumbers there was a significant difference between the leaders and the rank-and-file members with regard to union membership of their fathers. Sixty-five per cent of the metal workers' leaders were the sons of union members, as against 23 per cent of the members; in the case of the plumbers the figures were 83 and 53 per cent, respectively. The difference was also suggestive in the case of the miners, 80 per cent of the leaders having had union members as fathers, as against 69 per cent of the rank and file. There was no difference between the two groups in the steel local, however. In the case of the knitting mill an inverse relationship existed, in that half of the general members, but only a third of the leaders, were the children of union members. Perhaps women, who comprised the great bulk of the knitting mill employees, are influenced more by their husbands than their fathers with regard to unionism. In any event, union membership of the father is only one factor in a highly complex social situation.

one of the leading officers of the steel workers had been active in his union and also in the socialist movement. Another, whose father had been active in the United Mine Workers, observed that "I attended union meetings with my father before I was ever inside a church." Among several leaders who stressed their ideological attachment to the labor movement was an officer of the metal workers, who stated that the opportunity to become active in the union was the chief reason why he entered the company's employ. "You have a clear conscience in making this a better world to live in," he said; ". . . being active in the union means everything to me."

Political considerations, as in any other type of organization, have a profound effect upon the opportunities to become a leader. In the case of the plumbers some years earlier, a group that was organizing a slate of candidates to oppose the incumbent officers invited promising individuals who were well known and widely respected in the trade to join their caucus and accept a place on its ticket. In the steel and metal workers' locals, both of which have a rather high degree of factional organization, caucus heads are always looking for natural leaders who will bring support to their slate in the periodic elections. Sometimes the choice is made on the basis of a candidate's appeal to the membership at large, more often because of the votes he will bring to the entire ticket from his department or from some special interest group, perhaps racial or ethnic, scattered through the plant. The vice-presidency of the steel local traditionally goes to a Negro. In some cases, especially where the slate-making is controlled by a few individuals and the election is not expected to be close, a candidate may owe his selection to friendship with one of the leaders or to the payment of a political debt. The victorious slate, in turn, tends to carry all those upon it into office, whether or not each is better qualified than his opponent for his particular office. While political considerations of this sort may not insure the election of the most competent officials, either in the union or in the nation at large, they are perhaps inevitable accompaniments of the democratic process.

The variety of factors that have been discussed, as has already been evident in some of the cases cited, occur in various combinations. Personal qualities such as aggressiveness, intelligence, and tact may make a worker a popular and respected figure in his work group, just as a high level of skill and long years of service may add to his prestige. Whether he emerges as an officer of the local, however, depends upon such factors as his interest in the union, his hopes for advancement, his reaction to conditions in the plant and to his treatment by supervisors, the performance of the incumbent union officers, and the needs of the slate-makers for a representative of his department or ethnic group to complete a ticket that might win the election. While motivational factors and personal qualifications determine potential leadership, actual emergence as a leader depends upon the political opportunity available in one's department or in the local as a whole.

The Rewards of Leadership

However they happened to become active in their unions, those who continued as leaders received some satisfactions or rewards that led them to run for re-election, some many times. In certain cases, as with the business agents of the plumbers, there were obvious advantages in the high salary, the assurance of steady income, the power and prestige, and the opportunity to dress well and do clean work. The top posts in the steel and metal workers' locals, while offering little in the way of pay, gave incumbents a fair amount of power and prestige. All the other offices, including the leading ones in the other three locals, had to provide other satisfactions if officers were to seek re-election.

Many officers were kept active by the desire to win improvements for their fellow workers. "I get satisfaction in seeing that people get what they should" was a typical response. An officer of the steel workers' local spoke of the help that he was able to give outside as well as inside the mill: "You go to bed at night and if you accomplish a few things during the day you can sleep with yourself. Even petty things are big things in this business. You do a good deed. If you can get a ticket fixed for a fellow or get a man out of jail, it's a good thing." Members of minority racial or ethnic groups were particularly alert to instances of discrimination, and eager to protect their people's rights and enlarge their opportunities. As a Mexican officer of the steel union said, "It gives me a chance to do something for my people. As a griever, I can make sure that we continue to fight discrimination."

Other leaders spoke of the feeling of power their offices gave them. One referred to "the satisfaction of keeping the foremen in line." Often this feeling of power was associated with the opportunity to treat supervisors as they had once been treated by them. As an officer of the steel workers expressed it: "I get a chance to rub it into the supervision when they make a false step. I feel that it's up to the active people to keep the company on the ball. It gives me a feeling of satisfaction that they can't get away with what they did before the union came in." Often the way in which two or more factors were combined in a single response was significant. Thus one leader of the steel workers' union, asked what he got out of continued activity, replied, "Not a damn thing but a headache." Then, after a slight pause, he added: "I get plenty of satisfaction. It's worth a lot to be able to tell a boss to go to hell— one thing I could never do before. Also serving my fellow workers."

Others valued the recognition they received from company officials, or the prestige they enjoyed among fellow workers. "You always carry prestige as a departmental steward," a metal worker asserted. Another leader, a top officer in his local, referred to the sense of power he enjoyed in the internal politics of the union.

A safety committeeman in the steel plant plainly showed pride in his ability to deal with a top company representative on terms approaching equality: "I'm a safety committeeman; I get in to see the superintendent who makes 100,000 a year. I sit down and maybe put my feet on his desk. All the assistant superintendents and foremen remain standing until he comes in and tells them 'Gentlemen, be seated.' I . . . tell him what I think. After he dismisses the supervisors we decide what to do." The desire for recognition, prestige, and power so evident in this statement indicates clearly the rewards this worker receives from his union activity.

More tangible rewards were enjoyed by many of the officers. Sometimes it was only a small monthly payment, perhaps just enough to cover the cost of the extra telephone calls and meals away from home that union work made necessary. Even if no such sum was paid, time lost from work on union business—often a welcome relief from the monotony of the regular job—was paid for by the union. When union conventions or conferences were held, there was the chance to take a trip at the union's expense, to get acquainted with officers of other locals, and to meet leading officials of the national union. Only occasionally did an officer frankly admit that his supplementary income from the union helped keep him active, though motivations of this sort were frequently imputed to factional opponents. To a steward in the metal workers' union, work at overtime rates was a welcome ac-companiment of union service: "I found out that by getting into the political end of it with the union I get the overtime. Under the contract the steward has to come in even if only one man is called."

Differences between Leaders and Rank-and-File Members

The foregoing discussion of leaders has pointed to some significant factors in their backgrounds, experiences, motivations, and personali-ties that help to explain why they emerged as officers of their local unions. In these respects they were somewhat different from their fellow workers who remained rank-and-file members. Their union offices, in turn, have intensified the differences by giving them differ-ent roles to play, exposing them to different influences, and providing them with experiences rank-and-file members seldom have.

With regard to their attitude toward job and company something of a paradox was apparent in the case of the leaders of several of the locals, since they tended simultaneously to derive greater satisfaction from their jobs than the other workers and yet to be more highly criti-cal of their employers. Yet perhaps this paradox can be resolved if it is remembered that officers tended to be more highly skilled than the rank and file. Highly skilled work is more pleasant, less closely super-vised, more varied, and better paid; and since the skilled groups fur-nished a disproportionately high percentage of leaders in most of the locals, it is not surprising that union leaders like their jobs more than ordinary members do.

In the cases of the steel, metal, and knitting mill locals, conflict situations helped explain the presence of aggressive types of workers in the leadership groups. Among the telephone workers, though a somewhat different relationship existed, the union leaders tended to be drawn largely from long-service employees who were somewhat dis-illusioned with company policies. In the case of the miners the fact that control over collective bargaining and strike policy was in the hands of the national union leaders may have helped to preserve close relationships at the local level and to produce local leaders who re-flected the generally high opinion the miners held of their employer. The plumbers represented a wholly different situation from any of the others, in view of the dominant position of the union in the industry.

Though statements highly critical of their employer were very rare among the general members of the metal workers' union, fully a fourth of the leaders expressed such uncomplimentary views as, "I think they are deceitful," or "They are a cheap, chiselling outfit." Most of the leaders, while not going to such extremes, criticized the company far more than ordinary members did. Sometimes it was evident that experience as a union officer had helped produce a more critical attitude, as in the case of the leader who said: "As a union representative I know how they operate and it's hard to like anything about them when you have to deal with them." The leaders of the steel workers' union, similarly, were far more critical of their employer than were the rank-and-file members, their major objections being the company's attitude toward the union and the behavior of supervisors. While some of the leaders, like most of the rank and file, thought highly of the company, others could think of nothing about the company that they liked. "I feel that it's the worst company a man can work for that I know of," one said.

Local union leaders, as might be expected, showed a closer attachment to their union and a higher estimate of its achievements than was true of the rank and file. Of course it must be remembered that their estimate, in an important sense, was an account of their own stewardship and achievements. Their greater emotional involvement in the union's activities and also their greater knowledge of its problems and attainments may likewise have influenced their responses.

One of the areas where sharp differences in attitude could be observed between union leaders and rank-and-file members related to the internal political life of the organization. Leaders on the whole were more emphatic in their assertions that members could bring about changes within the local; they were far more convinced, especially in large locals, that organized support was necessary to get elected to office; and, particularly in the steel and metal locals, they strongly supported organized factions as essential to the democratic process, while the other members tended to disapprove of factions as divisive, causing unnecessary wrangling and impairing the unity essential to success in dealing with management. Rank-and-file members might feel incapable of factional activity, but this would hardly be the case with union leaders, who had risen to office by the successful use of such techniques. Perhaps there was also an element of defensiveness in the reactions of some of the leaders; knowing that charges of undemocratic practices were likely to be aimed at them, some of the leaders may have been more vehement than objective in their appraisals.

In the larger locals the leaders, with their greater political experience, were more conscious of the advantages an organized slate afforded in the way of publicity, finances, and the pooling of strength. A Negro leader of the metal workers' local, who owed his own union office to factional support, emphasized this point: "From a political point of view, it's necessary to line up with a faction. As an individual you would have to get around to all departments and that would be impossible. Working with a faction, you get support from the plant as a whole. As an individual you get only support from your department and friends."

Those who held a favorable view of factions were for the most part leaders or active members of the farm equipment and steel locals—men who understood the political realities of their unions and who themselves were active in the factions that had won control. The plumbers' leaders, more like their constituents, tended to dislike factions or to have reservations about their operation. Perhaps this difference might be due to the fact that rival factions were in existence in the steel and metal workers' union, some of them led by men who held union posts; as union officers they could hardly disapprove of their own activities as faction heads. With the plumbers, on the other hand, one group was solidly in control, enjoying strong support from the great bulk of the members. To these leaders factional activity could easily appear as harmful to organizational unity, if not as a potential threat to their positions.

It was interesting to note that the strongest support for factionalism was found among the leaders of the metal workers' union, although the strongest opposition to it came from the rank and file of that local. Perhaps one possible explanation lay in the vigor of factional life within that local, a condition which the leaders tended not to criticize because they thought it healthy or inevitable or because they were the persons responsible for its existence. A further explanation might be found in the members' view of the union as a collective bargaining agency whose effectiveness might be impaired by internal strife, a view that the leaders perhaps helped to strengthen by their constant appeals for unity and solidarity against the employing company. The leaders saw no contradiction between such slogans and the bitter struggle for power within the union. They saw the union both as an agency for bargaining with the company and as a governing body, control of which was to be won by political means; the other members, less sophisticated, were not so conscious of this distinction and feared that the methods employed in the political life of the local might weaken its effectiveness in dealing with the company. To some, "politics," whether in the state or the union, had an evil connotation, suggesting crooked deals, mudslinging, and unscrupulous striving for power. For the leaders, moreover, the union's political life was a matter of the utmost consequence in its own right, whereas to the other members it was of little intrinsic interest and wholly incidental to the important function of winning improvements for the workers.

Differences between the leaders and the rank and file in all six local situations were strongly marked regarding the proper scope of union activities. Leaders tended to view the union as functioning properly over a wider area than did the rank and file, who conceived of the union more as an agency dealing with problems growing out of employment in the plant. In the case of union activities affecting city, state, or national politics, the difference in attitude was particularly great, with a far larger proportion of leaders favoring such activity and many more members rejecting it as interference in an area properly reserved for individual decision. With regard to participation by the union in community and social affairs the leaders were somewhat more favorably inclined than were the rank and file; the most striking difference here was in motivation, the members tending to view the activity in terms of its value to them as individuals or as employees, whereas leaders were more concerned with institutional prestige and the building of union loyalty.

There were also sharp differences in attitude from one leadership group to another, depending on the characteristics of the occupational group and the forces tending to elevate one type of union member rather than another into positions of leadership. Leaders in the steel and metal locals, for example, were almost unanimously interested in political activity and generally supported it with enthusiasm. The plumbers' leaders, in contrast, were somewhat hesitant about political action and gave it only moderate support. On the one hand they knew that their local had to be influential locally in order to protect its interests with regard to the building code and the appointment of inspectors, and they were urged to support Labor's League for Political Education, sponsored by the AFL; on the other hand they were very reluctant to engage in political action, a composite of the conservatism of skilled craftsmen combined with pessimism as to the extent to which the voting behavior of members could be influenced.

Union leaders also differed from the rank and file in estimating the consequences of the union's disappearance. While the general membership usually foresaw lower wages, deterioration of working conditions, and a return to the arbitrary authority of foremen, the leaders were generally more extreme; they were more certain that these results would follow and they predicted even more dire consequences. Whereas a minority who did not predict these evil results could usually be found in the general membership, it was rare to find one dissenter among the leaders. To these predictions the leaders often added another—their own discharge. Only among the knitting mill workers were fears of reprisal prevalent among rank-and-file union members.

Leaders of the steel workers' union listed wage cuts, speed-ups, arbitrary discharges, loss of security, favoritism instead of seniority, discrimination, and dictatorial rule by foremen among the evils they foresaw. One compared the disappearance of the union to the imposition of slavery. Another said that it would be "like losing the war, losing the country." Many leaders of the plumbers found it difficult even to conceive of their trade without their union. "That would be impossible—it couldn't happen" was a frequent response. Most of the leaders asserted that utter chaos would envelop the trade. Leaders of the telephone workers, on the other hand, could readily conceive of the loss of their union, though many of them expressed the hope that it would soon be replaced by another.

Relations with Supervisors

Leadership groups in both the steel and metal workers' locals tended to be highly critical of their companies' promotion policies. The leaders were convinced that favoritism was the most important factor, with ability of much less consequence; the rank and file, while rating favoritism or "connections" high, thought that ability or educational background were much more significant factors. Many leaders also asserted, far more frequently than did rank-and-file members, that promotions often were made from among the ranks of active union men, provided they had the other qualifications. As an officer of the steel union said, "They try and accomplish two things with one stone by getting a good man for supervision and getting rid of an active union man." Another officer of the same local asserted that: "Guys who win lots of grievances are usually picked as foremen. It's that way in my department, anyhow. I've won lots of grievances from them and they want to get rid of me by making me a foreman. They think they can buy me off." All the leaders did not agree on this point, however, some declaring that "people who don't believe in the union very much" get promoted. Officers of the metal workers' local, while noting a tendency for supervisory positions to be offered to union leaders, gave somewhat different explanations, placing more emphasis on the company's realization that ability and leadership qualities were to be found in the union officer group.

In view of these opinions, it is not surprising that the officers of the steel and metal workers' unions were far more confident than the rank and file of their chances for promotion to supervisory jobs. There was sound basis for this confidence, for many could point to offers already made. Despite their greater opportunities, however, they expressed far less desire to accept positions as foreman. To some degree the leaders' responses may have been influenced by their present role, by the belief that they should disclaim any desire to rise into management ranks lest they be suspected of using their union offices to advance their own careers at the expense of the interests of the general membership. Yet it was also apparent in many cases that the job of foreman was defined negatively, and in other instances, fewer in number, that acceptance of such a promotion would imply an unwelcome change in their entire set of social attitudes and interests.

Many union leaders who asserted that the foreman's job was unattractive pointed to the small amount of authority. "The job is miserable," some said; others asserted that "foremen get nervous breakdowns" or that they didn't care to be an "errand boy" without the power to initiate policy. Several were afraid of losing the union's protection, fearing that if they left the bargaining unit they might later be discharged for their past militancy on the picket line or their part in wildcat strikes. Still others identified too strongly with the union to consider becoming management representatives.

Several of the leaders felt that as union officers they had more power than they would possess as foremen, since they now could raise questions directly with higher officials of the company and force some changes. One of the officers of the steel union asserted that "the foreman doesn't have much chance to get anything unless we help out," and gave this illustration: "There was a lack of heat in our department, but the foreman wasn't able to do anything about it. So the men slowed down production until they threw more heat into the place. The foreman was called on the carpet and we got some more heat."

Most of the leaders of the metal workers' union reported that they were well treated by their foremen, who respected them because of their union office. Some of the steel union leaders made similar comments, pointing out that "anything I suggest is given deep consideration" or that the foremen consulted them as union representatives before making decisions. "If anything goes wrong," said one grievance committeeman, "he [the foreman] gets hold of me right away and that way we save a lot of trouble." There were even cases where union officials and foremen made "bootleg" settlements of issues without writing out formal grievances, settlements that might violate management policy and create inequities that workers in other departments might never learn about. A former grievance committeeman in the steel plant thus summarized his technique in dealing with foremen: "The foremen aren't perfect and if he's tough on a certain individual you make it tough on him, the first mistake he makes. And they make mistakes, too. We overlook lots of mistakes they make that we could nail them on, if they treat the men okay. But we could make their lives miserable if they're rough on us and they know it. So we work it give-and-take with the foremen."

9

MEMBERSHIP PARTICIPATION
AND UNION DEMOCRACY

In its origin and function the labor union purports to be an instrument of democracy. It usually comes into being as a protest against managerial decisions in an authoritarian industrial structure where power is concentrated at the top and employees either follow orders or are dismissed. The union, by introducing collective bargaining, brings an element of democracy into industry. In a society in which democratic values are widely accepted and stressed, this appeal is an important one; should the union prove to be undemocratic, its moral position is weakened, just as its claim to represent the interests of its members is suspect.

Democracy in the trade union context may be defined in a variety of ways. If it is defined to mean active participation by the members in forming policy, there is relatively little democracy in the labor movement. If the test is the responsiveness of the leaders to the desires of the members, an opposite conclusion is reached: most unions are democratic, at both the national and local levels.[1] In our view, however, democracy requires more than this; the essential factor is the ability of the rank-and-file members to affect decisions, to replace leaders, and to change policies. By this test all six of the local unions were democratic. For the members to control the union or even exercise influence within it they must participate in its affairs to a significant extent. For this reason questions about the types and amount of membership participation are critical to the labor movement.

[1] See the discussion of this topic in Sumner H. Slichter, *The Challenge of Industrial Relations: Trade Unions, Management, and the Public Interest* (Ithaca, N.Y.: Cornell University Press, 1947), pp. 111–12, 114.

Attendance at Local Meetings

One important measure of participation in local unions is attendance at the local meeting, the body which normally has the power to make top decisions. In this respect there were enormous variations among the locals studied. By far the best attendance occurred in the case of the plumbers, whose semimonthly meetings usually attracted between 500 and 1,500 of the 4,400 members. This is a remarkable percentage, seldom attained in the labor movement except in time of crisis. Also high in attendance was the very much smaller local of knitting mill workers. No comparable figure can be given for the time the field work was under way, since a strike was then in progress; two years later, however, when a brief return visit was made, about a fourth of the membership of 135 attended routine meetings, the number rising to half when the ILGWU official who serviced the local was expected.

In the other four cases attendance was far lower, more at the levels usually found in the American labor movement. The routine monthly meetings of the metal workers usually drew only 50 to 125 members out of 3,000, although crisis meetings might attract from 600 to 1,000. Routine meetings of the telephone workers seldom attracted more than 50 out of a membership of almost 1,300. The steel local of almost 14,000 members could not attract more than 100 or at most 150 members to routine meetings, and only about double that to crisis meetings, at least in recent years. Routine meetings of the miners' local attracted between 10 and 20, out of a membership of about 285, with the attendance rising to about 50 or 60 at crisis meetings. The miners' case was hardly comparable to the others, since their union was so highly centralized that very little authority remained in the hands of the local. Meeting attendance is generally low in the labor movement, however, even where the local union has considerable authority and negotiates its own contract.[2]

Half of the telephone workers who were interviewed said they never

---

[2] Most other studies of union meeting attendance have found it to be rather low. Sayles and Strauss, for example, found that attendance in a group of medium-sized, established, industrial locals (with membership from four hundred to four thousand) was usually between 2 and 6 per cent (Leonard R. Sayles and George Strauss, *The Local Union: Its Place in the Industrial Plant* [New York: Harper & Bros., 1953], p. 173). Much the same is true in Britain, where Roberts estimates that branch (local union) attendance is usually between 3 and 15 per cent, with a heavy concentration between 4 and 7 per cent. B. C. Roberts, *Trade Union Government and Administration in Great Britain* (Cambridge, Mass.: Harvard University Press, 1956), p. 95. Other students of unionism, both in this country and in Britain, are in general agreement on this point.

went to union meetings; and a fourth of the steel workers, the farm equipment workers, and the coal miners also had never attended a meeting, although in these three cases, on the average, the degree of identification with and loyalty to the organization was rather high. As many steel and farm equipment workers said that they almost never went, and even more of the coal miners made similar reports.

Many reasons were given for the low attendance in these four locals. Workers pointed to the inconvenience of the meeting time, conflicts with their working schedules, the distance from their homes to the meeting place, or other interests or activities. Many of those who owned their own homes preferred to spend their free time working around the house, or at any rate gave this as their reason for non-attendance. Others pointed to the demands on their time made by their families. Some were baffled by parliamentary procedure or lacked the speaking skill or self-confidence required to address a meeting. Many with other native tongues could not express themselves well in English, and some were unable even to follow a meeting. Still others who failed to attend felt that union meetings were of little consequence to them or that they could get whatever information they needed from other sources. Among the telephone workers, as one might expect in an organization largely made up of women, home and children interfered with meeting attendance. Among some of the steel workers there were complaints about the occasional disorders to which the meetings were subject; "there's a clique in there that shouts you down when they feel like it," one said. Often these assigned reasons were mere excuses; many workers admitted frankly that they simply were not interested in routine business meetings.

Many of those, particularly among the steel and metal workers, who reported that they seldom or never went to union meetings, were somewhat apologetic. "I know I really should go," many of them said. Responses of this type were seldom met with among the telephone operators, who usually stated simply that they lacked the time. In the case of a small number of telephone operators this was combined with an unflattering opinion of active members. As one operator put it: "I used to go to more union activities than I do now. But I never was really active in the union. I only went to four meetings since I've been in the union [5½ years]. If there was something else that came up the same night as the union meeting, I'd go to that. It wasn't really that interesting to me. There are some people who do go to all union meet-

187

ings, but they're fanatics." In the other locals a member who attended all union meetings was more likely to enjoy the respect of the inactive membership; certainly he would not lose stature.

Large numbers of workers not attracted to routine union meetings make an effort to attend when a crisis occurs or when something important to them is under consideration. Sometimes a member will come to air a grievance affecting only himself. If a critical point has been reached in collective bargaining negotiations or if a strike vote is contemplated, the attendance will swell; at other times a problem affecting a single department will bring a large turnout of its workers. If the department is a sizable one, the attendance of a substantial portion of its membership may have a strong, perhaps decisive, influence on the disposition of the issue. A small department, on the other hand, may well feel defeated in advance; a maintenance man in the metal plant, for example, felt that he and his co-workers were at a perpetual disadvantage: "In certain departments, like our department, we couldn't do nothing because there aren't enough men working there. But in production, they can do almost anything they want because most of the men are there. For us it doesn't even help going to vote in the general elections."

It seems clear that the four locals with low meeting attendance rather than the two where it is high are more representative of tendencies in the American labor movement as a whole. In the case of the knitting mill the fact that the local was still a new one may have been a factor; coupled with this is the fact that the visiting union official who attracted the largest attendance was the one who had been in charge of the organizing drive, the strike, and subsequent collective bargaining negotiations. Still another factor tending to favor a high ratio of attendance was the small size of the local, which guaranteed that everyone would know everyone else and made it more likely that members inexperienced in public speaking would find it easier to join in the discussion. As against these factors, the opportunities for frequent and informal contact with officers and other members in the shop made it less urgent for these members to attend meetings than for workers in a larger plant or in a local whose members worked for a number of employers. Only the future can show whether high levels of meeting attendance persist as the local grows older and as more of its founders are replaced with new employees.

The attendance record that remains highly unusual, in terms of absolute numbers as well as percentage of members attending, is that of the plumbers. And yet it is clear that the functions of the union meeting as the highest decision-making authority in the local, and the place where officers' reports on collective bargaining developments are heard, were not alone responsible for the high attendance. Whereas the meetings of the other locals performed these functions and little more, the pressures that drew plumbers to their union meetings were far more varied. The meeting was the place to learn about economic trends in the trade, about the number and nature of the new jobs likely to be opening up within the local's jurisdiction; in an industry where jobs were so often of short duration, this was a factor of great importance which had no counterpart in factory or telephone employment or even in the somewhat insecure and unstable coal mining industry. New materials or techniques developing in the industry or new interpretations of the building code were likewise of interest to all members.

Since the plumbers worked in widely scattered locations, moreover, the meeting was the most convenient place to find one's business agent if there was a problem to be discussed with him. While the business agent spent much of his time visiting the jobs within his jurisdiction, he was able to make only occasional trips to the larger jobs, and might not get to some of the smaller ones at all unless a serious problem arose. By way of contrast, all the other groups of unionists studied could raise a problem with their steward or other union officer without leaving their place of work. For the plumbers, in addition, the union meeting served a social function by giving members an opportunity to see old friends now living and working in distant areas of the city. Because of their common craft identification and their lifelong commitment to the industry and the union, the bonds between plumbers who once worked together were very likely far stronger than between two factory workers who once were employed in the same department.

Attendance at meetings is related also to the manner in which business is carried on. Under the present group of officers, meetings of the plumbers are conducted in a democratic fashion, with opportunity for members to speak if they wish. This was a factor that encouraged attendance, whereas some years before, when the local was under more dictatorial control, participation of the general membership was discouraged. A veteran of forty-one years in the local, who made an effort to attend all its meetings, referred to this factor, among others: "The only time I don't go is when I'm sick. You go to see the people you haven't seen for a couple of months. Meet your old-time friends and find out what's going on. In the olden days, the union was different. Just one clique went and if you tried to say something, you got knocked down. Now, if anybody wants to speak, he does so and there's no hard feeling." Despite the democratic character of the meetings, their function as an agency of communication, and the opportunity they provide to see old friends, a fourth of the plumbers reported that they almost never attended. Most of these, however, were now supervisors or in business for themselves, or else were quite aged men who had attended meetings regularly when they were younger.

Repeatedly workers emphasized the fact that they participated actively and vigorously when their self-interest was affected, when some problem touched them directly; how narrowly or widely they defined this area of self-interest, however, depended upon many factors. In large plants, with their variety of processes, their sharp differences in the levels of skill, and the spatial separation of groups of workers, the area of self-interest tended to be narrowly conceived, to be limited largely to the department in which one worked or the type of skill one represented. Only when the contract was being negotiated, when a strike was contemplated or in process, or when officers were being elected were large numbers likely to feel that their immediate interests were involved; or, put another way, was self-interest likely to be conceived in broad enough terms to include the entire local.

Among the plumbers and the knitting mill workers, on the other hand, a wider identification was achieved, each worker feeling that what affected anyone else was likely to be his business as well. In the case of the knitting mill workers the small size of the plant, the close interpersonal relationships of the work force, and the recent strike helped produce this result; among the plumbers there was an identity of craft interest hardly possible in a factory, combined with a lifelong commitment to a trade and perhaps to a single local. The miners, similarly, were a highly homogeneous group with common identification and interests, but their greater chances to talk with each other, both on and off the job, made the meeting less necessary for that purpose; and the centralization of authority in the national and district union officers correspondingly reduced the area of decision-making available to the local union.

Among the relatively small number of rank-and-file members who made an effort to attend all or almost all of the union meetings, several types seemed to stand out. Some were quite ambitious, hopeful of advancement to a union office or to a foreman's position; others felt that promotion within the management hierarchy was blocked to them, perhaps unfairly. In a few cases workers with superior educational backgrounds were among those who attended regularly, though they disclaimed ambitions to rise within either the union or the management hierarchy. Still another type were workers who were dissatisfied with the company, anxious about their work situation, or critical toward their foremen. Another group felt a high degree of loyalty to the union for having won a grievance or concession for them or considered it their duty as members to attend, perhaps combining with this a fear that the union would back them in the event of a grievance only if they had shown proper union support. Still others felt insecure and in need of union protection, such as members of minority groups; and still others wanted to know what went on in the union and found union notices and plant gossip insufficient sources of information. These motivations, needless to say, hardly occurred singly, but rather in varying combinations.

Other Forms of Participation

The steel and metal workers' locals, both operating in large plants with a variety of specialized departments, had group or departmental meetings in addition to regular local meetings. These departmental meetings proved useful when problems arose that were peculiar to or limited to particular departments, saving the time of the local meeting for issues affecting workers in the plant generally. In both local unions more rank-and-file members were apt to attend group or departmental meetings than regular local meetings, since the problems under discussion were more likely to be those affecting them immediately and directly. Sometimes metal workers' departmental meetings were held in the plant lunchroom or locker rooms during the lunch period, with virtually all the workers affected present. Departmental meetings held in the union hall after working hours attracted far smaller attendance, though the hall was just across the street from the plant. Among members of the steel workers' local there were frequent complaints of factional bickering and endless talk, at group meetings as well as at meetings of the local. "They chew the fat and get nowhere and I figured what's the use of wasting time." Another factor tending to increase attendance at group or departmental meetings was the greater informality, which encouraged workers who spoke poorly or who were baffled by parliamentary procedure to raise questions or express their views. The departmental meetings served the incidental purpose of explaining peculiar departmental problems to union officers who worked elsewhere in the plant, and constituted a form of pressure upon them to obtain the action or relief that the workers affected by the problem desired.

Meetings, important as they may be, are but a single form of participation in union affairs. Another form, also of great importance, is voting for union officers. There were many workers, indeed, who asserted that they had performed their most important obligation by taking part in the election; having chosen good officers, they now felt that it was up to the latter to conduct the business of the organization—barring only crisis situations, in which the general membership could be expected to take an active part. The plumbers constituted something of a special case in that their local had had only three contested elections over a twenty-year period, candidates being elected by acclamation when all offices were uncontested. There had been ample opportunity, however, for rival candidates to be nominated in the elections held every third year.

In the metal workers' local elections, held annually, between 70 and 85 per cent of the members voted. The plumbers showed as high a percentage of participation in their rather infrequent elections in which there was opposition. The knitting mill workers had had an 80 to 85 per cent vote in their elections, though high participation was easy because of the small numbers involved and the newness of the union. Elections in the locals of telephone and steel workers were held every other year, and in both cases about half or somewhat less of the membership voted. In the steel workers' election held while the field work was under way, approximately forty-seven hundred votes were cast, about a third of the eligible voters. Because the coal miners' local was a new one, the president held his office by appointment of the subdistrict director. Regular elections for a two-year term of office were scheduled to be held soon. In locals in the area usually 60 to 70 per cent of the members voted in local elections.

Among the racial minorities in the steel and metal workers' locals there was a larger percentage who voted regularly in union elections than was true of the white majority. This was probably caused by the concern of minority groups lest they suffer discrimination at the hands of prejudiced supervisors or fellow employees and their desire to insure the election of union officers pledged to a policy of nondiscrimination. Within the steel workers' union, according to one of the Mexicans, his fellow countrymen constituted an informal group in support of candidates who would be of assistance to them: "Every election they had I voted. I got to know some of the fellows and decided to support them. There are a few candidates who the Mexican people get together and support. We don't mind supporting officers and candidates if we know they'll help us out."

In each of the locals there was a sizable minority that voted irregularly, as when there was a hotly disputed factional contest or when friends or fellow workers from their departments were candidates; sometimes they were motivated by an issue important to their department or by friendship, and at other times they were urged by a special interest group to support candidates committed to a particular set of policies. Others, for whom union elections held only marginal interest, voted when it was convenient, but would not miss a ride home or go out of their way in order to cast a ballot. Others, like some citizens in local, state, or national elections, voted chiefly when they were aroused by officers whose actions—or whose failure to act—they disliked.

The small number who never voted in union elections gave reasons similar to those given by citizens who fail to exercise their right of franchise; among these were indifference, ignorance of the issues or the candidates, unwillingness to be inconvenienced, and the view that one vote never made much difference in the results. Some had a passive attitude toward the union and were willing to accept any group of officers that the majority wanted. Others, including some plumbers working in one-man shops, had completely isolated themselves from the activities of the organization.

Besides attending meetings and voting in elections, members may participate in union affairs by serving on committees. There were general complaints by the officers that too few members showed an active interest in the organization and were willing to accept responsibility. Many of the officers asserted that they were always on the watch for promising new material and that they tried to develop people who showed interest and ability by appointing them to committees. Most of the members shared this view, to the extent that they had any opinion on the subject, though there were complaints that favorites of the officers or members of ruling cliques or factions monopolized committee appointments. Large numbers of ordinary members, needless to say, had neither knowledge nor opinion on the subject. The prevailing view of both officers and members, however, was that participation in committee work was easy to achieve provided one showed some interest and promise.

Among the inactive members of the steel, metal workers', and coal miners' locals there were a considerable number who asserted that their interest and activity had been greater in the past, whereas there were very few who reported that their interest and degree of participation had risen. Perhaps this should not be surprising, since the metal plant was relatively new and since unionism in the steel plant went back only to the 1930's, when pay was very low by present-day standards and when arbitrary treatment by company officials was possible. Unionism in that industry was established in a wave of protest in which masses of workers participated, at a time when complaints against the companies were widespread, and when unionism was a crusade to some and a new and exciting experience to all. It could hardly be expected that the tempo of internal union life would continue at the same rate after the worst abuses had been remedied and after the union had settled down to a more mature and more routine existence. Among the plumbers and the telephone workers, on the other hand, there has been relatively little change in the level of union activity over a long period of time; it has remained high among the plumbers and low among the telephone workers, particularly among the operators.

Among the workers whose activity in the union diminished over a period of time there were some who once were dissatisfied with conditions in the plant, but whose sources of dissatisfaction had been removed; though they have become relatively inactive in the union, they have retained a high degree of loyalty to it. Others, becoming ambitious to rise to a management position, feared that continued union activity might prove a handicap. Still another group had specific complaints against the union to explain their diminished activity. Some were dissatisfied with the operation of the grievance procedure or felt that union officers were too quick to propose strike action. Others disagreed with the political complexion of the leadership, criticized the local's racial policies, or believed that the officers were dishonest or interested only in themselves. Sometimes frustrated ambitions for union office, along with disillusionment with the leadership of the union, played a part.

There were a number of workers who never had been active, other than to pay dues, vote in elections, and participate in strikes. Yet among such workers there were all degrees of reactions to the union, from strong approval through indifference to opposition. Some of those who strongly favored unions felt that the officers were good men and that, having elected them, there was no further reason for activity. Others felt that they themselves lacked the qualifications for leadership, such as education, aggressiveness, or the ability to speak freely, and hence remained inactive. Others asserted that union activity was a rough and rather unpleasant business, with heavy demands on one's time and no commensurate rewards for taking everyone else's troubles on one's own shoulders. Some were unwilling to take the time that union activity demanded from their homes and families or their other interests. There were a few who were inactive because they viewed their stay in the industry—or perhaps in the ranks of wage-earners, regardless of industry—as temporary. There were also a few who had hopes for promotion to supervisory posts and who feared that union activity might injure their relationship with the company. Finally, there were some, forced into the union against their will by legal or social pressure, who remained indifferent or even hostile to it.

Behind the various types of formal union activity referred to there is a vast amount of informal activity.[3] The conversations that take place on the job, during the lunch period, or on the way to or from the plant may be considered participation in union activity to the extent that the collective bargaining agreement, the grievance procedure, union politics or other internal union developments, or group action against the employer under union leadership are discussed. The worker who complains to his steward about his rate, the member who asks another what happened at the union meeting, the employee who pauses at the bulletin board to read a union notice, the old-timer who suggests to a new employee that he join the union, the group that gripes during the lunch break about working conditions and agrees that the union ought to do something—all these members are engaging in informal activity that is an important part of the local's operations.

[3] This point has been developed by Joseph Kovner and Herbert J. Lahne. See their article, "Shop Society and the Union," *Industrial and Labor Relations Review,* VII (October, 1953), 3–14.

The officers and active members constituting a large part of the attendance at the formal meeting may take action representing the will of the membership because they are exposed daily to the informal pressures of fellow workers who express themselves with vehemence whenever they are strongly affected by some development in the plant. Where members work singly or in widely separated small groups, as is the case among the plumbers, there is less opportunity for such informal activity and less likelihood that the opinions expressed there will influence the formal union meeting unless the members themselves attend. This is an additional factor that helps to account for the much larger meeting attendance enjoyed by such unions.

In a small shop, particularly where workers are not sharply divided by differences of skill, the informal shop society is best developed and exercises most influence at the formal union meeting. In a large factory, however, with a wide variety of departments separated both spatially and in terms of function, and perhaps with different shifts as well, there tends to exist not one but several informal shop societies, with somewhat different and sometimes conflicting interests. Each such grouping then may function as a pressure group within the union, sometimes "packing" the meeting to exert maximum influence on the officers or on the issue under consideration. Whether present or not, unified groups of this sort, particularly if they are large or of strategic importance in production, cannot be ignored by officers who want to have an effective union and who also want to be re-elected.

Some Factors Affecting Participation

Of the many factors affecting union participation, several seem particularly worth stressing at this point. One is the change—that seems part of the life cycle in many unions—from a high level of participation in the formative period when the grievances that led workers to organize were keenly felt; the union was then a novel experience and the drama of the first strike and the first contract had tremendous impact upon the lives of the workers. In the case of the steel workers' union, old-timers who came to the sparsely attended meetings were fond of telling about the early days when the meeting hall, which could hold six hundred to eight hundred people, was jammed and a loud-speaker carried the proceedings to an overflow crowd on the sidewalk. Only the local of knitting mill workers was still in this stage when the field work was conducted.

Another factor, evident to varying degrees, was the decline in authority of the local meeting as a decision-making body. To document this statment properly would require studies over a period of time, which we were not able to make. Yet it was perfectly evident, particularly in the case of the coal miners' local, that a once-flourishing internal life had ended with the centralization of power in the hands of the national office. Collective bargaining is now handled at the national level without even the adaptation of the contract to local conditions that is characteristic of some industries, and strikes are turned off and on with the dispatch of telegrams from the United Mine Workers' headquarters building in Washington. It should be borne in mind, however, that bargaining at the local level is not possible in a highly competitive industry such as coal mining, where a single seam can be mined at a variety of points, where wages are a very large part of the costs of production, and where a national product market exists.

Not since 1933, in addition, have the Illinois miners possessed the right to elect their own district officers. Consequently the local's area of decision has been narrowed until it functions for the most part as a channel of communication. It still has problems of routine local administration, to be sure, but these are not matters of much interest to the bulk of the membership. Except for grievances and a chance to hear the communications from national and district officers, there appears to be little that would attract the average coal miner to a meeting of his local.

The other three locals with low attendance ratios also lacked full control over the negotiation of collective agreements and the calling and ending of strikes. The telephone local formed part of a national bargaining unit of long-lines employees of AT & T, and the metal workers bargained through a council representing the various plants of the company organized by the UAW. In both these cases the locals gained strength by bargaining with their employers jointly, though at the price of reducing their freedom of action and their power to make decisions.

The steel local was somewhat different in that it signed its own contract with the company; the basic pattern, however, was set in the union's negotiations with "Big Steel," although scope for negotiations existed in the adaptation to local conditions and in the other variations from the pattern, usually minor in nature, that appeared. Strike action in the industry has usually been on a nationwide basis. The steel industry, it should be remembered, was organized in the late 1930's by SWOC, a fact which gave the national heads much more influence over strike and collective bargaining policy than would likely have been the case if the locals had appeared earlier and then had combined to form a national structure.

All of this is not to assert that participation is automatically high where a local controls its own strike and collective bargaining functions, but merely that more members are likely to attend local meetings if important decisions affecting them are made there. It should be noted that in all three of these cases strikes, though sometimes national in scope, were approved by majority vote in each local union; and collective agreements, though in some cases embracing a wider area than the local union or negotiated in the shadow of a national pattern, were submitted to a ratification vote at the local meeting before going into effect.

Even where the local retains full control over its collective bargaining policy, however, the power to negotiate must be delegated to a small group of leaders. The general membership may participate in the formulation of bargaining demands and in the acceptance or rejection of proposed settlements. It is inevitable, however, that the key officials who engage in the give-and-take of bargaining should trade off the proposals that they think unrealistic or of little consequence for the ones that in their view are more significant. It is also inevitable that their recommendations on the acceptance or rejection of management offers or the ratification of an agreement tentatively reached should usually prevail. These factors reduce the scope of the decision-making authority of the local meeting, making its functions communication and ratification; some of the members, feeling that the real decisions are made beforehand by the officers, may conclude that their attendance even at crisis meetings is of little consequence. Nor should it be forgotten, in the case of large locals such as the steel locals, that the attendance of a substantial proportion of the membership would make it virtually impossible for business to be conducted in orderly fashion.

There was some degree of appreciation among all members, whatever their degree of participation in union activities, that decisions often were made only in a formal sense at local meetings. Before an issue of any consequence reached the local meeting for discussion and vote, it was usually considered at some length by a committee and was probably the subject of discussion at an executive board meeting and of a recommendation by the board to the membership. Since the officers and key active members were customarily members of the executive board, the most influential speakers at local meetings were persons who had already committed themselves on the issue and whose views were already well known to their associates. Only where there was disagreement among the leading officers and committee members, unresolved by the more lengthy discussions available within the committee framework, were the differences likely to be fought out on the floor of the local meeting.

Where active factional organization existed, as in the steel and metal locals, committee or executive board differences of opinion were likely to form the subject of local union debate when the leaders of the various factions could not resolve their disagreements earlier. Where there was general agreement between the rival factional leaders on an issue, or where an acceptable compromise could be worked out, there would usually be a unanimous committee or board recommendation to the local meeting, a perfunctory discussion, and an overwhelmingly favorable vote. Behind the executive board or committee meeting, in turn, there were often informal discussions of troublesome problems by the key factional leaders, who often reconciled their differences and worked out an acceptable policy in the union office or at a neighboring bar.

In such cases the executive board or committee faced no problem, since the rival factions supported the program their leaders presented; and the membership meeting, in turn, could witness only the occasional and sporadic protest of disaffected individuals. The average rank-and-file member, hardly ever attending meetings and taking no active part in factional life, might be unaware of this clashing and reconciling of opposing views prior to the local meeting; to the union leader, on the other hand, the formal motion at the full union meeting is but the culmination of a long process of decision-making.

Still another factor is the low degree of participation typical of many organizations to which Americans belong.[4] It is against that background, rather than by reference to an ideal but unrealized standard, that union participation should be considered. Religious bodies, politi-

[4] See, for example, Bernard Barber, "Participation and Mass Apathy in Associations," in *Studies in Leadership,* ed. Alvin W. Gouldner (New York: Harper & Bros., 1950), pp. 477–504.

cal groups, parent-teacher associations, neighborhood improvement associations, social clubs, fraternal orders, veterans' associations—these are but a few of the many organizations competing with union activities for the free time that members are willing to set aside from family and household duties and from hobbies or recreation. The union touches a peculiarly vital part of the worker's life in that it affects his standard of living, his treatment and his satisfactions during working hours, and it should therefore receive correspondingly more attention than do many other groups to which he belongs. Yet to the worker the union may represent but another one of a number of activities, all of which he may find it impossible to attend. In all of them a relatively small group of officers and active members carry most of the responsibility, while the bulk of the membership assents to the decisions they make. He may not think it unusual or undesirable that his union functions in the same fashion.

Democracy in the Six Local Unions

In all six cases the membership overwhelmingly considered their local union to be democratic, a view which we shared. There was general agreement that meetings were conducted properly and elections held regularly and managed honestly. As a metal worker characteristically observed: "The union is run pretty democratically. The majority vote takes it. If the people come out at meetings they can do anything they want in running the union. If they don't come out for the meetings, they have to like what they get." Many of the plumbers pointed to the meeting as the agency through which policy could be changed:[5] "They can get up on the floor of the meetings held every two weeks and tell their complaints, which they have been doing. If they want a change, somebody can get up and make a motion to that effect. They can talk to any business representative or any official of the union and tell them what's wrong and things will get straightened out."

Workers also generally looked upon the local elections as a way of effecting policy changes. Factional organization in the steel and metal workers' locals assured frequent contests for offices, contributing to the beliefs of the members that their locals were democratic. Among the

---

[5] For an analysis of factors making for responsible leadership and democracy in building trades unionism see George Strauss, "Control by the Membership in Building Trades Unions," *American Journal of Sociology*, LXI (May, 1956), 527–35.

plumbers, where contested elections were few, there was general agreement that officers who did a good job were not likely to be defeated, and perhaps not even opposed, for re-election. Informed members emphasized, in addition, the support won by incumbents as a result of the power at their disposal: "Anybody can run, but I don't know how much chance he'd have of getting elected. You naturally build up quite a following when you hand out jobs. You get an awful lot of people obligated to you. . . . It's not that they build up a following themselves—it's that the following naturally comes to them. That happens in politics or any place. When you're in, you're in; and that's very much so in the union. It's very hard in any union and I've seen it in the coal mining union, too. Unless the guys in office do something very bad . . . then it's very easy to get thrown out. But when an officer has been in for a long time, he's either been awful good or awful careful."

A democratic device open to members of the metal workers' local was the power to recall departmental stewards: "If they don't like the steward, four men can go over to the union hall and sign the man out; the majority rules, and there isn't anything the steward can do about it. . . . We recalled one guy six months ago because he knew he was going to quit and didn't give a damn for us and the company knew it and started pushing us around; so we went over and signed him out." The union rules provide that a recall meeting of a department must be held upon petition of five workers; if two-thirds of those present vote for recall, the office is declared vacant and a new election is held. The recall provision does not apply to local-wide officers such as shop committeemen or executive board members, who can be removed only under the trial procedure prescribed by the constitution of the international union.

The unusual practices of the local with regard to nominations for union office are worthy of mention. Under a motion adopted prior to each election, notices are posted in the plant and in the union hall listing the offices to be filled and stating in effect that all union members in good standing are automatically nominated for all offices. Members wishing to accept nomination are then required to indicate by registered mail which office they are seeking. Names of candidates are placed on the ballot, with no favored position assured incumbents, and voting machines are used as a safeguard against dishonest counting.

Sometimes workers listed still other ways of registering protest or influencing decisions. Such techniques included daily contacts with department stewards, "buttonholing" plant committeemen or other officials, and informal meetings of groups of workers with key local officers. Among the telephone workers, where union loyalty was weaker than in the other locals, the suggestion was made frequently that dissatisfied members could drop out of the union or threaten to do so. Such action was not possible in the other cases because of union-shop clauses or because of the strong group pressure exerted upon non-members. However, a few of the metal workers pointed out that dissatisfied members could resign from the union when this was opportune, or bring in another union when the contract expired. The rival unionism that prevailed in the industry when the interviews were conducted made such action a real possibility if a large enough proportion of the membership became dissatisfied.

Occasionally a worker expressed doubt that the membership could change local policy, despite the existence of a formally democratic structure. An interesting minority view of this sort was expressed by a twenty-six-year-old telephone operator, now inactive in the union, who had served as a union steward: "If they'd come to the union meetings they could talk about their problems and get some action. But that's just the spiel I give them when I'm a steward. I don't really believe it. It's a lot of hooey. You go to meetings and they talk a lot of double talk and they don't pay any attention to what we say. I'd give them a line as a steward, but in my heart I don't really believe it. But I still believe in the union—they do stand back of you if you get into trouble." Some of those who felt skeptical about the possibility of bringing about desired changes placed the responsibility on inactive members like themselves for not attending meetings: "I pay my dues, and it's my job to see that I get my results for that—see that the men do their job right, who are in office. . . . I don't do anything about it, though. I think it's my responsibility, but somehow I never do anything."

Structural Factors Affecting Democracy[6]

It is interesting to contrast the frequent contests for office, particularly in the steel and metal workers' locals, with the absence of such contests among the plumbers, although the offices at stake were far

[6] For a fuller discussion of this topic, as well as of some other aspects of union democracy, see Joel Seidman, "Democracy in Labor Unions," *Journal of Political Economy*, LXI (June, 1953), 221–31.

more desirable in the latter case. It is not enough to say that challenges to incumbents were less likely to be successful among the plumbers, so that those ambitious to achieve office were unwilling to run; again the question is why this was the case. The reasons, in our opinion, include the structure of the industry, the communication channels within the industry and the local, the duration of jobs and the control of hiring, and the powers and prestige of the officers. Perhaps the contrast can best be made by suggesting different combinations of these factors, as they were encountered in the situations studied, that had an impact upon election contests in particular and upon union democracy in general.

Structural factors are most favorable for the development of democratic local unionism in the case of a small local, such as that of the knitting mill workers or the coal miners, all of whose members are employed at a single location. Under such circumstances most of the members know one another, see one another frequently on the job, and are likely to be affected by much the same problems. In a local too small to need or be able to afford a full-time official, there can be no great difference in income, socia prestige, or even knowledge and power between union leaders and union members. In cases such as these the union officers work alongside their members as equals, listening to their views and complaints, and sharing their experiences. The employer does the hiring, the jobs are of relatively long duration, and the union leader usualy has little power, except in relation to the grievance procedure, to affect the worker's ability to get and hold his job.

Abuses of local union administration seldom appear in a local of this type. The financial rewards of union office are very slight, since payment for lost time leaves the officer no better off than if he had worked in the plant, and the small monthly grants usually do little more than pay for the extra expenses to which the officer is put. Since the rewards are not great and the pressures and annoyances are many, the union officer seldom wishes to remain long in office. Even if he does, he lacks disposal of the favors necessary to build a political machine, and he is not in a position of power over the members. As a result of all these factors, there is a high turnover of positions, including the top ones, in locals of this type. While limitations upon democratic procedure may exist even in locals of this general description, conditions are optimum for the development of an effectively functioning democracy, with officers generally responsive to the wishes of the membership.

If the local has thousands rather than hundreds of members, either because the plant is very large as in the case of the steel local or because the members of the local are employed in a number of plants, conditions are somewhat less favorable for a high degree of democracy, though safeguards do exist which prevent a dictatorial regime from coming into existence and perpetuating itself. Because of the size of the local and the volume of its business, one or more full-time officials may be required to conduct the business of the organization, creating a gulf between these key officers and the membership. Full-time union officials, as has been indicated in an earlier chapter, find the executive, middle-class type of occupation of union leader far more rewarding, in psychological as well as material terms, than their work in the shop.

Moreover, the membership, fragmented into a number of separate plants or departments within a large plant, is in no position to develop a collective will or even to make its influence directly felt upon officials more important than shop stewards. There is no informal shop society, as in a small plant, existing in the background of the union meeting and imposing its wishes upon it. Union members see their chief official in his office or at the union meeting, in an environment that he dominates—not in the shop, where, as equals, they are both subject to the discipline and the other conditions of work imposed by management.

While the full-time local officer has the incentive to build a political machine to perpetuate his tenure of office, the chief question is whether he can control enough rewards and punishments to attract and discipline a following of active unionists, while producing enough benefits and sufficiently monopolizing the channels of communication to command a majority vote of the rank-and-file membership. It is precisely here that the head of a large industrial local such as the steel workers is weak. The favors at his disposal in the way of offices or committee appointments that yield small incomes, compensation for lost time, or prestige are too few to permit a stable political machine to be built, and both rank-and-file members and ambitious active unionists are secure in their jobs, barring misconduct of some sort.

Under such circumstances an active member who has a following in his department becomes a political power to be courted when election time comes, and shifting combinations of these departmental leaders may determine control of the local and election to the choice jobs. Indeed, a popular departmental leader whose job or union activity makes him known to the entire membership of the local has a good chance to displace the union head, who is liable to lose popularity precisely because he is in the union office rather than the plant, cut off from informal contacts with large numbers of workers and enjoying physically easier work at a somewhat higher income. In locals of this type democracy is likely to be achieved, partly by direct responsiveness of union heads to the wishes of the members and partly through the interplay of a number of informal groupings, each representing a different plant, department, or craft within the local.

If turnover is rapid among the heads of small industrial unions and moderate among the heads of large ones, it is small indeed, and sometimes nonexistent, among the heads of craft unions such as are found in the building trades in the big cities. The building tradesman usually finishes a job within a very short time and must then go to work at another location, for the same or a different contractor. A number of business agents are needed to police these short-lived and scattered operations, and considerable power must be given them to stop the job in order to enforce union rules. Craftsmen refuse to work with one who lacks a union card, and the other building trades halt the job if any group not affiliated with the building trades council is employed. The union controls entrance into the trade through an apprenticeship system and enforces discipline through a closed-shop arrangement that has persisted despite the Taft-Hartley Act. There is no informal shop society on a scale large enough to matter, and, in any event, no union official with any degree of power is a member of it.

Since in such a local the leader's job is full-time—and at a good salary, since building tradesmen are well paid—the union head has an incentive to maintain himself in office; and the full-time jobs he controls, either by appointment or by the power to determine the composition of the winning slate in local elections, give him the nucleus of a machine. His connections with contractors, most of them economically weak compared to him, and with other building trades leaders help give him power over the livelihood of his members, who may be unable to remain on their jobs against his wishes or those of his business agents, and whose jobs in any event hold little promise of permanence. The full-time union officers, the only ones in contact with the scattered membership, have a near monopoly over the means of communication. If, in addition to all these political assets, they bring substantial economic benefits to the members, as the leaders of the plumbers have done, they are almost impossible to defeat in an election. Under these circumstances an active unionist who is ambitious for full-time office is more likely to support the officers and await his turn for recognition by them than court almost certain defeat by running against them.

While the plumbers' union is a democratic one, despite the absence of opposition in most elections, the conditions under which the industry operates permitted autocratic leaders, who enforced their rule by violence, to control the local in the past.[7] Yet they were defeated by the present group of officials in an election, indicating that some democratic safeguards exist even in autocratically controlled local unions of this type. Unless elections are skipped or held under grossly fraudulent conditions, the administration in power must periodically submit itself to the membership for re-election. Even if the slate as a whole is returned to office, a business agent who has made himself especially unpopular may be defeated. Partly because the members work in such scattered locations, there is a greater tendency to attend the union meetings; these meetings, in turn, act as a check on autocratic behavior by business agents, serving as something of a substitute for the informal shop opinion that exists elsewhere.

Much depends on the extent of member dissatisfaction, which in turn may largely reflect the level of material benefits the leadership is able to provide. If substantial dissatisfaction exists and if the leaders cannot be deposed by democratic means, the members may drop out or form a rival organization, depending upon whether or not they can keep working in the trade if they leave or are expelled from the organization. In some cases appeals to the international union officers or to the courts may play a part in removing autocratic and unscrupulous leaders.

Requirements for Local Union Democracy

The discussion so far has emphasized structural factors such as the size of the local—really the possibility of face-to-face communication among members—and the security of the job in relation to the problem of union democracy. Conditions of this sort, needless to say, are only a few of the influences operating in a complex social situation. They are limiting rather than determining, in that they set the stage favorably

[7] In the longshoring industry in New York City the daily hiring through the shape-up, plus the control of the hiring boss by the union, are among the factors that have permitted autocratic and unscrupulous leaders to maintain themselves in office for long periods.

or unfavorably for the development of democracy. Other factors operating in the situation may bring about a high degree of democratic control despite unfavorable structural elements or produce a low degree of democracy in an otherwise favorable environment.

It has already been suggested that an organization as large as a typical local union, with the volume of business that it must dispose of under pressure of time, cannot possibly decide all matters at local meetings. The officers must be empowered to handle a large number of routine items as they come up, according to general rules that have been adopted and subject to a report to the body on their actions. The executive board must be authorized to take such action as is necessary between meetings of the general membership and to prepare recommendations for the body to act upon. Collective bargaining negotiations and the formulation of strike strategy must be delegated to small groups if they are to be performed efficiently; here democracy is satisfied if there are instructions in advance from the body, and reports to and ratification by it before action is completed.

More than this, union democracy requires full and open debate on the floor of the local, with the right of members to disagree with leaders on policy issues without the opportunity for the officers to cause harm, either by discipline within the locals or by jeopardy to their jobs, to those members who criticize them. For this to be true members must enjoy job security, and the disciplinary procedure within the union must be fairly administered. Democracy also requires the frequent and regular election of officers, elections in which rival groups have approximately equal opportunity with the incumbents to present their candidates and their programs to the membership. While officers deserve reasonable compensation for their services, their salaries should not be so far above their earnings in the trade as to give them a financial incentive to crush democracy in order to remain in office. The requirements for local union democracy may therefore be summed up as follows:

1. The officers must exercise restricted authority, subject to instructions from and periodic reports to the membership.
2. The members must have the supreme power—the right to decide important matters whenever they choose to do so.
3. Freedom of speech, including freedom to criticize, must be safeguarded.

4. Disciplinary procedures within the union must be administered fairly.

5. The members must enjoy job security.

6. There must be frequent, regular, and free elections.

7. Freedom to organize groups within the union must be safeguarded to insure choice among rival candidates.

8. Rival groups must have approximately equal access to the membership.

9. The salaries of officers should not be too far above their earnings in the trade.

Democracy will also be aided, as the earlier discussion has shown, if the local is not too large, if the members have opportunity for face-to-face contacts in the course of their work so that the officers do not monopolize the channels of communication, and if the members have approximately equal pay and status. Since these conditions are not possible in all industries or in all locals, however, they are not presented as conditions of democracy, though they exert an important influence on the degree of democracy likely to prevail.

Observers of the labor movement have long been aware of a duality in the nature of the labor union that hinders the development of a high and sustained degree of democracy. The union is primarily a collective bargaining organization that develops as a counterbalance to management's economic strength, and needs discipline and internal unity if it is to bargain effectively and conduct strikes efficiently. Democracy, on the other hand, implies the recognition and protection of internal divisions of interest or opinion. Which is to be emphasized—democracy and internal division or discipline and internal unity in the face of the external threat posed by the employer? Years ago A. J. Muste called attention to the dilemma of the local union in trying to combine the social structure of the democratic town meeting with that of the army.[8] Much the same dilemma confronts the democratic nation in time of war or other national peril.

[8] A. J. Muste, "Factional Fights in Trade Unions," in *American Labor Dynamics,* ed. J. B. S. Hardman (New York: Harcourt, Brace & Co., 1928), pp. 332–33.

Factionalism[9] in Unions

The question of factionalism raises this dilemma in acute form. Except perhaps for very small locals, where all members know each other and have ample opportunity for face-to-face contacts, some degree of organization is necessary if alternative programs are to be put before the membership and if present officers are to be effectively challenged. This, however, implies a caucus or faction—and this in turn means internal division that may be viewed as harmful to the unity necessary for collective bargaining success. In the view of the leaders and active members of the steel and metal workers' locals factional organization was necessary to local democracy, whereas in the eyes of most inactive members it was a development to be deplored.

The plumbers were unusual in that factions had been instrumental two decades earlier in ridding the local of undesirable leaders and that the nucleus for political organization still existed in various clubs serving only social purposes. While there was, as a result, some appreciation of the need for political organization, the prevailing view both among rank-and-file members and leaders was that factional organization was undesirable. It should be noted, however, that leaders had a very different interest in this respect; while the members were concerned with collective bargaining gains, the officers were more interested in the assurance of continued re-election so long as no organized opposition existed. In the other three locals there were no organized factions or caucus meetings, though informal slates sometimes appeared in the telephone union elections.

Relatively few of the rank-and-file union members supported factional organization as fundamental to the democratic process, as necessary to keep union officials alert and responsive to the desires of the membership. The far more typical attitude was one of disapproval because of the internal conflict that resulted. Some disliked factionalism because of its connection with politics, which they viewed as a corrupt-

[9] This word, unfortunately, carries undesirable connotations to many of unnecessary internal conflict, destructive opposition, even disloyalty. We use the term, rather, to mean constructive political opposition, in which there is equal loyalty to the union but legitimate differences on objectives or the means for attaining them. We do not use "two-party system" or some such phrase, because so many union political groupings tend to be shifting and temporary. As we use the term, factionalism includes all political groups within a union, from informal and temporary ones to the permanent party structure such as exists in the International Typographical Union. It includes any group seeking to advance a program, influence policy, or obtain power within the union.

ing force whether inside or outside the union; and others, reacting against factionalism with little knowledge and a vague prejudice, associated it with rackets or with Communists. Occasionally an inactive member, coming to a meeting of the steel or metal workers out of curiosity or because he had a problem in his department, was antagonized by the factional conflict he saw there. Even those who felt that caucuses and factions might be necessary in crisis situations, or perhaps inevitable at election time, generally viewed them as undesirable because divisive and preferred to have them inoperative most of the time. Yet even some of those who disliked factions conceded that they served a useful purpose by keeping a close watch on each other; and there was general agreement, in view of political realities, that one who wanted to be elected was wise to align himself with an organized group.

One would not expect to find many national union leaders, outside the ranks of the International Typographical Union, who supported factionalism. A typical view was that expressed by Matthew Woll, for many years one of the leading vice-presidents of the AFL: "Factionalism tends to destroy and weaken the organization and seeks to divide the membership in general into distinctive groups and my own judgment is that it does not make for the free and democratic expression of the rank and file."[10] Such views are not surprising if one bears in mind that the national union head, for reasons that have been discussed, is assured of permanent control unless rival political organization is sanctioned. His position is one of power, sustained by his control of organizational machinery and means of communication. Rival centers of power can develop only if the members are free to organize meetings to present an opposition view, circulate their program to the rank and file, and nominate and campaign for slates of candidates in the elections. Without these rights, adequately protected and implemented, union democracy at the national level is a formal right of little practical consequence.

Other objections advanced against factionalism are that it focuses attention upon internal union affairs rather than the collective bargaining relationship with management, that union policy decisions become political issues to be decided by emotion rather than by reason, and that union appointments under conditions of factionalism are determined more by political considerations than by merit. Some of these objections, it should be noted, can be made with equal force against a

[10] In a letter to one of the authors, dated October 21, 1948.

system of rival political organizations in the state. It is true, beyond question, that factionalism has sometimes weakened unions to the point where they could not function effectively; often in such cases, however, the factions were loyal to an outside organization, as in the case of the Communists, rather than to the union movement. It has also been noted that factionalism may create insecurity on the part of union leaders and encourage aggressive action by them against management.[11]

Factionalism, however, can and often does make a positive contribution to union democracy. It keeps the members informed of issues and provides opposition that adds interest to meetings and elections; it helps develop leadership ability independent of the administration; it gives the members an opportunity to choose among competing programs and rival candidates for office; it increases the importance of the membership meeting as a decision-making body; it makes the officers careful of their actions and holds them accountable for their conduct of union affairs; and, for all these reasons, it tends to increase the interest, knowledge, and extent of participation of the members.

Democracy in the National Union

It has been argued, both by some union leaders and by some students of the labor movement, that democracy should be sacrificed when it conflicts with attainment of the collective bargaining objectives of the union; these arguments, it should be noted, center on the national or district rather than the local union. John L. Lewis, for example, has opposed restoration of district autonomy within the United Mine Workers on the ground that efficiency would thereby be lost. In a characteristic speech, at the 1936 convention, Lewis denied that district self-government was a question of principle:

I trust that the Convention, in considering this matter (autonomy) will consider it for what it is really worth and what it means to the organization. It is not a fundamental principle that the Convention is discussing. It is a question of business expediency and administrative policy as affecting certain geographical areas of the organization. It is a question of whether you desire your organization to be the most effective instrumentality within the realm of possibility for a labor organization or whether you prefer to sacrifice the efficiency

[11] See, for example, Clark Kerr, "The Collective Bargaining Environment," chap. 2 in *Causes of Industrial Peace under Collective Bargaining*, eds. Clinton S. Golden and Virginia D. Parker (New York: Harper & Bros., 1955), p. 17.

of your organization in some respects for a little more academic freedom in the selection of some local representatives in a number of districts. These are the issues which are involved.[12]

Lewis has also argued that elected officers are not necessarily good and that the International Executive Board is better qualified than the members to determine what is good for them. He has constantly asserted that the union has achieved its current strength and effective bargaining position under the policy of provisionalism.

One of the leading students of the American labor movement, Philip Taft, is also among those who stress union discipline and bargaining strength rather than internal democracy. He argues that discipline is necessary for effective union functioning, that national officers need broad powers, and that they use their powers wisely. Concerned as he is with union strength rather than with democracy, Taft has little patience with factionalism.[13] A recent British writer, V. L. Allen, has questioned whether the participation of union members, beyond their willingness to become and remain members, is pertinent. It is possible to assert, as Allen does, that "the end of trade-union activity is to protect and improve the general living standards of its members and not to provide workers with an exercise in self-government," and to conclude that internal democracy, while desirable, is not essential so long as the workers are free to join or leave as they see fit.[14]

One may feel otherwise, however, if one also supports unions as constituting a democratic influence at the plant level and a democratic force in society that helps to offset the power of big business and big government; if one holds democracy to be a desired goal in itself, to be sought in voluntary organizations as well as in the larger society; if one is concerned with workers' power to control their union as well as collective bargaining effectiveness; and if one thinks that workers should

[12] *Proceedings of the Thirty-fourth Constitutional Convention of the United Mine Workers of America* (1936), p. 122.

[13] "Mutually warring factions are a luxury most unions cannot afford." Philip Taft, *The Structure and Government of Labor Unions* (Cambridge, Mass.: Harvard University Press, 1954), p. 239. In his view, adequate safeguards for union democracy exist without factional organization.

[14] V. L. Allen, *Power in Trade Unions: A Study of Their Organization in Great Britain* (London: Longmans, Green & Co., 1954), pp. 15, 10–11. Where unionism is compulsory, however, Allen argues that the union structure should be democratic and that this should be assured through government intervention (*ibid.*, p. 64).

be protected from the arbitrary acts of union leaders as well as from those of management. These are values and objectives that the authors accept.

It should also be noted that union discipline is in the interests of management as well as of union leaders. Until a union is recognized it may permit its shop stewards or other local leaders to stop or slow down production whenever a grievance arises and they are unable to obtain prompt action. Once management enters into a contract with the union, however, it usually insists that the union prevent such tactics and use the grievance system instead.[15] This means that the union must be more disciplined, which in turn means more power in the hands of the officers over the stewards and rank-and-file members. While discipline is possible under democratic control, it often lends itself readily to the growth of union autocracy.

The question as to whether a union, particularly at the national level, can long expect to remain democratic was raised in a penetrating analysis by Will Herberg,[16] himself a union education director of long experience. Herberg observed a tendency for union members to participate actively at first, but for lively factional conflict to be followed by the consolidation of power in the hands of a successful leader; in time a bureaucracy develops, with the end result a single political machine monopolizing power within the union. This argument represented the application to unions of Robert Michels' thesis that an "iron law of oligarchy" governed the internal life of large-scale voluntary organizations.[17] A number of more recent writings have documented the "iron law of oligarchy" in various national unions, both in this country and in Britain.[18]

To this "iron law of oligarchy" the International Typographical

[15] The Taft-Hartley Act, by increasing union liability for contract violations, has led to increased control by national union officers over the administration of local contracts. Though one of the objectives of the framers of this measure was to strengthen the rights of members against union officials, the total impact of Taft-Hartley has been to intensify the trend toward union centralization.

[16] Will Herberg, "Bureaucracy and Democracy in Labor Unions," *Antioch Review*, III (Fall, 1943), 405–17.

[17] Robert Michels, *Political Parties*, translated by Eden and Cedar Paul (New York: International Library Co., 1915; reprinted by the Free Press, Glencoe, Ill., 1949).

[18] For a recent study of a branch of a British union, the Transport and General Workers, from this point of view, see Joseph Goldstein, *The Government of British Trade Unions* (London: Allen & Unwin, 1952).

Union, with its unique two-party system and its tradition of political freedom, has been the outstanding exception, offering a challenge to students to explain its differences from the rest of the American labor movement. S. M. Lipset and his colleagues,[19] after a careful study of the union and its members, trace its unusual democratic practices to a number of factors, including the prevalence of small shops in the industry, the fact that the industry is not competitive from one city to another, the many opportunities presented in the chapels and in occupationally related institutions to develop leadership skills,[20] the lack of an appreciable gap in pay or status between officers and members, the job security of the members and the security of the union in the industry, the homogeneity of the membership in terms of skill and pay, and the beliefs that have developed in the union as to the legitimacy of political opposition.

Powers of the National Union Head

The national union leader is in a wholly different position from the head of a local union. Whether the local union is managed in a democratic or autocratic fashion, the local leader is at least close at hand and known personally to many of the members, and he deals with issues the local members can understand. The national head, on the contrary, is far away, negotiating with employers' associations, lobbying in Congress, ruling on important economic and constitutional issues arising in the union, and in other ways handling problems far beyond the experience of local members. Usually he has at his disposal, among other political resources, a staff of international representatives, organizers, and other employees, plus a union paper or magazine that presents his policies and actions in the most favorable light. Whereas an active member in a local may make himself known to the membership and attempt to unseat the local leader in the next election, in the case of the national union this requires publicity, finances, and organization that only a combination of powerful locals can make available.

[19] Seymour Martin Lipset, Martin A. Trow, and James S. Coleman, *Union Democracy: The Internal Politics of the International Typographical Union* (Glencoe, Ill.: Free Press, 1956).

[20] Shepard found, in his study of the Toronto District of the Amalgamated Clothing Workers, that the shop-chairman system performed a similar function in the development of leadership skills. Herbert A. Shepard, "Democratic Control in a Local Union," *American Journal of Sociology*, LIV (January, 1949), 311, 312.

Since the head of a large national union has the power to fill a number of union jobs and to dispense other favors, to reward the faithful and punish the disloyal, he is usually in an excellent position to build a political machine which he can then use to insure his remaining in office. Among the international representatives or organizing staff he has a number of lieutenants, each assigned to a strategic area within the union and each with a network of locals he has helped organize or has serviced in other ways. These staff members, in addition to their regular duties, may serve as channels of communication or agencies of control.

Another important set of powers at the disposal of the national union head relates to discipline within the union.[21] The president has power, under conditions specified in the national constitution, to revoke the charters of local unions and to appoint administrators to handle their affairs. Power over individuals is given by vague clauses in union constitutions prohibiting "improper conduct," "disturbing harmony of meetings," or "insubordination or just and sufficient cause."

Added to these powers is the unparalleled opportunity the national head has for keeping his name before the members. If the union is an important one, his members read about him in the daily press or hear his name on radio news programs. In addition, he has the union newspaper or magazine, which is usually sent to the home of every member and which is edited by an official whom he appoints. Small wonder that the union publication functions as a sort of house organ for the national administration to support its policies and to publicize, in the most favorable light possible, the actions of the president and his chief lieutenants. It is a rare union whose constitution opens the union press to the opposition, as does the International Typographical Union, during the political campaign preceding the election of national union officers. It is not strange, considering all these powers and advantages possessed by the union president, that he is seldom ousted from office and that often no formal opposition to his re-election appears.[22]

[21] For good discussions of this problem see Clyde Summers, "Disciplinary Procedures of Unions," *Industrial and Labor Relations Review*, IV (October, 1950), 15–32; Taft, *op. cit.*, chap. 4 and Supplement; and Benjamin Aaron, "Protecting Civil Liberties of Members within Trade Unions," in *Proceedings of the Second Annual Meeting, Industrial Relations Research Association, 1949*, pp. 28–41.

[22] Taft, *op. cit.*, chap. 2, contains a great deal of material on elections in national unions.

Variations in National Unions

Just as local unions vary greatly in the conditions that foster democracy or permit the growth of autocracy, so variation exists among
the national unions—though the power and influence of the national
head must be judged in relation to the heads of powerful locals, not
rank-and-file members. The local leaders are in the strongest position
with respect to the national head where they possess economic power
in their industries and within the union, measured in terms of functions
and finances. Industries that are decentralized in an economic sense,
such as construction, retailing, and the service trades, are most favorable to local leaders from this point of view. In such industries, where
collective bargaining usually remains a local function, the national
office is likely to have only a small percentage of the members' dues
and a correspondingly small headquarters staff. In industries where
economic conditions foster national collective bargaining or pattern-
following, however, the essential bargaining power may be transferred
to the national officers, leaving local officers only the less significant
functions of applying the contract to local conditions and operating the
grievance machinery. Where this happens a larger percentage of the
funds goes to the national office, which correspondingly increases the
size of its staff.

A union with a number of large and powerful locals is more likely
to preserve democracy in its national affairs than one in which the
local units are small and weak. The local that is large and wealthy
enough to employ its own staff and conduct its own collective bargaining activities is largely independent of the national officers; it provides
a training ground beyond the control of the national heads for the
development of leaders, and an independent base of political support
for a local leader. A small and weak local, on the contrary, is more
likely to depend upon the national officers for financial support, help
in negotiating contracts, and other services, and its delegates are therefore likely to support the administration at conventions.[23] This yields
something of a paradox, in that the small local that is most likely to
be democratic in its internal structure may unwittingly support a
bureaucratic regime at the national level, while the large local with

[23] The authors are indebted to Brendan Sexton, UAW educational director, for
pointing out many of these factors, which also have been observed by Lipset and
his colleagues in their study of the ITU. See Lipset, Trow, and Coleman, *op. cit.*,
chap. 17.

full-time officers may be dictatorial in its internal operations and yet be a force for democracy in the national organization.

Still other factors to be considered are the age and tradition of the union and whether or not a successful revolt can occur if the conditions for peaceful replacement of officers do not exist. Here legal as well as economic factors are important; one must know which unit holds the contract with the employer and whether or not a seceding or expelled local can win bargaining rights under the rules of the National Labor Relations Board. In the service trades and in many manufacturing industries a single local may revolt successfully and even maintain itself as an unaffiliated local if it is unable to join another national union. In the building trades or in coal mining, on the other hand, a revolt must be widespread to have much chance of success.

While the International Typographical Union is easily the most democratic among the powerful unions of the American labor movement, some of the lesser unions should also be mentioned in this respect. Many of the unions of government employees or of professional workers, for example, are conducted in democratic fashion. Reasons to account for this tendency are not hard to discover. In the case of government employees job security usually exists, often based on civil service regulations, and members suffer no economic loss if their union membership ends. Since the main weapon of these unions is the legislative lobby rather than the collective bargaining agreement and the strike, dues are low and the number of full-time union officers is small. The delegates to conventions, as a result, are independent in relation to the union head, who has neither rewards nor punishments at his disposal and who must rely on persuasion rather than economic or legal coercion to keep up his membership. As a consequence proposals by the administration tend to be freely debated at conventions and sometimes defeated, delegates are inclined to speak their minds freely, and close votes are frequent.

Unions of professional workers tend to be democratic for a different reason: since the members enjoy high pay and status because of their professional work, a full-time union position does not appear as desirable as it does to a manual worker; indeed, the pay is often no more and the prestige in the eyes of the public may be less. Consequently the officer's incentive to build a political machine to retain union office may be lacking, as may be the control over rewards and punishments necessary to discipline a following.

In the six cases studied the problem of democracy at the national union level was acute in only one, that of the coal miners. In addition to the spread of provisionalism, the UMW leadership has strengthened its control by making it virtually impossible, through constitutional devices, for an opposition movement to be organized. Article XXI, Section 3, provides that:

Any member guilty of slandering or circulating, or causing to be circulated false statements about any member or members, circulating or causing to be circulated any statement wrongfully condemning any decision rendered by any officer of the Organization, shall, upon conviction, be suspended from membership for a period of six months and shall not be eligible to hold office in any branch of the Organization for two years thereafter. The above shall be construed as applying to any local officer or member reading such circulars to members of a Local Union, or who in any way give publicity to such.

This article has apparently been interpreted to limit the circulation of information which in any way challenges the authority or decisions of the officials, district or national. In addition, Article XIV, Section 20, provides that "It shall be illegal to contribute funds for the promotion of the candidacy of any candidate for office within the Organization." Since the International leadership has the power to revoke charters, appoint district officials, prohibit the circulation of information in opposition to any official, and prohibit the contribution of funds to promote the candidacy of any official, it can build a machine to perpetuate its control with little chance of an effective opposition movement being organized.[24]

In the other five unions, despite the political advantages of the national union head, there were pressures that helped to keep the officers responsive to the desires of the members. Whatever the difficulties in the way of rival candidacies, there was always the chance that one might be successful if the incumbent's record of performance was bad; in the case of the CWA, in addition, the workers might drop their union membership if they were sufficiently dissatisfied. Yet responsiveness of officers to the wishes of members and the winning of material benefits, though they will assure a contented membership,

[24] The attitudes of the miners toward provisionalism and toward John L. Lewis are described above in chap. 2. For a fuller discussion of provisionalism and related issues in the UMW see the authors' article, "The Coal Miners: A Study of Union Control," *Quarterly Journal of Economics*, LXVIII (August, 1954), 415–36.

are not enough to satisfy the requirements of democracy. For this the members must also possess the effective power to change the policies and the officers they dislike, without jeopardy to their jobs or to their rights within the organization. Unless such democratic rights exist the moral position of the union, as a force created to bring democratic influences into industry, will be seriously weakened.

10

THE SCOPE OF
UNION ACTIVITIES

If the workers we interviewed are at all representative, previous chapters have shown that the members of American labor unions believe that their unions perform important functions in representing their interests on the job, in helping to determine their pay and working conditions, in improving their security, and in regulating the treatment they receive from supervisors. If the union is accepted by the worker as a legitimate and necessary institution—as seems overwhelmingly to be the case—it is because of the contribution it makes toward protecting his rights and advancing his interests in the employer-employee relationship.

Once one leaves the work place, however, the question arises as to what function, if any, the union should properly perform. At one extreme is the belief that the union should restrict its activities to those directly and immediately affecting the employer-employee relationship, while at the other is the view that the union, as the basic organization of workers, should help to satisfy their needs as less privileged members of society or to solve problems confronting them as members of their communities. In between these extremes is the view that the union should engage only in those activities outside the plant—such as lobbying for labor legislation—having a direct effect upon its ability to organize and engage in collective bargaining.

No hard and fast line can be drawn between the worker as employee and the worker as citizen, or between the collective bargaining or in-plant functions of unionism and the wider community. The extent to which improvements can be achieved by collective bargaining depends upon a variety of factors—including, among others, the state of the law, the attitude of the police and of other public officials in the event of a strike, and the morale of the workers. Their morale, in turn, is affected by the extent to which union members have become a cohesive group, sharing common values and participating in common activities outside of work. Social activities may help create a solidarity that enhances collective bargaining strength, and community activities may win respect and prestige for the union that may prove an asset in strike as well as in other situations.

Political activity, similarly, may affect minimum wages, safety legislation, or the basic labor law that defines the rights and obligations of unions, as it may also have an impact upon the behavior of the police when a picket line is being maintained. In a more immediate sense the interests of an occupational group may be affected by the actions of local or state authorities, as the interests of the plumbers, for example, are involved in the licensing arrangements for their craft or in the building code. In a wider sense the interests of workers as citizens are strongly affected by such matters as taxation, the level and type of public expenditures, and a variety of other measures where they need some sort of agency to represent them if their interests are to be made known effectively to legislators and administrators.

Social Activities

The question as to whether unions should engage in social activities raised fewer problems with union members than did the corresponding questions relating to community and political activities. Getting acquainted, being sociable, and making friends are culturally valued. Even those who do not care to attend social events are rather unlikely, unless the expense is great, to oppose their sponsorship, since they offer harmless pleasure to those who participate. Picnics are particularly valued, since they provide opportunity for entire families to engage in recreational activities at limited expense and to become acquainted with the families of fellow workers. The lower the family's income, the more important this type of recreation may be. Dances for the younger members and Christmas parties for children may likewise be important for the groups involved.

Among the plumbers, the metal workers, and the knitting mill employees there was general approval of union-sponsored social affairs, without much concern with them as devices for strengthening the union. The interest was usually in the purely social values of meeting fellow workers from other departments or shops and in enjoying one's self in their company. The plumbers, a closely knit occupational group, were primarily concerned with seeing old friends who worked in other parts of the metropolitan area. The basic identification expressed spontaneously by most plumbers was with members of the trade rather than with the union, though admittedly the two concepts might merge in the minds of many members. The great interest of the plumbers in social contacts within their trade suggests that such activities may most easily be promoted where common skills and experiences create common interests, where the basis for identification exists independently of union affiliation.

In the case of the metal workers the interest in social affairs lay largely in the opportunity to meet employees in other departments of the plant. Their very heterogeneity, however, created problems, since some of the white workers did not want to mix socially with Negroes, though they usually supported the idea of equal rights on the job. Because of the color issue the local had had much less success with dances than with picnics. The statements of many of the metal workers, shifting readily from "union" to "factory" or "company," suggested that they were concerned with social affairs with co-workers without regard to sponsorship, and that many of them might have been as receptive to events sponsored by the company as to those under union auspices.

In the case of the small local of knitting mill workers all employees knew each other to some degree, though there still was interest in the friendships that social affairs could stimulate. Some associated social activity with the close relationships they had developed during the strike, in contrast to the impersonal atmosphere existing earlier in the mill. A woman in her fifties, a rank-and-file member, put it this way: "Well, I think maybe a party once in a while would be kind of nice. It keeps them together, all of us working people—and if you keep them together they are nicer with each other. Like now after the strike, everybody is so nice with each other, you can talk to everybody. . . . It's maybe because they know each other now; before the strike you never had a chance to meet even those who work with you in the same department." Many stressed the importance of getting acquainted, building friendships, and developing an understanding of each other. One woman approved of the sponsorship of social events by the union "if the company doesn't—it's always nice to get together and get to know people." Clearly she was concerned with social relationships, without caring whether the company or the union sponsored them—and, incidentally, derived some benefit in terms of loyalty. What was explicit in her response was implicit in those made by some of her shopmates; the general concern was with the work group rather than the union members as such, though it should be remembered that the two were almost synonymous in this case.

The telephone workers differed from these other three groups in that they were generally indifferent to the idea of union-sponsored social affairs. This does not suggest an indifference to social functions involving fellow employees; rather, their need for such contacts was satisfied through social events sponsored by the company, which enjoyed considerable prestige in their eyes. Being concerned with the social values to the participants rather than the benefit in loyalty or morale to the sponsoring organization, most of the workers saw little need for the union also to become active in this area. Indeed, some preferred to have the company rather than the union sponsor social events, an attitude doubtlessly related both to the high prestige of the company and to the low degree of union consciousness on the part of this white-collar group.

In each of these four locals there was a very small number of rank-and-file members who supported union-sponsored social activities because of their contribution to the strengthening of union morale. At the other extreme there was an occasional member who opposed social affairs because of a lack of personal interest, because such affairs were considered beyond the proper scope of union activity, or as a waste of union money.[1]

From the point of view of the union the motive for sponsoring social events is not merely to satisfy the recreational needs of members and their families at a low cost. If this were all that was involved, management-sponsored events, supplementing commercialized recreation and the efforts of individuals, might fully satisfy the need. The union's motive is to build a deeper attachment to the union, to foster a sense of identification with the work group and with the union that will translate itself into solidarity and determination should a collective bargaining crisis occur or a strike be called. Indeed, it is during a strike, when the morale of the rank-and-file members is of vital importance to the union's leaders and when strikers with free time and lack of funds

---

[1] The question about social activities was asked in a different form in the steel union study, so that the results are not comparable. It was not asked of the miners.

pose critical problems, that social functions' are most likely to be sponsored by the union. Often the motivation for parties is to bring out the wives of members so that they can hear the union's version of events or simply enjoy themselves under the union's auspices and so develop a friendly attitude toward it. In an organizing drive aimed at youthful workers social events are likewise apt to be a deliberate part of the strategy, since young people, eager for fun, will respond more readily to dances and parties than to meetings.

This is not to say that members or their families will necessarily be attracted to social events sponsored by the union. Some may prefer to be alone or with a few selected friends, others may have rather specialized recreational interests, and still others may prefer commercial entertainment. A few may feel themselves to be the social superiors of most of their fellow workers and may not care to mix with them after working hours. Many white workers may prefer not to bring their families to social events if appreciable numbers of Negro workers are to be present. Social events are likely to be best attended where the union membership forms a fairly homogeneous group in terms of skill and pay as well as educational background and race or national origin.

Community Activities

Like social affairs, community activities are usually non-controversial[2] and generally valued in our culture. Most rank-and-file members were therefore willing to approve of union participation in community activities, although the union had been formed to deal primarily with in-plant problems. In all five cases where the question was raised—it was not asked in comparable form in the case of the steel local—there was general agreement that it was desirable for the union to interest itself in community affairs. A variety of such activities was suggested as meriting union concern and co-operation, from items such as community fund drives or blood-bank donations to such needs as improved recreational or transportation facilities.

Many of the plumbers, members of a group dependent in part on a licensing system and building code, saw a value to the union in the good will that community activities would foster. In the other cases

[2] Some activities at the community level, such as rent control or the treatment of minority groups, may be highly controversial. The questions relating to community activities, however, were generally interpreted to mean non-controversial matters of the community chest type.

only a rare rank-and-file worker was concerned with any value that might accrue to the union.

Despite the non-controversial nature of most community activities, in no case was there anything like unanimous support for union participation in them. In each instance there was a minority, often substantial in size, opposed to community activities as beyond the proper scope of union affairs. The usual view of this sort, found among the plumbers as among the other groups, was that the union had been formed to deal with in-plant problems and that it should not permit other activities to divert it from its main goal. Workers with such views did not object to community fund drives and the like, but wanted workers to participate as individuals rather than through the union. Occasionally there was also an objection to union participation in community affairs on the ground that not all workers lived in the municipality where the plant was located.

The six locals were in very different situations with regard to community problems and potential union influence in dealing with them. The steel plant was located in a medium-sized city and the metal plant in a small municipality, both of them part of a vast metropolitan area from which the labor force was drawn. Only a portion of the union membership had an interest in the community in which they worked, except for such matters as public transportation facilities and discrimination in lunchrooms. Where the union head was himself a nonresident, as was often the case in both locals, he was in a weaker position than a local resident would be in efforts to bring pressure on behalf of the union. Yet both locals were in a potentially strong position to exert community influence, since they could speak for large groups of people in their respective towns.

One of the most important community issues to confront the steel local in recent years was the decontrol of rents, an issue in which the union members, most of them tenants, should have been vitally interested. Yet the local made only a very weak and ineffective effort to represent its members on this issue. Its leaders made no effort to mobilize members against decontrol, utilizing neither union meetings nor the union newspaper for this purpose. When the local's president appeared before the common council to oppose the decontrol bill, he was shouted down by a large and well-organized landlord group on the ground that he lived outside the city. In this group there were many union members, including a few active stewards, all of whom were under the leadership of the large real-estate operators in the town. While the mayor was deciding whether to sign or veto the bill he learned that the local intended to support a rival candidate in the forthcoming primaries, and this may have helped him decide to sign the decontrol measure. In part the local's performance may represent mere political inexperience or ineptness; in part it reflects divided interests within the local; and in part it represents a concept of union functions that relegates non-collective bargaining issues to a minor role.

The plumbers and the telephone workers were similar in that both locals existed in large cities. Yet the telephone workers' jobs had no particular relationship to community problems or community sentiment. Unlike other telephone employees, who bargain with an operating company subject to state regulation, this local was made up of AT & T employees whose wages and conditions of work were determined through a national bargaining unit. Telephone workers, moreover, comprise a very small proportion of the workers in any given area, and can hardly expect to exert substantial community influence in their own right.

The plumbers, while not more numerous than telephone workers in any town, had far stronger traditions of attempting to influence community action. Their concern with such political-community matters as the building code, as well as with their trade's prestige with the general public, inevitably led them to look upon the community as vital to their well-being. Once such an attitude is established and a group is led as a result to define the scope of their union's activity broadly, it is relatively simple to engage in further types of community activity.

The other two locals of knitting mill workers and coal miners were located in very small towns, far from a metropolitan area. Even in their small town, however, the knitting mill workers comprised a relatively small group. Nevertheless they possessed far greater potential influence in their community than could have been the case in a larger city, and their experiences with police, city officials, and public opinion leaders during their strike had given them an appreciation of the importance of community sentiment during a crisis.

The coal miners, on the other hand, lived in an area where miners provided a large proportion of the public officials. While a town is no longer made up primarily of employees in the nearby mine, as in the days before the automobile, the area is predominantly a coal mining one and this was reflected in municipal and county elections. Indeed, the miners may have felt little need to approach community problems through their union because union pressure was hardly necessary on union leaders or active members who doubled as town officials.

Whether they live in small towns or big cities, however, there are a number of ways in which workers are affected by community affairs. Besides such matters as transportation, the building code, and public opinion during strikes, there are such items as strike relief, welfare agencies, housing, recreation, education, neighborhood police protection, street lighting, and a variety of other community services that affect workers as citizens. In recent years an increasing number of unions have become active in such areas.[3]

Activities of this sort, besides helping to improve the community, bring union members together with other citizens in problem-solving situations unrelated to industrial conflict; they also raise the union's prestige in the community, provide opportunities for more members to be active in matters concerning them, and so help to develop leadership skills. While these activities are a step removed from the core functions of the union, they may serve incidentally to increase the number of rank-and-file unionists with leadership experience, and thus make a contribution to membership participation and union democracy.

Political Action in the Six Locals

If union community activities fail to obtain complete support from workers, it is not surprising that excursions into the political arena should arouse far greater opposition. Political activity is almost always controversial, concerned as it is with the structure of power in the community and in the nation.

[3] For a description of a very active and successful union community relations program, involving the use of neighborhood community stewards, see "How 'Community Action' Succeeds in St. Louis!," *International Teamster*, March, 1956, pp. 7–11. For community-welfare activity of another sort see the report on UAW activities in Windsor, Ontario, in C. W. M. Hart, "Industrial Relations Research and Social Theory," *Canadian Journal of Economics and Political Science*, XV (February, 1949), 53–73. Suggestions for planning a program of union community activities are contained in a pamphlet by Alice H. Cook, "Labor's Role in Community Affairs: A Handbook for Union Committees," issued by the New York State School of Industrial and Labor Relations in August, 1955. The National CIO Community Services Committee has also issued material relating to union counseling, community services committees, labor representation on community agency boards, and similar topics.

The six locals, it should be noted, were in rather different situations with regard to political action. Two of them were peculiarly in need of political influence, the miners at the state and national levels for the passage and enforcement of safety legislation and the plumbers at the city level for the adoption of favorable provisions in the building code and the appointment of friendly inspectors. All the others, as industrial-type locals including workers with various skills and incomes, needed some favorable legislation concerning the right to organize, social security, and the like, though none was in a depressed industry and therefore dependent on legislative action rather than collective bargaining. Friendly behavior by police, city officials, and judges in time of a strike was important to some extent to all the locals, though the solidarity of the miners and the lack of skilled replacements for the plumbers put these two unions in the most independent positions.

So far as the opportunity to influence local elections was concerned, the miners and the steel workers were in the strongest positions. The miners, indeed, had little need to organize for political purposes through their union, since there were relatively few other sources of livelihood in their towns or in the county where the mine was located. Coal miners, usually active members if not officers of their locals, were officials of the mining towns and of the county because they were among the natural leaders of the dominant occupational group, which was almost solidly organized into the United Mine Workers. Under these circumstances there was perhaps little more that the UMW could do with regard to local elections in many municipalities, though there were doubtless other municipalities—and larger political units, such as congressional districts—where vigorous political leadership by the union might have had a greater impact.

The steel workers' union, as the largest labor organization in a strongly unionized town, was potentially an important political influence in the community.[4] Union influence was weakened, however, by the tendency of the local to make independent indorsements during political campaigns, with little co-ordination with other locals of the same union or with other CIO unions in town. The fact that most union leaders and perhaps half the members lived outside the city

[4] For a fuller discussion of the steel local's political behavior and influence see the authors' article, "Political Consciousness in a Local Union," *Public Opinion Quarterly*, XV (Winter, 1951–52), 692–702.

weakened the interest and effectiveness of the local in community political affairs.

In recent years the Democratic party has been in almost unchallenged control of the city where the steel plant is located. The Democratic machine is viewed as undesirable and corrupt by many of the local's leaders; they doubt, however, that they could defeat the machine's candidates and in any event have never tried to organize their members with that end in view. Members of the local who have been active in Democratic politics, it is believed, would probably support the machine, not the local, in the event of a clash. Under these conditions the local has generally supported the Democratic organization's candidates for city office in return for their benevolent neutrality in time of union-management strife. Except in the area of collective bargaining, however, the company has been able to exert influence within the community to get whatever it desired.

The steel workers overwhelmingly agreed that the police treated the union well. Only 3 union members out of 108 said that the police were neutral, and not one said that the police favored the company. An important union leader asserted that favorable police treatment was due to a "deal" made with city officials. "We don't have any trouble with the cops," he added. "They help us on the dues inspection lines. I remember the last picket line we put around the mill. I was arguing with some guy that didn't want to join the union and a cop came up and asked what the matter was and said to the guy: 'What do you want to do, cause trouble here? Join the union.'"

The police have not always been so friendly to the union, however. During the 1937 strike the influence of the police and of the entire city administration, headed by a Republican mayor, had been exerted against the union's strike efforts.

An overwhelming majority of management officials shared the belief of union members that the police were sympathetic to the union. When no labor dispute was involved, management officials had no criticism of police conduct, and those whose duties brought them into contact with the police found them friendly and co-operative. "But when there is a strike," said a general foreman, "they're on the union side." Asked how the police treated the union, a member of the top management group replied: "With kid gloves. The police have never interfered with the union . . . regardless of how illegal their activities are. . . . Whenever there was trouble [in the last strike] you couldn't find the police within miles. . . . Evidently they have an arrangement—whenever the police are there all is quiet; the baseball bats are all put away."

The national heads of the six unions responded very differently to the question of political action. The strongest lead by far in the direction of union activity was taken by the officers of the UAW, one of the national unions most interested in active participation in political life at all levels. The national leaders of the ILGWU and the Steelworkers likewise engaged in sustained efforts to increase the political awareness and effectiveness of their members. Leaders of the telephone workers and the plumbers were rather less active in this field—the telephone workers perhaps because the primary job of building a strong collective bargaining organization was still in process, the plumbers perhaps because the political influence most valuable to their members had to be exerted locally within whichever party was dominant.

Despite these differences in their needs for political influence, the opportunities open to them, and the attitudes of their national union leaders, the rank-and-file members of the six locals showed a high degree of uniformity in their attitudes to union political action. In four of the cases a clear majority rejected union action; in a fifth case—that of the metal workers—half did so, and in only one local, the steel workers, did slightly more than half favor political action and then usually with reservations. Since the CIO has had a strong interest in political action from the time of its formation and since the AFL has similarly been quite active politically since the passage of the Taft-Hartley law in 1947, it is evident that either a failure of communication or deep-seated resistance on the part of rank-and-file unionists or both have played a part.

In each of the four locals of coal miners, plumbers, knitting mill workers, and telephone workers a clear majority of the rank-and-file members interviewed answered in the negative some form of the question, "Should unions be active in politics?" The question did not specify what was meant by "politics," leaving the respondent to make his own interpretation. This led to some ambiguity in the answers, since a number of those who said they opposed union political activity nevertheless approved of lobbying for favorable legislation or indorsing pro-labor political candidates. It was a greater degree of political involvement that met with such widespread opposition.

The grounds advanced for opposing union political action were quite similar in these locals. The reasons most frequently assigned were that politics constituted a private matter, that unions should restrict themselves to in-plant problems, and that politics was a corrupt business that unions would do well to avoid. Less frequently it was also argued that union heads would become too powerful, that dissension would arise within the organization, and that retaliation might occur if candidates opposed by the union were nevertheless elected. As one of the plumbers put it, "It never helps at any time to bet on the wrong horse, whether it is for two bucks or for a local." There was opposition to being told how to vote—as against being given information and allowed to make up one's own mind—and fear that somehow this would occur if the union engaged in political action. The plumbers, incidentally, were familiar with a limited amount of political activity, since candidates for city office were invited to membership meetings to present their views. Despite the importance of the licensing system and the building code, however, most of the plumbers rejected union political activity at the municipal as strongly as at other levels.

The great majority of the rank-and-file unionists were completely uninformed about the CIO's Political Action Committee and the AFL's Labor's League for Political Education, and most of them opposed the idea of having such organizations after it was explained to them. Some CIO members who did not favor political action nevertheless contributed a dollar to PAC "to be sociable with the fellows" or because the union urged them to. Fully half of the inactive members of the steel local, when asked for their views on PAC, responded with variations of "What's PAC?" or even "Who's he?" Such political activity as the local carried on was largely undertaken by the leaders and active members, leaving the vast majority of inactive members uninvolved and almost completely untouched. If this situation was at all typical—at least of large locals of mass production workers—it helps explain the weakness of union political efforts.

In each of these locals there was a substantial minority of rank-and-file unionists who favored political action, the number rising to just above half in the case of the steel local. The activity consistently favored by these workers was the support of friendly candidates and favorable legislation. Many of those who expressed opposition to political action favored these two types of activity, however, so that majority support or something close to it was achieved in several of the other locals. Those who supported union political action saw a meaningful connection between politics and the collective bargaining problems faced by the union. Several pointed out that all other large organizations were in politics and asserted that unions had to engage in similar activity for their own protection. Some of the members of the UMW wanted to send coal miners to the legislatures so that their point of view on safety legislation and other matters could be presented properly.

Some of the metal workers, perhaps influenced by the political pronouncements of Walter Reuther or other UAW leaders, supported union political activity because they saw possible benefits to workers in general or to the people as a whole. The overwhelming tendency, however, was to define occupational interests and problems rather narrowly and to support only those political activities directly related to collective bargaining or occupational problems. Often those who favored political action expressed reservations as to the types of action that should be engaged in or the issues in which the union should interest itself. Some of these made it clear that they wished to operate within the traditional two-party system, avoiding anything "pink," and others insisted that the rights of the individual be respected.

In each of the six locals there was a substantial number either undecided about union political action or with no opinion on the subject. The number of such workers was understandably high among the knitting mill workers, who were so new to unionism, and among the telephone workers, whose relationship to the labor movement was most tenuous. Even in the case of the steel local, however, one worker out of six could express no opinion.

Though some surveys of members' political attitudes have yielded results similar to ours, two recent studies have shown somewhat greater support for union political action. In their study of the attitudes of the members of District 9 of the International Association of Machinists in an Illinois area, the Rosens found that 55 per cent of the rank and file thought the union should always or usually take an active part in politics, 24 per cent wanted it to do so sometimes, and the remaining 21 per cent seldom or never. There was overwhelming sentiment (81 per cent) for the support of candidates who backed legislation good for labor, but divided opinion as to whether the union should discuss politics at local lodge meetings (31 per cent favored doing so usually or always, 35 per cent sometimes, with the remaining 34 per cent opposed). There was overwhelming opposition to having unions tell members whom to vote for or ask members for donations for union political action.[5]

A study of the UAW membership in Detroit showed 78 per cent approving of the union's working for Stevenson in the 1952 campaign, and approximately half of them trusting the voting recommendations of labor groups in particular. Newspapers and business groups, by way of contrast, were trusted by only 9 and 7 per cent, respectively.[6] Some of the differences between these results and ours might be due to the phraseology of the questions; in the case of the auto workers, part of the difference is probably the result of the active political education and campaigning carried on by the UAW staff in the Detroit area.

Factors Affecting Labor Political Action

To the extent that they are typical of American labor, the political attitudes of the workers in these six locals contrast with the widespread participation of the labor movement in politics in other highly industrialized countries, particularly in western Europe. Perhaps attention might be paid very briefly to some of the factors influential in America that have contributed to this difference.

In countries with a homogeneous population and relatively rigid barriers between social classes there is a strong tendency to form political parties on the basis of class distinctions. In the United States this is true to a degree, in the sense that most of those in the upper income and social groups support the Republican party, while most workers and low income people are allied with the Democrats. Yet the political division in this country is far more complicated, since racial and ethnic differences, along with sectional rivalries and the heritage of a bitter civil war, have all played a part. Protestants, farmers, business and professional men, and descendants of the older settlers tend to be Republicans; low income urban dwellers, Catholics, Jews, Negroes since the New Deal days, most of the newer ethnic groups, and the overwhelming majority of southerners tend to be Democrats.[7] Political allegiance is more complicated than economic interest, though economic interest

[5] Hjalmar Rosen and R. A. Hudson Rosen, *The Union Member Speaks* (New York: Prentice-Hall, Inc., 1955), p. 37.

[6] Arthur Kornhauser, Harold L. Sheppard, and Albert J. Mayer, *When Labor Votes: A Study of Auto Workers* (New York: University Books, 1956), pp. 100, 105.

[7] For an able analysis of our political alignment see Samuel Lubell, *The Future of American Politics* (New York: Harper & Bros., 1951).

is a major component. Once a particular political loyalty has developed, it may take a crisis to shake it.

In the United States there is an unusually high degree of economic-social mobility, as one would expect in a relatively new country with vast natural resources and a rapidly rising population. As industrialization has developed a new urban middle class has steadily grown, in proportion as well as in absolute numbers, drawing many of its recruits from the sons and daughters of the skilled industrial workers. Meanwhile the ranks of the less-skilled workers in industry were filled with immigrants or our own surplus rural population, white and Negro; this has given us a heterogeneous working class population, poorly prepared for joint political activity. The heterogeneity of the population, the internal divisions within the ranks of workers, the relatively high degree of social mobility, and a widespread psychology of individualism have all contributed to make union political action more difficult to achieve in this country.

Our political structure, moreover, with its complicated system of checks and balances, was designed to prevent quick action by a temporary majority. The division of authority among forty-eight states and the federal government, with further division within each among the executive, legislative, and judicial branches, makes it far easier to block than to achieve change. Since office-holders are elected for different periods of time—in the case of the federal government, two years for representatives, four for the president, and six for senators—even a clean sweep of all offices in a national election may not permit action by the victors; and if it did, an unfriendly judiciary, holding office for long periods if not for life, might declare certain legislation invalid or interpret it in ways unintended by its sponsors. The federal power, which is peculiarly important in an interconnected economy, is limited by constitutional restraints, while state action with regard to many issues of interest to workers is impeded by the fear of putting local industry at a disadvantage or by the desire to attract new industry. All of this has operated to make labor political action more cumbersome, less inviting, and less effective than in many other countries.

Economic action, however—at least for certain groups—promised far greater rewards than workers in most other countries could hope to achieve. The traditional aloofness of the AFL from political action is not unrelated to the fact that skilled workers, who have always dominated the organization, were able to take care of their most urgent needs through collective bargaining; and this, in turn, was a reflection of the wealth of the expanding American economy, which, by giving industry a generous margin of profit and enabling it to raise prices without sharp reduction in volume, permitted substantial bargaining gains to powerful unions. The building trades, long the backbone of the AFL, operated in a series of separate local markets, a fact that facilitated gains through economic action. The possession of the franchise by most workers before industrialization was far advanced, the organization and leadership of early unions by men primarily interested in collective bargaining, the greater productivity of American enterprise, and the higher living standards that could be won for workers through economic pressure all played a part in giving the American trade union movement its distinctive cast.

Less-skilled industrial workers, by way of contrast, depend to a greater degree upon the national government. Lacking the economic power of craftsmen, they were unable for the most part even to organize until a friendly New Deal adopted a favorable basic labor law; once organized, they were dependent in varying degrees on the federal government for favorable legislation dealing with minimum wages, unemployment and old age insurance, and other matters affecting their living standards. From its start the CIO has been active in the political field to supplement the more limited gains its members could achieve through collective bargaining. It took the passage of the Taft-Hartley law, with its threats to all unionism, to convince the AFL that it too had such a great stake in government legislation that it was essential to mobilize all the political influence it could muster.

Once relatively aloof from the economic sphere, the American government is now increasingly involved, exercising a substantial and growing influence; because of the dangers of war, and the need to keep the economy functioning at high levels of employment and production, this involvement is more likely to increase than to diminish. Unions cannot ignore this development, since to do so would be to expose government and the public to pressures from management without providing any counterpressure from the labor movement. The problem is no longer whether to engage in political activity; it is, rather, to work out the most effective method of operating in the political arena and to learn how best to interest and activate union members in order to achieve maximum results.

So far as the great body of union members is concerned, important questions are whether and under what circumstances economic pressures will take precedence over other influences on their voting behavior, and whether they will accept to a greater degree their union's influence or guidance in political matters. If living standards continue to rise, if workers share equitably in the increasing productivity of industry, if employment continues to be high, and if the opportunities for upward social mobility, at least from one generation to the next, continue to be good, then other issues might well supersede the economic ones in the minds of many, perhaps of most, workers. Should the reverse prove true, however, then economic factors could be expected to take precedence over the other influences having an impact on voting behavior.

To the extent that unions can produce economic gains, along with protection and security, through collective bargaining, most workers may continue to feel that the primary purposes for which they joined their union have been achieved. If continued economic gains are threatened by political factors, however, the meaningful link between politics and unionism will be forged, and workers will likely be prepared to expand the scope of union activity to include political action. Unions may indeed engage in political action anyway, but until such action is viewed as legitimate, indeed as essential, by the masses of members, it will have relatively little effect on their voting behavior.

In this connection the relations between union leaders and union members, the degree of effective democracy within the unions, and the type of union security clause in effect will all have an influence. Union leaders in America are more powerful than their counterparts in the democratic countries of Europe, with more instruments of control over their members. It is not surprising, therefore, to find among many American workers an undercurrent of antagonism toward their paid leaders and a reluctance to increase their power. If genuine union democracy can be achieved at the national as well as the local level and civil liberties assured within the union,[8] the members may be more ready to engage in new activities that increase the influence and power of their union heads.

[8] Some way may also have to be found to protect the rights of the political dissenter, the member who does not support the candidate or party indorsed by his local union. See the discussion of this question in Kornhauser, Sheppard, and Mayer, *op. cit.*, pp. 295–97.

A Labor Party?

In four of the cases—those of the coal miners, the plumbers, the metal workers, and the knitting mill workers—union members were asked whether they thought labor should have its own political party instead of supporting the existing parties. Considering their widespread reluctance to support labor political action in general, it is not surprising that the workers overwhelmingly rejected the idea of a labor party. The strongest support for one came from the metal workers, where one out of five favored the idea;[9] only a tenth of the miners and of the plumbers reacted favorably, and among the knitting mill workers the percentage was only moderately higher. Half of the knitting workers, new to the labor movement, did not know how to answer the question.

Much the same reasons for opposing a labor party were offered by the three experienced groups of unionists—the metal workers, the miners, and the plumbers. Most workers felt that the existing parties were doing their jobs satisfactorily, that too much power would lead to corruption or other evils in the labor movement, or that a labor party would somehow become too radical. Images of communism, socialism, dictatorship, Soviet Russia, Nazi Germany, or labor-influenced Britain were associated by various workers—and negatively—with the idea of a labor party. In addition, there were some feelings that other elements in society were entitled to representation in a political party and in government, that too few qualified persons were available within labor's ranks, and that a labor party could not win elections. Among the knitting mill workers the ideas were less well crystallized; there was a widespread fear, however, of separating labor from the other groups in society, of losing the sympathy and help of other people.

The relatively small numbers who favored the formation of a labor party argued that more could be done for workers through a party of their own that was not dependent upon the good will of other parties, and that one could be sure that its candidates would favor labor. It was

[9] Part of this support may have been due to the influence of Walter Reuther, whose statements in support of a labor party under certain circumstances were referred to by some of the workers. In his study of Local 688 of the Teamsters in St. Louis, Arnold Rose found that 45 per cent of the members, an unusually high proportion, wanted their union to help start a labor party sometime in the future (*Union Solidarity: The Internal Cohesion of a Labor Union* [Minneapolis: University of Minnesota Press, 1952], p. 84). This high degree of support probably reflected the unusual background of the able leaders of the local, as well as the political education carried on by them over a long period of time.

also suggested that the formation of a labor party would incline the other parties to make concessions to labor.

The labor party issue is hardly a live one in the United States at the present time because of the close working relationship between the labor movement and the Democratic party. In some areas, such as Detroit and other automobile manufacturing centers in Michigan, the unions have become an integral part of the Democratic organization from the precinct level up. In many other industrial states there is also a fairly close relationship between the union movement and the party.[10] Democratic national conventions include a substantial number of active unionists—about two hundred in 1952[11]—as delegates or alternates. So long as both union leaders and rank-and-file unionists see an important difference between the Democratic and the Republican parties, it is unlikely that a move to launch a labor party would attract substantial support.[12]

Even if the differences between the two major parties were somewhat less than at present, it would not be easy to persuade large numbers of union officers to organize a new party. The average local officer, who must face a new election in a year or two, is necessarily concerned with building a record of achievement that will improve his chances of success. The formation of a new party is a long-run venture, however, which may not yield results for some time. Long-range planning is a luxury, if possible at all, for the leader whose union may go down to defeat unless the police are neutralized, or who may himself be defeated in the next election unless he achieves substantial bargaining gains in the meantime. Where tenure in office seems assured for a relatively long period of time, as is the case with most national union heads,

[10] For a description of various of these relationships and an analysis of their operation in the 1950 local, state, and congressional elections, see Fay Calkins, *The CIO and the Democratic Party* (Chicago: University of Chicago Press, 1952).

[11] Max M. Kampelman, "Labor in Politics," in Industrial Relations Research Association, *Interpreting the Labor Movement* (1952), p. 171. Kampelman's article is a very good analysis and review of labor political action.

[12] Kornhauser and his associates found that 53 per cent of their sample of UAW members in Detroit saw an important difference between the two major parties, 35 per cent did not, and the remainder did not know or failed to answer. Of those who were above average both in prolabor political orientation and in political interest, however, 75 per cent saw an important difference; since these are the active unionists most directly involved in the union's political decisions, Kornhauser and his associates conclude that the chances for the establishment of a new party on the initiative of these members are very slight (Kornhauser, Sheppard, and Mayer, *op. cit.*, pp. 163, 240).

there is more opportunity to engage in long-range political planning; even here, however, the union head must balance the immediate loss of political influence with old-party legislators and administrators against the possibility of future gains that a labor party might achieve.

Nor should it be forgotten that unionists and members of their immediate families, though numerous enough to affect most elections and to constitute the balance of power in many, are by themselves a majority only in highly industrialized and strongly unionized areas. In the nation at large they have hopes of achieving majority status only if very substantial numbers of the growing army of white-collar employees are unionized. In any event, blue-collar workers in industry do not constitute, with their families, a majority of the electorate, and they are less likely to do so, in view of the rapid rate of technological advance, in the future. This means that a new party with the potential of becoming a majority must appeal to white-collar as well as to manual workers, and is in a better position if it can attract agricultural support as well. It must also be remembered that a lower percentage of manual workers, particularly of those with less education and income, tend to register and vote than is the case with other economic-social groups.

There are, in addition, a number of legal obstacles that any new party would have to face, along with some handicaps to a party based on labor that are inherent in our political system. In a number of states it has become increasingly difficult for a new party to get on the ballot. Since proportional representation scarcely exists here, a candidate usually has to be able to defeat his rivals in a single electoral district in order to be returned to office; in many other countries, by way of contrast, a substantial minority party is assured of some representation, so that no one need feel that his vote for a minority group constitutes "throwing his vote away."

Our system of electing the president, moreover, focuses attention every four years on the personalities seeking that office at the expense of local issues and aspirants for lesser office, and it also places a premium on the coalition of forces that is large enough to attract majority support to its presidential candidate. The allocation of seats in the federal Senate and in the various state legislatures, in addition, overweights the rural or small town areas against the urban, and thus acts as a handicap to a party that inevitably would find its greatest support in the cities. As against all these difficulties, there is the opportunity to exercise influence within the ranks of the Democratic party, and to nominate candidates through its conventions or primary elections who are acceptable to labor.[13]

There are, however, a number of offsetting advantages that would accrue from the formation of a labor party, should the Democratic as well as the Republican party prove generally unresponsive to the wishes of the labor movement. There is much to be said for controlling one's own party, for being able to present candidates and programs without the need to conciliate rival and sometimes unfriendly groups. The Democratic party, like the Republican, is hardly a national organization, but rather a loose federation of state and local groups held together under the same label by the hope of electing candidates and obtaining patronage. Labor's influence within the party varies, and will continue to vary, from state to state and from city to city, depending on the resources that unions have in the way of votes, political workers, appealing candidates, and funds that the party organization needs in order to win elections. In some areas labor will be courted, in others disregarded, and in still others it will have to fight at the primaries in order to make the candidates it supports the official standard-bearers of the party. Yet political experience shows that it is hard to interest the public—and this would include union members—in primary contests. Still another factor, should labor prove largely successful within the Democratic party in the North, is that the congressional seniority system usually gives the powerful committee chairmanships to conservative Democrats from the one-party South. A final consideration is that the formation of a new party, if it showed promise of success, would probably frighten the older parties into substantial concessions.

[13] A fuller discussion of the reasons that impel labor to function as a pressure group rather than through a labor party will be found in Avery Leiserson, "Organized Labor as a Pressure Group," *Annals of the American Academy of Political and Social Science,* CCLXXIV (March, 1951), 108–17.

11

A TYPOLOGY
OF UNION MEMBERS[1]

The interviews show that a wide variety of factors may influence a worker's view of unionism. His family background, including his father's occupation and any experience that his parents or other close relatives have had with unionism, may affect the attitude that, as a young worker, he brings with him. His employment experiences—his pay and working conditions, his treatment by supervisors, the degree of security he enjoys, his advancement or failure to advance—in turn may profoundly influence his view of his employer and his reaction to his union. Moreover, his experiences within the union—the union leadership, the economic and social functions performed by the union, its success in solving members' problems, and the way union officers may have handled any grievances in which he was involved—are likewise important, as is the bargaining relationship between the union and the company.

The age of the union and the strength of union tradition in the industry may likewise exert a strong influence, as the entering worker is exposed to the attitudes of the older members of the work force. It may make a substantial difference whether the particular worker experienced at first hand the conditions that preceded the development of the union and participated in the initial struggles or whether he was merely told of earlier conditions and of organizing strikes by older members. It may matter, similarly, whether the new worker learns about the union from union leaders or strongly pro-union rank-and-file members or whether his information comes from the lukewarm or the indifferent. Economic factors affecting the industry and the particular

---

[1] This chapter is based in large measure on the authors' article, "A Typology of Rank-and-File Union Members," *American Journal of Sociology*, LXI (May, 1956), 546–53.

enterprise may likewise be important: whether the industry is expanding or declining, whether the company is prosperous or marginal, whether the company is a pattern setter or a pattern follower in the industry. The size of the plant, its location in a small town or a metropolitan area, the steadiness of its operations, and the general attitude of the community toward unionism may all play a part. Finally, aspects of the worker as an individual—age, sex, education, degree of skill, racial or ethnic background, and level of aspiration—may all play a part in determining the worker's attitude toward the union.

Many of these factors will also influence the worker's participation in union affairs. While meetings are attended, for the most part, by those very favorably inclined toward the union, there will be many absentees who likewise hold the union in high regard. Yet there may be a two-way relationship between the worker's part in union affairs and his attitude toward the union. The more favorable his attitude, other things being equal, the more likely he is to attend meetings, serve on committees, read the union press, and be friendly with like-minded members. The more he engages in such activities, in turn, the more he is exposed to union influence and the more he is likely to be attached and appreciative. Anything that affects participation, such as what shift he works on, home duties that interfere with his attendance at union functions, or the time and place of union meetings, may therefore have an indirect influence on his attitude toward unionism.

We have tentatively distinguished seven types of rank-and-file union members: (1) the ideological unionist; (2) the "good" union man; (3) the loyal but critical member; (4) the crisis activist; (5) the dually oriented member; (6) the card-carrier or indifferent member; and (7) the unwilling unionist. In some cases the types tended to merge, making the count somewhat arbitrary; but, on the whole, the cases were grouped into types separated by major differences, relatively minor differences being permitted within each.

The Ideological Unionist

The ideological unionist, the extreme case of enthusiasm and devotion, is distinguished from the others by an articulate political and social philosophy, intensely held, oriented toward social change. The ideological unionist sees the union primarily as an instrument for furthering his doctrine. Usually sympathetic to one or another of the leftist philosophies, he sees management as an oppressor and union-management relations as an aspect of a class struggle, with both contenders in the grip of larger social forces. While most union activities necessarily center about the employer-employee relationship, the broader goal of a different social order appears to the ideological unionist as one toward which workers should ultimately strive. The strengthening of the union is an important objective, and any heightening of class consciousness is welcomed.

The ideological member supports all traditional union goals and activities and is anxious to extend their scope as widely as possible to include political and community life as well as the employment relationship. He is anxious to gain support and prestige for the union as a collective bargaining agency, as an instrument of the working class, and as a possible basis for a political labor movement. He may argue that a strike is not lost, whatever its immediate result in collective bargaining, if, through it, workers have shown unity and strength, won greater confidence in themselves, and gained increased respect from management. He is more willing than most other members to consider personal sacrifices in order to strengthen the union. Nevertheless, he may be critical of union leaders who do not conform to his standards of union activity; he may object to their lack of militancy, to tendencies toward business unionism, to political activities such as the AFL-CIO's Committee on Political Education, which he may consider inadequate or even a distortion of the union's proper political goals. Even his criticism of the union, however, is likely to be tempered with an explanation of its shortcomings or praise for its achievements.

The ideological unionist is far more likely than any other type to know something about the history of the labor movement and to be informed about actions taken by the international union with which his local is affiliated. He is likely to reject sharply any suggestion that he might accept a foreman's position, stressing his devotion to the union, his distrust of management, and his unwillingness to accept management ideology. Particularly if he is a member of a group of union leaders, he views his job in the plant as of secondary importance compared to his job in the union and his concern with the labor movement. Very few such workers are found except in metropolitan centers, where radical groups have strength; and the number has been decreasing as the depression period of the 1930's, along with the radicalism fostered by it, fades farther into the past. The number of union members of this

243

type is very small, probably not exceeding 2 per cent at the highest, but where they exist they tend to participate actively in union affairs and frequently become candidates for office.

Where the union leadership group is ideologically oriented, the member of this type who achieves leadership is likely to retain his point of view. In other cases the pressures and responsibilities to which he is subject as a union leader may tend to change him, in time, into the "good" union man that is next described. Where the union environment is hostile to his point of view, the ideological unionist may become part of a minority faction, and eventually turn into a critical or disillusioned member. One such case appeared among the plumbers.

The "Good" Union Man[2]

The "good" union man is devoted to his union, accepts its goals fully, and supports all its objectives. Often strongly emotional, he supports his union's strikes without qualification and pickets willingly and enthusiastically. Typically, he gives strong support to the union shop, seeks to sign up new workers in the union, and plays an active part in union meetings. Except under very rare circumstances, he respects the picket line of any bona fide union. Whereas other workers may picket because they feel it their duty, the good union man, in addition, supports picketing as necessary to demonstrate and protect the power of the union and win the wages or working conditions for which the strike was called. He understands and supports union rules and regulations beyond mere obedience.

Like union leaders and ideological unionists, but unlike other types of the rank and file, the good union man seeks to protect and advance the union's prestige and power. Again like them, he gives the union full credit for achievements and criticizes it with reluctance and sympathetic understanding, disparaging those who adopt a self-centered attitude toward it. But, on the other hand, he has no desire to change the existing order. While he opposes management during collective bargaining negotiations or strikes, he does not see employers as class enemies, though he may be more hostile to his own employer than are most of his fellows or have mixed feelings.

[2] This term is used by many union leaders and active unionists to describe this type. We have used quotation marks here to make it clear that we are using the term purely descriptively, without value orientation.

However, the good union men among the plumbers were noticeably different from their counterparts in the other unions, in that they were not markedly aggressive toward employers. Instead, as is characteristic of the plumbers, they took pride in the harmonious relationships prevailing between the masters and the journeymen. Plumbers, aware of their union's economic strength, are not afraid of their employers, most of whom are small contractors with relatively little economic power. The ideological unionist has reacted unfavorably to the established social order and views unionism as an agency of social change, but the good union man looks to his union to do no more than improve working conditions.

Though the good union man can accept a position in management more readily than can the ideological unionist, he has doubts about it. He may say that management would not consider him because of his known pro-union stand; or he may think he would be suspect in the eyes of his fellows.

Most active unionists, those who serve as stewards and pressure their fellow workers to join the union, are good union men, as is a proportion of the inactive rank and file. The number of good union men is unlikely to exceed 10 per cent of the membership, and in most locals will probably be under this figure. Good union men, with a sprinkling of ideological unionists, make up the leaders and the active groups. Good union men are the type usually preferred by leaders when an office is to be filled. Where ideological unionists comprise the leaders, however, they usually give their support to rank-and-file unionists who share their political and social orientation.

Though the circumstances that produced the good union man cannot be specified from our limited data, a strong pro-union family was responsible in some cases, and in others it was close contacts with union leaders. Sometimes members of minorities—in our sample, Negroes and Mexicans—turn to the union as an agency to get jobs and fair working conditions for their people. Still others seem to have been motivated in large part by frustrated ambitions. The good union man was found among skilled and semiskilled, young and old, whites and Negroes.

There is evidence that, as unionism has become more firmly established and as local treasuries increase, the dedication characteristic of the good union man in the past has given way to an expectation on the part of many that lost time will be paid for any union service performed, and that some compensation, even though quite small, will accompany union office. There is obvious danger to the labor movement if its minor officials, who are primarily good union men, view union office and committee work not simply as an opportunity for service but also in terms of monetary reward.

The Loyal but Critical Member

The loyal but critical member resembles the two types already discussed in his devotion to unionism but differs sharply in his appraisal of his local. He may criticize the leaders for inefficiency or incompetence, for dishonesty or corruption, for conservatism, for dictatorial tendencies, for constituting a clique, for separation from the rank and file, for lack of militancy in dealing with employers, for siding with the employers against the rank-and-file union members. He may be equally critical of the members' apathy, lack of militancy, ignorance, or self-centeredness. He is likely to support strikes and picketing and to assert that he would never work in a non-union shop. He urges extending union activity beyond collective bargaining to include political and community action.

Loyal but critical members ranged from the relatively active or potentially active who objected to certain policies to those who, hostile to or disillusioned with the leaders, had withdrawn from union activities while still believing in unionism on principle. To this class belong those former members of the Progressive Miners of America who returned to the United Mine Workers in defeat and who cannot forgive John L. Lewis for his autocratic control. Others of the type were identified with a minority faction or were antagonized by the leaders' handling of a specific issue. With a change in leaders or in the relationship with management, the loyal but critical member may again become an active and enthusiastic unionist. The loyal but critical member is most likely to achieve leadership if and when an opposing faction wins control of the union.

The Crisis Activist

If the union membership is conceived as a ring of concentric circles surrounding the leaders and the active group, the layer of normally inactive members closest to the center is made up of "crisis unionists."

Here belongs the member who supports the union, but without being involved emotionally as are the ideological unionist and the good union man. Though interested in the benefits the union confers, he is hardly concerned with its internal life or its prestige. In the miners' union, which is dominated by the national union officers, the good union members supported centralized decision-making, even where undemocratic practices were involved, as assuring returns in wages and working conditions. Most of the crisis activists, on the other hand, were completely detached, being not even aware, for example, that their key district officials were appointed instead of being elected. Yet they supported the union wholeheartedly because of its contribution to their welfare. The crisis activist views the union primarily as an agency of collective bargaining and sees little reason for political activity unless it contributes to collective bargaining success. He conceives of the day-to-day operations of the union, the routine business between crises, as the business of the leaders. "Let the officers run the union," he is likely to say, "that's what we elected them for."

Workers of this type are passive supporters most of the time, but they attend meetings in critical periods and willingly serve their turns on picket duty. They usually observe union rules without protest but are less emotionally involved and understand less than ideological unionists or good union men. The union is something external to them with which, at least during times of industrial peace, they have little feeling of identification.[3] They see the union as an agency to which one regularly makes payments and from which, in turn, one obtains substantial benefits from time to time. They rarely discuss their duties to the union spontaneously, as good union men do, but rather the potential benefits and rights that they think should flow almost automatically in return for the payment of dues. When questioned, crisis activists usually admit that they *should* attend meetings and see to it that the union is run properly; they readily confess, however, that they often permit other commitments, such as those to family or friends, to come first unless there is a crisis in the union or in union-management relations.

---

[3] Crisis activists and also the various types of less active members discussed later speak of the union as "they," as contrasted with the use of "we" by the leaders and many of the active members. Good union men may use either term, depending upon their degree of activity in the union. The use of "we" or "they" is a function of the worker's role or activity in the union rather than his attitude toward it—though there is an obvious relationship between attitude and activity.

Whereas the good union man and the ideological unionist, active in the internal life of the union, tend to support factionalism as necessary to democracy, crisis unionists and also other types of inactive members usually oppose it as selfish and as harmful to the interests of the members. They do not usually consider joining a union as an aggressive step directed against management but rather as a defensive reaction against management abuses, actual or potential. Viewing the strike as a last resort against management's unfairness or unreasonableness, they tend to react unfavorably to overly aggressive union leaders.

Though this type was apparent among the plumbers and among the other union members studied, there were some noticeable differences in behavior or attitudes. Most striking was the fact that among the plumbers the type under discussion, elsewhere relatively inactive, went regularly to meetings. The explanation is that, whereas among miners or factory workers there were inevitable contacts with fellow workers on the job or on the way to or from work, the plumbers worked for the most part in widely scattered shops, with several men in each. The meeting therefore served a social function and also as a channel of communication whereby one learned about developments in the trade, including employment opportunities.

Crisis activists, who go to meetings "when something important comes up," may mean, by "important," collective bargaining negotiations, union elections, and other local matters; others, using the same phrase, may mean only issues of immediate personal relevance. Some may see the union as winning positive gains, whereas others may think of it merely as serving the restraining function of keeping the employer fair and preventing inequities and injustices. Some may pay union dues in the same spirit that one pays taxes: in order to have a policeman on the beat, in the hope that his mere presence may make his services unnecessary. Some think the dues are as high as is necessary to insure union strength and finance union services, whereas others may believe them far too high. Many crisis unionists proved critical of the leaders' political efforts, though differing substantially as to what was legitimate, some insisting on avoidance of politics and others arguing that unions should indorse candidates and give them financial or other support. Crisis unionists differed also in their general attitude to union leaders, from complete confidence to considerable distrust.

Crisis activists are very numerous among rank-and-file unionists, probably outnumbering any other type in many locals. We hesitate to suggest percentages of members who may belong to this or any of the other intermediate types, however, because these tend to shift fairly readily from one category to another depending on the specific situation—on the local's success or lack of it in collective bargaining, the quality of the local leadership, the satisfactions or disappointments that union membership brings. The ideological unionists and the good union men at the one extreme, and the unwilling unionists at the other, tend to be more deeply committed to their views and to constitute more stable groups.

The Dually Oriented Member

In the metal workers' local and among the plumbers there were members who, while giving support to the union in all essential respects, viewed production and efficiency from the point of view of management.[4] The metal workers so minded tended to be skilled workers in responsible positions, such as layout inspectors, maintenance workers, utility men, or former supervisors. Many of them could reasonably hope to achieve supervisory positions. Among the plumbers, who permitted supervisory personnel to retain union membership, such members were likely to be supervisors, present or former owners of small shops, or sons of master plumbers. These men held the union in high regard and gave its policies and programs generally strong support; yet they felt that its activity should be confined to collective bargaining and were most reluctant to strike. In their attitudes toward the union some resembled the good union man or the crisis activist; others—the plumbers in particular—were more like the loyal but critical member.

The point of view toward the company and productive efficiency typical of the dually oriented factory worker is far more positive than

---

[4] Our use of the term "dually oriented" involves a meaning quite different from that intended by the term "dual allegiance" in Theodore V. Purcell, *The Worker Speaks His Mind on Company and Union* (Cambridge, Mass.: Harvard University Press, 1953). Using as his test acceptance of both company and union as institutions and allegiance to their objectives, Purcell found that 73 per cent of his sample of employees gave dual allegiance (pp. 263–64). It seems quite likely that most of our good union men, loyal but critical members, and crisis unionists would show dual loyalty in his sense. A Cornell University research project, using a definition on the whole similar to Purcell's, found dual loyalty to union and management prevailing under conditions of conflict as well as co-operation (see Lois R. Dean, "Union Activity and Dual Loyalty," *Industrial and Labor Relations Review*, VII [1954], 526–36).

that found among many ideological unionists and good union men, who may value the employer for providing such benefits as steady work, good pay, security of employment, and fair treatment. Indeed, long-term employees who have had a choice of alternative sources of employment have usually found some such advantages in their place of employment or they would probably have left it.

The dually oriented factory worker usually questions the seniority principle as harmful to efficiency. He may accuse the union of undermining discipline. Plumbers of this type understood the impact of union rules upon the plumbing business as a whole and were prone to criticize the restrictive, "make-work" aspects. Inevitably, there was some ambivalence toward the union and its policies, particularly on the part of the owners of small shops. Yet even these respondents, in the manner characteristic of the dually oriented member, viewed the union as essential within its traditional scope. Dually oriented plumbers, like all plumbers, came to union meetings fairly regularly, if only because the union remained the best center for information about conditions in the trade, whereas the dually oriented metal workers were usually inactive. No member of this type was found among the miners, perhaps because of their limited opportunities for rising into supervisory ranks.

The Card-Carrier or Indifferent Member

Beyond the crisis unionist and dually oriented members are those who are completely unconcerned about unionism, who have no feelings for or against it, who join the union because they have to or because they wish to be part of the group. Most of the card-carriers whom we met had joined the union under such circumstances, but it does not follow that all who join under similar circumstances are indifferent members. They may change. A number of good union men, including several who rose to leadership, had joined the union because of legal or social pressure and remained card-carriers for their first months or even years of membership.

Workers of this type join the union if most of their fellow workers are members, but fail to do so if the shop is predominantly non-union. In either case they are indifferent to the institution, caring more for shop fellowship. Sometimes workers who see themselves as only temporarily in the labor market—as young women who plan to be employed only until they get married or start to raise a family—are indifferent union members. So, too, are those who are completely satisfied with their jobs and opportunities and see no threat from management, against which unionism might provide a defense. Workers of this type carry union cards but do not participate in union functions except where unusual circumstances or pressure from their fellow workers may force them to, and they have no sense of their duties or obligations as union members and are indifferent and uninformed.

The Unwilling Unionist

There are occasional members, forced into the organization against their will by legal or social pressures, who see no advantage in unionism and who, left to follow their own free will, would promptly drop out. They are critical of unionism in general. A member who has been "bumped" into an undesirable job under seniority rules fostered by the bargaining agent may adopt this attitude. Or he may feel that he does not need the union because of his peculiar skill, willingness to work hard, or ability to get along with his supervisors. He may even see himself as an unusually proficient worker who would be rapidly advanced by management if only the union's seniority regulations did not block his progress. If he has ideas of entering into business for himself, he is apt to think unionism unnecessary for him.

The unwilling unionist is likely to view union leaders with hostility and suspicion and to sympathize with management where handicaps are imposed on it by union demands. He may criticize union leaders for dishonesty, for favoritism, or for dictatorialness, as he may blame the union for undermining efficiency or for protecting the interests of a few at the expense of the other members. Usually, he will oppose most strikes as unnecessary and reject all union activities not directly concerned with collective bargaining over wages and working conditions. Yet he may admit, perhaps grudgingly, that unions have brought about some improvements in wages, working conditions, or treatment of workers by the supervisory staff. We found several unwilling unionists among the metal workers, one among the plumbers, and none among the miners.

At one extreme within the group may be a very few convinced anti-unionists, the counterparts of the ideological unionists. They give the union no credit at all for improvements on or off the job and see the union as an unfair, oppressive force, perhaps dominated by Communists, racketeers, or other undesirable elements. The convinced anti-unionist has deep feelings on the subject, just as the ideological unionist does; and, unlike many workers belonging to intermediate types, he does not readily change views as a result of greater experience.

The typology here presented, based on a very limited number of cases, is meant to be suggestive only. It would be interesting to know whether the types that appear in the locals studied occur in other locals, faced with other problems in other industries, and also whether, if the same basic types reappear, they will adopt somewhat different attitudes and behavior in response to special conditions—much as the peculiar conditions surrounding the operation of the plumbers' union have produced some variations, even though the types remain distinguishable. It would also be important to know how and to what extent specific conditions within the trade and the union affect the distribution of types within each local—whether, for example, a change in the type of union leader or in the nature of union-management relations will produce a redistribution. A number of union members with whom we spoke had progressed from one type to another as a result of their experiences within the plant or within the union; much more needs to be learned about the circumstances and direction of these shifts.

The typology of members may throw light on some aspects of the present-day American labor movement, as well as on some of its coming problems. If union leaders are chosen almost exclusively from among the first two types, which, between them, comprise a very small proportion of the total membership, then a gap between the orientation of leaders and members is inevitable, especially since experiences, once leadership has been assumed, are bound to widen the gap further. It appears very unlikely, moreover, that there will be any widespread and sustained participation by members in union affairs except in crises. This, in turn, hinders the growth of a functioning and effective democracy within the union movement. The presence of large numbers of the inactive types of unionists helps to explain the overwhelmingly favorable vote that a union may win in a National Labor Relations Board election, though the union may find it difficult thereafter to muster a quorum at a meeting. Conversely, the low level of participation at meetings does not demonstrate that the members see no value in the union.

Even where the union can win few improvements in wages, working conditions, and security, the ideological unionist and the good union man will continue to give the union strong support, search for ways to increase the union's prestige, and criticize their fellow workers who show only a lukewarm interest in the union. For them the union will remain a key institution regardless of the particular experiences on the job. The rest of the membership, however, may see little reason to be concerned with unionism under such circumstances. For the crisis unionist in particular, occupational experiences are crucial for his degree of involvement in the union; his approach is usually pragmatic, and hence his participation and also his loyalty suffer if no problem develops which he looks to the union to solve.

Yet the union, far from being unique in this respect, is faced with a problem similar to that confronting many other types of organizations. In most groups a handful of officers and active members fully accept the institution's norms of behavior, devote time and energy to its work, and concern themselves with its growth and prestige, while the bulk of the membership gives more passive support and becomes active only in crisis situations. In the union, as in other large organizations, the small group of officers and active members have the problem of activating the crisis members, of creating situations that will increase loyalty to the organization and give new meaning to its norms and goals. For new generations of members especially, it is important that such situations exist, to provide meaningful experiences for them and to bind them emotionally to the organization.

The ideological unionist and the good union man are likely to seek the views of union leaders, not only within the narrow sphere of union-management relations but in far wider areas as well. Other workers, however, may identify with other groups in or out of the plant and respond to the views of other leaders in the community. In time of union-management strife the union may also become a reference group for other types, such as crisis members, providing them with a feeling of identity and a source of attitudes and opinions. Yet this may be restricted sharply to the area of union-management relations, with any attempt by union leaders to broaden their area of activity, such as into politics, regarded as illegitimate.

In times of industrial peace the union may not be the most important reference group for most workers even with regard to union-management problems. The union is in the strongest position when the most highly respected members of the occupational group are good union men, preferably holding union office. Often, however, the most influential members of the occupational group may be less firmly attached to the union and subject to its influence only at certain times and with regard to limited areas. Indeed, the reference group accepted for certain purposes by the dually oriented worker may be composed of management officials.

The attitude that union leaders assume toward management—their degree of aggressiveness, their willingness or reluctance to threaten or call strikes—will also command different degrees of support within the union, depending in part upon the distribution of the types. Similarly, support for institutional demands such as the union shop will increase as the percentage of good union men grows, whereas other members will be much more concerned with using the union's bargaining power to win wage benefits and other immediate gains for themselves. Since only a few of the types believe the union should engage in political action, success in politics will depend in part on the local distribution of types. One of the most important attributes of the successful union leader is knowing how to convince unwilling, indifferent, or crisis unionists that the union has a more important place and a deeper significance.

12

SOME PROBLEMS
AND POLICY ISSUES

If our methods of study have been well chosen, our observations and conclusions should be accurate with regard to the locals that we studied. We should like to go beyond this, however, and offer comments on some of the critical problems and policy issues with which the American labor movement is faced—problems and issues on which our material may have thrown some light.

One of the problems of the trade union is that it is a dependent organization, in the sense that it is created in response to problems existing in the employer-employee relationship. The degree of need for the union depends largely upon the level of wages, the state of working conditions, the degree of job security, and the type of treatment accorded workers by supervisors. The union, therefore, has little control over the factors determining the need for its existence. Membership loyalty, crucial to the union's survival as an effective bargaining agency, is likely to vary with the contribution made by the union to the members' welfare; but this will depend to a great extent on conditions that are initiated by management. All of this means that the union is basically an insecure institution likely to be troubled by the problem of membership morale.

The behavior of union leaders, in turn, is conditioned by the insecurity of the union. Leaders who cannot rely on the support of their membership are apt to react defensively or assume an aggressive pose. If the members have enjoyed a long period of satisfactory employment and income and an absence of overt conflict, their loyalty to the union and their willingness to sustain a strike may be open to question. This is not a desirable situation for the union leader, whose ability to obtain an important concession at the bargaining table may depend to some extent on the assessment that both parties make of the membership's union loyalty, determination, and fighting spirit. The union is in a more secure position when it makes a continuing contribution to the members' welfare, as by operating an employment service or providing health or welfare benefits, rather than depending solely upon infrequent collective bargaining gains or correction of management mistakes.

Hopes for Social Mobility

Another problem confronting American trade unions is caused by the widespread hopes of workers that they or their children will rise in the social-economic scale. Whereas in some of the older industrial countries of Europe those born into working-class families have had relatively little chance to rise into other social classes and, as a consequence, have developed strong ties to a working-class economic and political movement, in the United States a much greater degree of upward social mobility has existed—the result of the opening up to settlement of a continent rich in natural resources as well as of the traditions of democracy and of dependence on individual effort fostered in a frontier community. All of this has hindered the development in this country of the type of working-class solidarity found in industrialized areas of western Europe, increasing the insecurity of the American labor movement and creating an additional obstacle for it to overcome.

The interviews show that particularly among many young workers there are keen hopes for social advancement and a corresponding reluctance to view themselves as permanently tied to the working class and therefore to the union movement. Minority group members, such as Negroes, may often have a stronger attachment to the union than is usually the case among the white majority, since they depend on the rules embodied in the union contract to permit their entry into better jobs and to protect them from layoff in violation of seniority. They do not have the hopes of many white workers of advancement into management's ranks to dilute their loyalty to the union, and they fear that the union's disappearance would place their survival in industry, in the event of a depression, at the whim of each supervisor. Their attachment to their union, however, depends in large measure upon the way it treats them, upon the extent to which it adopts and enforces non-discriminatory rules in the union and in the plant. The fact of minority membership, however, makes the achievement of broader class identification more complicated. Workers who expressed a class-conscious philosophy tended to be European immigrants or the sons of immigrants, whose views were strongly influenced by the European social environment.

Despite the individualism and the hopes for upward social mobility that are so widespread in the ranks of American workers, the steady rise in the size of the business unit, the larger amount of capital required, and the high percentage of failures among small business enterprises have made it increasingly difficult and hazardous for a wage-earner to attempt to enter many lines of business. Acceptance of relatively permanent wage-earning status is apt to be accompanied by a greater acceptance of the need for group action to protect and advance one's interests in the employment relationship. Workers tend to settle early in life for the security of a steady job, depending on their mounting seniority to shield them against the hazards of the lay-off. The aspirations of factory workers are scaled down to industrial realities; for everyone who dreams of a business of his own, there are many who hope to move up to a better paying job at a somewhat higher level of skill or responsibility or at most to a foreman's position.

Most of those who dream of a business of their own know that it is but a dream and project their hopes for upward social mobility upon their children, hoping that an education superior to their own will open the doors to professional status, to managerial positions, or at least to white-collar employment. While these hopes for their children are part of the American dream, they frequently reflect the extent to which the parents have failed to realize their own hopes, the extent to which their own dreams have been shattered by disappointment and frustration. Nevertheless, social mobility persists, though it operates to a large extent from one generation to the next rather than within a single lifetime. Workers who lack hopes of upward social mobility for their children, on the other hand, are likely to look upon unions as a solution for their children's problems as well as their own. They are more likely to bring up their children with an expectation of permanent wage-earning status and an appreciation of the past achievements and potential value of the labor movement. The union is on much stronger ground where it receives support within the institution of the family, as the interviews of many miners, themselves raised in union mining families, show so clearly.

The small number of dually oriented members that we found among the plumbers and the metal workers illustrate the change in values that seems to accompany changes in status or in self-conception. The union plumber who may also be a supervisor, the owner of a small shop, or the son of an owner, has the problem of harmonizing the objectives appropriate to management with those of union members. The factory worker who is ambitious to rise into the ranks of management and who can see himself in the future as a management official is faced with a similar problem of reconciling conflicting values. The ambitious and highly mobile worker, indeed, may be unusually sensitive to the opinions of the group in which he has just arrived or to which he hopes soon to belong. His reflections of a management point of view may be seen in his emphasis on production, efficiency, and discipline, or in his critical reaction to union aggressiveness.

On the other hand, the worker who does not expect to rise into management's ranks or whose hopes to rise have been disappointed may develop into a strong supporter of the union. He may be quick to credit the union for its achievements or to excuse its mistakes, while any shortcoming on the part of management may strengthen his pro-union orientation. He may increasingly look to union officers, not just for leadership in relation to management, but for opinions over a wide range of matters. Some of the "good" union men we interviewed may be explained, at least in part, in terms of their realization that they were likely to remain permanently in the ranks of wage-earners. It should also be noted, however, that a number of good union men were offered management positions after they had held union leadership posts.

Effect of the Occupational Environment

The occupational environment has a powerful influence on the attitudes of workers to their union, to the structure of power within it, and to the range of problems with which it deals. Factory workers' views of unionism are molded by the relatively permanent ties to one employer, the authoritarian structure of management, the closeness of supervision, and the heterogeneity of the work force in level of skill, as well as in other respects. Conflicts of interest within such a group are bound to have an effect upon the union and its activities. By way of contrast, groups like the plumbers and the miners are relatively homogeneous in their occupational interests. The plumbers' fear of handymen, the need for constant policing of the trade, and the importance of the building code are among the factors responsible for the place of the union in the lives of its members and the broad authority they willingly grant it.

Miners accept centralization of their union partly because collective bargaining and striking in their industry cannot be carried on effectively except on a centralized basis. As a group that feels looked down upon by the general public, miners appear to draw some feeling of strength and power from their hard-hitting leader, though some of them, concerned with acceptance by the larger community, tend to disapprove of Lewis' more extreme utterances and activities. Whatever the occupational setting, the union will gain in membership support to the extent that rank-and-file members see the union's activities as directly related to their own personal interests and concerns; where this is not the case indifference or even hostility to particular activities may be the result.

Though protection in relation to management is the most important service that unions render to their members, some also offer a measure of protection against the insecurity caused by impersonal forces. The plumbers are a case in point; their union is powerful enough to affect the market for plumbers, to influence both the amount of work to be done and the number of men eligible to perform it. Factory workers, who also fear the layoffs that a business recession may bring, are generally powerless to do anything to relieve this basic insecurity, except to see that unemployment insurance is available or that supplemental unemployment benefits or dismissal wages are provided by contract.

The union may also function in some cases to relieve status anxieties of particular occupational groups. To miners the higher living standard that union wages make possible may serve a double purpose; in addition to being welcome in its own right, it serves as evidence that miners are like other people, enjoying the same conveniences and presumably entitled to the same respect. The power of the union helps bring attention and recognition to an insecure group. In the case of the plumbers the problem is a very different one, since it is created by the disparity between high earnings and low status. The union-supported slogan—"plumbers are like doctors"—serves to bolster the prestige of the occupational group and, incidentally, to justify its income level.

Expectations of Employer and Union: The Question of Loyalty

The prosperity of American industry and the domination of much of the economy by large firms make it likely that unionism will continue to play an important role. In profitable industries experience has shown that unions with bargaining power increase direct wages and fringe benefits, limited by the ability of the industry to pass higher costs on to the consuming public. Even where wage gains may not be possible, however, conflicting interests within large concerns, along with problems created by sheer size, are apt to raise issues of fairness and discipline, with need for a grievance procedure to review decisions and adjust disputes. Only in very small firms is there much likelihood that personal relationships between worker and employer will lead to quick and satisfactory solutions as problems arise. All of this suggests that unionism will continue to receive the support of large numbers of workers, even though management may increase its concern with problems of human relations.

In their expectations of their union, workers are likely to value most highly the feelings of protection and security that they enjoy—the job security, the protection from arbitrary treatment and from the threat of wage reductions or the deterioration of working conditions. Also important is the assurance that inequities will be corrected, that a qualified representative will present their case if they are treated unfairly, that a mechanism exists for the adjustment of grievances. Needless to say, workers also value the wage increases union pressure may achieve, whether to keep abreast of price rises in a period of inflation, match the gains achieved in comparable plants when productivity and profit margins are high, or raise their living standards at any time. Yet the interviews show that workers do not expect repeated wage advances, although it remains true that the achievement of a substantial wage gain is a most powerful argument for re-election. Observers who see only the wage effects of unionism, who evaluate the workers' expectations of their union solely in terms of higher wages—and therefore foresee continuing inflation as the inevitable result of collective bargaining in a full employment economy—fail to appreciate the important non-economic achievements of unionism or the value the membership places upon them.

Workers tend to have different expectations of employer and union, rather than to see them as conflicting bodies competing for their allegiance. The employer is expected to furnish a lasting job with acceptable wages and satisfactory working conditions; the union is expected to exert pressure for improvements, prevent arbitrary action by supervisors, preserve fairness among the employees, and correct abuses though collective bargaining and the grievance procedure. Workers widely recognize that the employer is in business to earn a profit, and that their employment is incidental to this purpose. However highly they rate their employer in relationship to other potential employers, they see no conflict in belonging to a union whose function it is to improve the treatment accorded them by the business enterprise. Conflicts in loyalty are most likely to occur in acute form in the organizing stage of unionism, as in the knitting mill situation, where strong ties to the employer had to be broken before a union could be formed. Where the union is established, however, both employer and union may be highly thought of, as was generally true in the other five situations studied, each agency being valued for its distinctive contribution to the workers' well-being.

In some cases, however, workers may have little use for either company or union, regarding them as necessary evils to be endured rather than as desirable institutions making a positive contribution to their welfare. The worker may view the entire work situation as unrewarding in itself, to be tolerated only because of the need for income. He may put up with the employer out of necessity, without internalizing the employer's goals or accepting his objectives—if, indeed, he understands much about them. Attitudes of this sort are unlikely to be found among plumbers or other skilled workers, who derive satisfaction from their work; and they do not occur, of course, among the dually oriented workers. Similarly, there are a number who derive no satisfaction from union membership, who do not identify with the union or internalize its goals. Among the indifferent and the unwilling unionists some will be found who see both company and union as external agencies that have little relation to the worker's own goals and values. Perhaps "dual disloyalty"[1] is the term that best describes workers such as these, the number of whom is increased by the union-shop clause.

Some workers, such as those who accept a class struggle interpretation of society, may reject management's goals and wholeheartedly

[1] This term suggests itself as opposite to the dual allegiance found by Purcell to be widespread among members of a packing house local. See Theodore V. Purcell, *The Worker Speaks His Mind on Company and Union* (Cambridge, Mass.: Harvard University Press, 1953), pp. 263–64.

embrace those of the union, while criticizing the union's objectives as too narrow, as seeking merely amelioration of the workers' lot instead of a different order of society. For every worker who adopts such views, however, there are very large numbers at the present stage of development of American industrial society who have no quarrel with the basic organization of society or industry, who look to the union for a more equitable distribution of business income and for insurance against improper treatment. What makes this view possible is the margin of fat in the American economy, permitting unions to obtain substantial concessions from employers through collective bargaining without endangering the profitability of the enterprise or the stability of the economic system.

Attitudes toward Strikes, Union Security, Political Action

Because labor-management strife makes headlines and because the strike or the threat of a strike is the ultimate sanction in the collective bargaining relationship, the union leader appears to the general public in his most militant aspect, just as the union is apt to appear the aggressor when a strike occurs. Yet most union leaders approach the strike weapon with caution; while a strike or the threat of it will activate crisis members and show all others that the union is trying hard to further their interests, the strike itself is unpopular with most union members unless they suffer from a deep sense of grievance. The ability of workers to sustain strikes is limited, both economically and psychologically, and the use of the strike weapon must therefore be rationed carefully. Yet even workers who dislike the strike in general or who feel that its use in a particular situation is unwise will likely respond to it if the union is powerful or if the opinion of their fellow workers gives it strong support. They will support a strike most strongly if it can be interpreted as a defensive weapon against the employer's effort to break the union or his unreasonable refusal to establish fair wages, a proper level of fringe benefits, or appropriate working conditions— although different interest groups within the union may often disagree as to the meaning of fairness in this context.

It would be a gross mistake to conceive of the union security clause as a measure forced by union leaders upon unwilling members. Union members show widespread support for the union shop, chiefly on the ground that all those who share in the benefits of the union contract should help defray the cost.[2] While the worker who is critical of the leadership or policies of the union in his plant should have an opportunity to earn a living, as should the worker who is opposed to unionism on principle, it must be recognized that there is no "right to work" in our society for people who are unwilling to accept the employment conditions that prevail. Yet the right of minority dissent, whether for religious or social reasons, deserves protection, particularly in the nongovernmental sector of our lives.

Until the serious depression period of the 1930's most union leaders de-emphasized the importance of legislation and the role of the labor movement in political affairs. The intervening quarter of a century has witnessed a sharp change in this respect. The CIO's Political Action Committee, the AFL's Labor's League for Political Education, the merged body's Committee on Political Education, and the close functional connection in many areas between the labor movement and the Democratic party make labor political action today something vastly different from the AFL's policy in Samuel Gompers' day of seeking, with limited resources and little vigor, to reward friends and punish enemies. Government now affects the labor movement in so many important ways—and the trend is ever more strongly in that direction—that it is unlikely that the union movement's interest in politics will diminish. The problem is no longer whether to engage in political activity; it is, rather, to work out the most effective method of operating in the political arena and to learn how best to activate the union membership and to exert their influence so as to achieve maximum results.

Union political influence is limited, however, by the attitudes of the masses of rank-and-file union members, who tend to view their unions as agencies established for somewhat limited purposes rather than as organizations to which they turn spontaneously for the solution of a wide range of problems confronting them as citizens as well as workers. Political facts and political traditions, social mobility and myths relating to social mobility, the greater productivity of American enterprise, and the higher living standards won for workers through eco-

---

[2] During a fifty-month period from 1947 to 1951 the Taft-Hartley Act required a union-shop authorization poll prior to the negotiation of a union-shop agreement. In the forty-six thousand elections held under this provision, covering some six and a half million employees, 91 per cent of the ballots were cast in favor of the union shop, which was authorized in 97 per cent of the cases (*Sixteenth Annual Report of the National Labor Relations Board for the Fiscal Year Ended June 30, 1951* [Washington: U.S. Government Printing Office, 1952], p. 10).

nomic pressure have all played a part in the development of an American working class with its present attitudes toward labor political action.

Where workers see a meaningful connection between the union and a particular objective, such as the neutralization of the police, the passage of improved safety legislation, or the adoption of a building code, they support the necessary activity even though it is political in nature. On the whole, however, they tend to oppose political activity as beyond the proper scope of the union's functions. In part they reject politics as corrupt or as introducing a divisive factor into the union, and in part they view the political area as one in which they have the right and duty to function as individuals.

A further complicating factor is that the worker functions in political affairs in his home neighborhood, where he is subject to a variety of influences and pressures. This is particularly important in the case of the white-collar workers, who tend to live in middle-class neighborhoods, and it grows in importance as the better-paid manual workers move out of purely working-class districts into more desirable residential areas. Union political influence is limited by the fact that workers make their political choices on the basis of a series of considerations, of which the union's position is but one; and in large numbers of cases its advice is ignored or even has a negative effect because its entry into this field is not considered legitimate.

Such attitudes, however, may be subject to change, just as union leaders' views of political action have altered. A shift in membership views may be expected if, under the economic conditions of the future, collective bargaining no longer produces substantial gains, or if government appears as a threat to the effective functioning of unions or as an agency that must be influenced if economic gains are to be achieved or maintained. For a labor party venture to receive mass support, however, a necessary condition is that the bulk of union members should see no substantial difference between the two existing major parties. For the immediate future, at least, the fears voiced in some quarters that labor may exercise dominant political power in the nation would appear to be groundless. The problem of labor leaders is at the other extreme—to persuade the majority of their members that the labor movement has a legitimate political role to play within the existing two-party system.

White-Collar Workers and Young People

The spread of unionism in the past quarter century, embracing the great bulk of production workers employed in large enterprises, raises problems of great importance to the labor movement. On the one hand there is the problem of fashioning organizing techniques that will prove attractive to those still unorganized, among whom white-collar workers, the fastest growing segment of the labor force, occupy a leading position. On the other hand there is the problem presented by the younger generation of industrial workers, who find unionism established in the plant in which they obtain employment and who join without emotional involvement, perhaps because membership is required under a union-shop clause or because of informal group pressure.

Key factors in any organizing effort are the existence of dissatisfactions and the presence of union representatives or sympathizers who are respected by the workers and who, building upon real or fancied grievances, can make group action—unionism and collective bargaining—appear as the solution. This involves creating a new in-group relationship that will exclude members of management and include other organized workers along with union leaders. This process is aided where the hope to advance has been frustrated, where relationships with top management are distant and impersonal, and where supervisors have exercised power in an arbitrary manner.

With regard to such factors, however, white-collar groups usually present problems to union organizers. They tend to react strongly to prestige symbols, valuing highly the better dress they wear and the better manners and higher education of those with whom they work; they are correspondingly more difficult to interest in unionism, which carries a connotation of working-class status. In addition they feel close to management, often part of it; they are usually treated with some respect and consideration; they dress and speak more like management officials than like production workers; and they tend to identify more strongly with the business enterprise that employs them and to be antagonized by the crude language and denunciations of the employer that are so typical of the union organizer with an industrial background. Moreover, the office employees of manufacturing concerns usually receive automatically the benefits obtained by the unions of production workers employed by their companies. For professional

265

employees there is the additional factor that unionism may appear as a threat to their hard-won and highly valued professional status.

White-collar workers, accustomed to more polite and more polished behavior than industrial workers, may be reluctant to join unions because they associate unionism with strikes and picketing or because they fear losing prestige among friends and neighbors in the middle-class communities in which they live. Should a strike occur white-collar workers may find picket line duty particularly onerous and may hope to avoid being seen by persons outside the work situation whose good opinion they value. The rough language and the violence that may accompany strikes—of less concern to most industrial workers—may present an important deterrent to unionism in the case of white-collar groups.

As against all of this, however, there are the frustrations that are a part of white-collar as of industrial employment, as well as the growth in the size of the business enterprise. Given the presence of dissatisfactions that are almost inevitable in a large organization, the telephone switchboard, the typing pool, the department store, and the large office all breed group consciousness and identification that form the psychological base of unionism. Even engineers prove interested in unionism where they find themselves working on assembly-line type projects, treated as members of a group instead of as individuals, with conditions of work and opportunities for recognition and advancement far inferior to those they had anticipated. The increasing routinization and rationalization of white-collar employment, the closer degree of supervision, and the reduced chances of advancement all tend to produce the group identification which may ultimately provide a foundation for unionism. Yet many organizers will have to modify their tactics and their language if they hope to attract large numbers of white-collar workers to unionism.

A union organizer is not likely to achieve much success by trying to convince white-collar workers that they are no different, or not much different, from workers in the plant. White-collar workers believe that they are different—a belief that has real consequences for them. To attempt to convince them otherwise is to seek to destroy or drastically alter their self-conception—and self-conception is guarded tenaciously. The union movement is unlikely to enrol large numbers of white-collar workers unless it caters to this self-conception and shows how it may become a basis for successful unionization.

The growing number of younger unionists who lack personal knowledge of non-union conditions presents another type of problem. As each local union grows older, the generation that built it, that experienced undesirable non-union conditions and participated in the struggles to establish an organization, is replaced by younger people who find the local union a going concern, associated with the job and accepted, perhaps, as casually as the personnel interview or the medical examination. These newer members, unless they experience critical strikes, are unlikely ever to be as touched emotionally or to be involved in the union as wholeheartedly as the group of workers who built the union. Particularly is this likely to be the case in industries in which collective bargaining has passed from the local's control into the hands of district or national officers, in which calls to strike or to return to work come from these higher officials, and in which picket line duty is perfunctory.

In factory employment where the union shop prevails, moreover, the new employee usually first learns of the union from a company representative. The applicant for employment is likely to receive from a personnel clerk not only the company's employment form but also forms for insurance, health, or other benefits—plus an application for union membership where a union shop is in effect, and perhaps also a dues checkoff authorization card. A company brochure may explain all the benefits that go with employment—without reference, needless to say, to union struggles to which some of those benefits may be due. As for the union, the prospective employee is told merely that he must become a member a certain number of days after starting work, as prescribed in the contract. Small wonder that the company is likely to be seen as the source of high wages, good working conditions, and attractive fringe benefits, whereas the union is apt to appear primarily as a deduction from earnings for initiation fee and monthly dues. With the union as with any other institution, moreover, the initial reaction is a peculiarly important one. In the minds of some new employees the distinction between company and union may even be blurred—the result of being recruited to union membership apparently by an agent of the company.

How many of the newer entrants into factory employment, introduced in this fashion to company and union, will develop the attitudes and values characteristic of the good union man? The union movement of the future will be but a pale image of the present one unless numbers of good union men are produced. Whether this occurs will depend, among other things, on the frequency and type of contacts between the younger worker and the good union men in his department. The local union officers, stewards, committeemen, and active members, who are drawn overwhelmingly from the good union man type, are the ones who can transmit to the new member something of the history and tradition, the goals and the values, of the labor movement. If this does not happen, the young worker is likely to have his ideas about unionism molded largely by the mass media, as modified by his own work experience and the views of his fellow workers.

All of this assumes that the good union men in the department understand the requirements of their role and play it consistently and accurately. To the extent that they depart from this—by failing to support labor political action, for example, or by ignoring the picket lines of other unions—the uncommitted recruits will get inadequate and faulty understanding of the labor movement and lack proper models for the development of the good union men of the future. The good union man is the key person in the transmission of the union's culture to succeeding generations of workers, among whom the leaders of the future must of necessity be found.

In this process the department steward plays the most important role, since he serves as the symbol of the union in the shop. Since the young worker's opportunity to interact with him may be limited, much depends on the manner in which the steward handles the first grievance or other critical situation in which the new worker may be involved. Unless the steward is an able and respected person who can interpret unionism sympathetically to the newcomers, moreover, the union may always appear to them as just another condition of employment, just another deduction from the pay check. There are exceptional situations, needless to say, as the strong union sentiment among younger miners and plumbers shows; in these cases, however, the union clearly makes a continuing contribution to the welfare of employees in terms of economic benefits, protection against the feared oppressive conditions of the past, or the need to bolster occupational status.

What attitude to the union is to be anticipated, however, where conditions such as these do not exist? There will always be work for the local union to do, needless to say, in the adaptation of the contract to local conditions and in the policing of the contract through the grievance procedure; and in any large organization there is a continuing need for a mediating or protecting agency between the individual worker and the employing company. Will larger numbers of the new industrial work force, nevertheless, become indifferent, if not unwilling, unionists? Or can the unions manage to learn about and help to solve their problems, encourage participation, excite their interest, and continue to produce the good union men who are the backbone of the successful labor organization? The answers to questions such as these will be crucial to the strength of the labor movement in the years ahead.

Some Policy Observations and Proposals

A vital policy issue confronting the union movement, and the public as well, is the excessive power that union leaders may be able to wield over the membership. While leaders in any type of organization are vastly more influential than rank-and-file members in the decision-making process, and like union leaders may dominate the channels of communication within the organization, union leaders are unusual in the powers of coercion they exercise over their members. This power of coercion exists because of the widespread use of the union security clause in this country, which may endanger a worker's job if he loses good standing in his union. The coercive aspect of the union leader's relations with his members should not be overestimated, however; the union head who produces a reasonable volume of economic and other benefits will win the support of large numbers of his members whatever his failings, so that coercion need be applied only to a critical minority. Yet it is at this point that violations of democratic procedure are apt to occur.

Because the union shop, while it builds union organizational strength, coerces the non-member into joining and increases the power of union officers over their members, it has long been the subject of controversy and a focal point of attacks on unionism. Since the passage of the Taft-Hartley law the fight over union security has shifted largely to the states, where so-called "right-to-work" laws, that would ban the enforcement of union security provisions, have been pushed with undiminished vigor. Whereas such laws, now in force in eighteen states, have the likely effect of weakening the power of unions when compared to that of employers, we see more promise in devices that seek simultaneously to keep unions strong and members protected in their rights and in their jobs. One such device is the so-called "revolving door" plan negotiated in the steel settlement of 1952, under which new employees had to apply for union membership when they were hired but had the option to withdraw by written statement several weeks later. The number exercising this right of withdrawal—perhaps 5 per cent during the first six months—was too small to have much impact upon union bargaining power, yet permitted the occasional person who was strongly opposed to the union to work in the industry. Since they also receive union benefits, however, it would be reasonable to require them to pay union dues or the equivalent.[3] The purpose here is not so much to increase union revenue—the amount would be small in any event—as to remove the financial incentive for not joining. It would serve the same purpose if the sum were to be donated to charitable activities.

Even more important is the need to provide safeguards against abuse of the disciplinary process within unions. Here the problem is that the same union officials usually serve as both executive and judicial officers; leaders of the administrative group, they occupy key posts in the judicial machinery before which their factional opponents may be brought. The result at best may be a lack of confidence in the impartial operation of the appeals machinery, and at worst the crushing of the right of political dissent. Recently, important progress has been made with the establishment by the Upholsterers' International Union and the United Automobile Workers of boards of prominent citizens to pass on disciplinary cases. Yet it should be recognized that the unions needing such machinery the most are the least likely to establish it.

It would represent even more substantial progress if such machinery were to be created by the AFL-CIO to function with respect to all its affiliated unions, just as the Federation since the merger has adopted codes of ethical practices that are binding on all affiliates. It is encouraging to note that the AFL-CIO has recently prepared a code to guarantee the democratic rights of members of affiliated unions, to encourage participation, safeguard the expression of opinion, and provide for due process and appeals in union trials. Yet the Federation's only penalty, other than the force of opinion within as well as outside of the labor movement, is expulsion, which might prove ineffective with some

---

[3] Along these lines see John V. Spielmans, "Bargaining Fee versus Union Shop," *Industrial and Labor Relations Review*, X (July, 1957), 609–19.

of the national unions most in need of reform. For this reason government action may eventually be desirable if it is designed to be corrective rather than punitive; in our view legislation should be delayed, however, so long as the labor movement shows active interest in self-reform.

The AFL-CIO is to be applauded also for its efforts to enforce higher standards of behavior on the part of officers of affiliated unions. It would be a healthy development, in addition, if the power of national union officers were subjected to greater checks and if the gap in pay between officers and workers in the industry were substantially reduced; some officers as a result might leave the union for managerial or governmental positions, but the union movement in the long run would be better off without leaders who respond primarily to financial incentives. Certainly the spirit of unionism would be improved and the gulf between leaders and members narrowed.

The single most important reform, if effective democracy is to exist within the national union, is to make it possible for opposition political groups to exist and function without fear that the union's disciplinary machinery might be used arbitrarily against them. For this to be achieved regular and frequent elections, along with assurance of an honest count of the ballots, are necessary, though equally essential is the recognition within the union movement of the legitimacy of political opposition and provision for reasonable access of opposition groups to the members. An administration group is in effect a faction that can seldom be defeated unless others have a corresponding opportunity to organize.

It is generally recognized that, if a society is to be democratic, citizens sharing a similar point of view on social issues must be free to unite into political parties, propagandize for their ideas, and present and support candidates in elections. Though the process often seems to involve more shouting than wisdom, more mudslinging and abuse than reasoned argument, no better way has yet been devised to make democracy work. We believe that similar considerations hold for the union, and that a faction in opposition to the union administration is no more disloyal to the union than a minority political party is to the state. Democracy is as important to a union as efficient administration or effectiveness in striking or bargaining, and ways must be found to reconcile these objectives.

Attention must be paid also to the more formal aspects of the union, to the mechanism created by it for the making of decisions. There is a real question as to whether the democratic ideology of the trade union movement, as expressed in its rhetoric, is compatible with its function in an age of mass unionism, of locals with many thousands of members. In such locals the meeting of all members is as poorly adapted to an effectively functioning democracy as the New England town meeting is to the needs of the modern metropolis. Once more than several hundred persons are involved, it is no longer efficient—indeed, often not possible—to transact business through mass meetings. The meeting of thousands of people may serve other functions, such as to whip up enthusiasm, demonstrate needs and loyalties, or transmit information, but it is not a promising device for the transaction of business.

The simple facts are that thousands of members will not attend routine meetings, that there would be no place to put them if they came, and that if a place were available the proper conduct of business would be impossible. The large industrial local, moreover, is made up of overlapping special-interest groups within the factory, based on such factors as skill, department, shift, age, sex, race, and national origin. The nature and function of the union meeting, shaped when membership groups were small and homogeneous, need redefinition in an age of mass unionism.

One can conceive of the local union as embodying not one but two distinct governments, each performing a different function for which an appropriate structure has been erected. One government, concerned with relations within the union, is formed in accordance with the local's constitution and bylaws, with its executive board occupying a position of key responsibility. The other government, concerned with relations with the employer, is symbolized by the collective bargaining agreement and the grievance procedure, and its functions are carried out by the stewards or the grievance committee. Though the personnel executing these two functions may overlap, their roles are different. The second government carries on its business at the workplace, where the members are found, and it is structured formally as a representative government.

The large local, in our view, should accordingly abandon the rhetoric of the mass business meeting and experiment instead with plans of representative government. Democracy could best be achieved if workers met for the discussion of issues in relatively small and homogeneous units such as departments, but if the local took action only through a body of representatives, each of whom was chosen by and responsible to a constituency of fellow workers. Those who attend routine meetings, indeed, are usually the stewards and other active members, who legislate with the interests and views of the workers in their departments in mind. It would be a gain if this were recognized and the formal structure of the meeting changed accordingly. Since the functions and authority of the stewards have declined as unions have matured and union-management relations grown more stable and routinized, perhaps the positions might become more attractive and the stewards revitalized if they were given an important place in the legislative structure of the large local. An additional gain would be the safeguarding of the local against legislation enacted by a special-interest group that packed the meeting or domination by an organized minority that attended meetings regularly.

A related issue is the necessity of sustained efforts by the local leaders to keep members informed of developments. Often the officers assert that the meeting is designed to perform this function and that they have no further responsibility to members who fail to attend. Since few members attend routine meetings, the result usually is a membership that is uninformed as well as inactive. It would be far better for the leaders to utilize every possible device, such as a local newspaper or departmental meetings, to insure that the members, though inactive, could be informed; the members would then have an intelligent basis for re-electing or defeating the officers at the next election. Sometimes officers fear to open channels of communication with the members outside the local meeting lest the employer would learn too much about internal union affairs; but management is usually informed on union developments, and in any event the leadership's overriding responsibility is to have an informed membership.

As for the strike weapon, we see no prospect of its elimination in a democratic society. Besides being an important right of workers, it is the ultimate sanction that gives force and meaning to union demands in the collective bargaining relationship. Its absence could only reduce collective bargaining to a meaningless interchange of opinions or compel the determination of disputes by a governmental agency. Because of the costs of going on strike, there is little danger that the weapon will be used frivolously where democratic controls operate within the union; on the contrary, serious problems and grave dissatisfactions are likely to lie behind every decision to strike. Therefore, despite the losses of income to the parties and the inconvenience to the general public, the right to strike should be jealously guarded.

Yet it must also be recognized that in an increasingly interdependent economy the curtailment of essential goods or services may cause severe loss to important segments of the public and in extreme cases may paralyze much of the economy. At some point the government must intervene to keep vital goods and services flowing, just as in time of war it cannot allow strikes to occur lest the nation suffer military disaster. In our view the government has tended to intervene before an emergency could be said to exist; the cause of free collective bargaining and the public interest would both be served if the government operated with more restraint, permitting the parties more often to fight out their differences and regarding the resulting inconvenience and loss—to innocent parties as well as to the disputants—as part of the price we pay for a free society.

The fear that the merger of the AFL and the CIO will create a "labor monopoly," with adverse effects upon business and the general community, appears groundless to us. While the merged federation exercises greater power over its constituent national unions than the AFL ever did, the bulk of the power, as of the funds, in the labor movement remains where it always has been—in the hands of the officers of the national unions. Organizing will be changed little by the merger, and collective bargaining not at all. The labor movement's influence in political matters, legislative developments, and community affairs should gain moderately as a result of the merger, with its substitution of a single authoritative voice for two separate and sometimes conflicting agencies. Internal administration should also be improved, as a result of the codes of ethical practices. While the elimination of union raiding is a social gain, some price is paid for this in the inability of a group of workers, dissatisfied with their present leadership, to find a home elsewhere within the merged movement.

Despite their relative lack of interest in labor political action, their rather low level of formal participation, and their general indifference to union institutional prestige, it seems clear that American workers as a group have a high regard for union achievements and value the protection and security that unionism affords. Evidence is lacking that they make demands upon their leaders for economic gains that the industry or the enterprise cannot possibly grant, except at the price of continuing inflation or growing unemployment. Job security, protection from unfair treatment, respect for human dignity, and effective grievance procedure, all of which exist where unionism does its job well, are enough for workers to feel that the union is a desirable institution. It is important, however, that essential democratic controls exist, that workers feel that the unions are their organizations, responsive to their needs and offering them opportunities for meaningful participation, if unionism is to retain a permanently strong hold upon their affections and loyalties.

APPENDIX

Methodological Note

In attempting a study of so broad a theme as the attitudes of American workers toward their unions, we were faced with a number of methodological problems. We had to adopt criteria for the selection of locals, isolate the particular problems to be studied, construct interview guides, and determine the sampling procedure to be used. We knew that we wanted to study a broad range of problems, with emphasis upon those discussed in detail in this volume, but we felt that an interview guide which would take into consideration the specific problems of each group could be constructed only after we had selected a local and become familiar with its history, its structure and methods of operation, its collective bargaining relations, its achievements and its problems.

We decided on one of the mass-production industries for the pilot study. At that early stage of our work we were most concerned with the problem of participation in union affairs, and we reasoned that that problem would be seen in sharpest focus in a large local of workers representing all levels of skill. Our early attempts to formulate our problems, however, convinced us that the extent and types of participation could be understood only in the light of the wider meaning of unionism to the worker, and for this reason the question of participation quickly became only one of many problems in which we were interested.

Steel was selected for the pilot project because of its vital role in the nation's economy and its concentration in the Chicago area, the latter permitting wide choice as to the particular local to be studied. In making the actual choice we went first to a union official at the district level, explained the purposes of the study, and asked him to suggest locals in basic steel that would raise typical sets of problems and that would have officers likely to co-operate. We preferred a local of workers employed by an independent company rather than one in a plant of a subsidiary of the United States Steel Corporation, in order to avoid complicating our pilot study by the issue of corporation-wide bargaining. The local that the district official suggested proved to be friendly and co-operative; indeed, that was our experience in the case of each local we selected for study.

Because our ideas at the beginning of the project were not definitely formulated concerning the particular problems to be concentrated upon and the specific techniques to be employed, it was our expectation that, by the time our work progressed to other locals, our objectives and methods would have shifted so much that the pilot study would not be comparable with the later ones. We planned, therefore, to use the pilot project merely to isolate problems and perfect techniques, with the resulting data used where appropriate for journal articles but not incorporated into the volume. Experience showed, however, that we had underestimated the time the pilot project would absorb and overestimated the differences our techniques would undergo. By the time the pilot project had been completed we had funds —and therefore time—remaining for the study of only five other locals.

For the second case study we wanted a local affiliated with the UAW-CIO in order to include this active and aggressive union in our project. We considered each of its locals in the Chicago area, observing the level of skill, the regularity of employment, and the characteristics of the work force before making a choice. In the automobile industry proper the plants available to us were final assembly units, in which the level of skill was low, the turnover high, and employment subject to great fluctuations. While all these factors presented interesting problems, we thought it preferable at that stage of our work to study a local whose members represented a wider variety of skills and felt more permanently attached to their employment. A contributing factor, though not the major one in our decision, was that members of the research team already possessed some background knowledge about the local of metal workers selected and its bargaining relationship with management, permitting the work to proceed more rapidly than would otherwise have been the case. This case was planned as the example of the militant, industrial local, replacing the steel workers' union. There were, however, a variety of important differences between the two situations, so that we finally decided to report on both unions in this volume.

For our third case we decided to study a local of highly skilled workers. We thought it best to go into the construction trades rather than into printing or the metal industries because the unions of building tradesmen have so long been the backbone of the AFL, and we decided against a local of railroad workers because they operated under separate federal labor legislation. The operating brotherhoods, in addition, were independent unions and we preferred, in this choice as in others, to be within one of the mainstreams of the American labor movement. Here, as at so many other points, we would have liked to take one local of each of the types we were considering, if only our time and resources had permitted.

Once we had decided upon the building trades, we discussed the selection with several persons, including labor attorneys who knew the background of many of the locals. Some we ruled out because they had admitted some less-skilled groups to membership, and others were not good choices because they were currently the subject of governmental investigation. In some cases the collective bargaining function was exercised by a district council, and we preferred at this time not to study a local with little bargaining authority of its own. Still other locals, we were told, were headed by men who might prove uncooperative, and so the process of elimination continued until the plumbers remained as the most likely choice. We would have preferred a craft in which there was no licensing system, simply because we wanted our case to be typical of the building trades as a whole, but at this point we had to balance considerations and make a choice. The officials of the plumbers' union, whom none of us had met up to this time, proved to be just as co-operative as those of the steel and metal workers' locals.

For our fourth case study we decided to look for a local composed primarily of women at moderate levels of skill, to help us try to assess the influence of sex upon attitudes toward the union. Our choice fell, after consultation with the responsible officers, upon a local affiliated with the ILGWU. Interviewing proceeded slowly, however, because the women, most of them middle-aged or older and foreign-born, had difficulty understanding the purposes of the study and were reluctant to schedule appointments. While we were pondering this problem the officers of the union told us about the knitting workers' strike that had just been concluded, and we decided to change locals and start work immediately in the small Wisconsin town, in order to study the impact of an organizing strike upon a group of moderately skilled women new to the labor movement.

We chose the United Mine Workers for our fifth case study primarily for two reasons: we wanted to see how workers raised in a one-industry area with very strong union traditions differed from other workers in their orientation, and we wanted to see the effect upon workers' attitudes of the concentration of authority in the hands of national union officials. Here again we had no contacts with local officers and first obtained the co-operation of higher union officials who described the various mine fields to us; when we had chosen a field in the central part of Illinois as most representative, they helped us select the local that seemed most promising for our study. Some we passed over because they were not typical in size, others because they were hardly working at the time or because there were reports that the mine might soon be closed permanently. The local that seemed most promising had two disadvantages for our purposes in that it was new and highly mechanized, factors that we feared might somehow affect the attitudes of the miners and make them less representative of the industry as it then existed. Since the miners had all transferred recently from older mines in the area, however, we decided that this factor would not affect our results to any appreciable extent.

For our final study we wanted a union of white-collar workers, and we considered all the unions in that broad area before deciding upon the Communications Workers of America. Once we had chosen the union, we discussed our problem with a representative of the national office, who described the composition, characteristics, and bargaining situation of each local within easy reach of Chicago. The local we selected was one that in terms of size, skill, and relationship with the company seemed fairly typical of the industry; and here, as in the other cases, the local officers proved friendly and co-operative.

We regretted that we were unable to study additional locals. We would have liked to have studied local unions in other parts of the country, especially in the South; to have done more of our work in small towns; to have gone into other types of skilled industries, including the railroads, and also into service trades; and to have included government workers and teamsters in the study. We recognize the difficulties in trying to generalize about skilled workers after studying only the plumbers plus a few craftsmen in large factories or in attempting to reach conclusions about white-collar workers as a result of observations of one local of telephone employees. Limitations of time and money, however, compelled us to terminate our field work when we had studied six locals.

For each of the locals a separate interview guide was constructed, varying in length from about sixty to more than a hundred questions and centering about the problems considered significant in each case. Many of the questions, dealing with such matters as the circumstances of joining the union or the projected consequences of the union's disappearance, appeared in all of the guides. In each case, however, some of the areas inquired about received more detailed treatment or wholly new problems were considered; thus craft problems were raised in the case of the plumbers, questions dealing with the organizing campaign and strike were stressed with the knitting mill workers, white-collar status and prestige was emphasized in the telephone guide, and with the miners attention was directed to the miners' community and problems of democracy. These problems, of course, were the ones that lay behind the selection of these locals for study. To keep the interviews down to reasonable lengths we had to compromise between the desire to ask the same set of questions, in order to have comparable material, and the desire to inquire fully into problems unique in each case. In some cases, though keeping the same problem in mind, we found it desirable to change the phraseology of the questions somewhat where experience showed that questions might be misunderstood or where we had failed to get the full and frank responses for which we had hoped.

Questions that could be answered "Yes" or "No" were avoided except as a way of opening up a subject, and care was exercised to avoid phraseology that suggested an answer or indicated a bias. Probing was employed systematically, its form being standardized wherever possible. In arranging the order of the questions we tried to start with non-controversial ones, saving those that touched on sensitive areas for later in the interview, by which time greater rapport could be established. We also endeavored, of course, to have questions follow each other in easy conversational order, so that the interview flowed smoothly, with questions dealing with a common subject grouped together. Interview guides were pretested and revised in the light of this experience before systematic interviewing was attempted. Two typical interview guides, those used with the metal workers and the miners, are reproduced following this note.

We recognize that opinions expressed in an interview may not constitute a very good basis for prediction of future behavior, since each concrete situation involves a variety of factors and pressures which influence conduct; and that statements of past behavior need to be viewed cautiously, since memory is selective and one's present orientation affects one's view of past events. Yet one learns about people by studying their responses to questions as well as by observing other types of behavior, and to the extent that time permitted we tried to do both.

In all cases samples were drawn from the lists of members maintained at the union office. The leadership group was segregated in each case; sometimes the rest of the members comprised the field from which a single rank-and-file sample was drawn, and sometimes they were first divided into two or three groups. Usually the names were arranged alphabetically, though sometimes, as with the steel workers and the miners, they were in order of clock number. We decided in each case what size sample would yield satisfactory results for our purposes and still permit us to finish the work in the time we had available. Although we made use of the union's records, we took care that no person other than the members of the research team knew which names were selected.

In the case of the steel local three groups—leaders, active rank-and-file members, and inactive members—were isolated for study. The leadership group was defined to include the 13 officers of the local and all the grievance men or "grievers," plus chairmen of key committees and past presidents. This made a total of 36 in the leadership group, of which 28 were interviewed. Active members were defined as those who had attended from four to seven meetings in the past year, and 24 of the 43 in this group were interviewed. Finally, a 1 per cent sample was taken of the union members who had not attended any meetings during the previous year, and interviews were held with 62 of the 128 persons forming this group. Interviewing was stopped when patterns of responses became repetitive, though a subsample of the remainder was first interviewed without any additional patterns of responses being discovered. The material thus obtained was supplemented by observations of the local over a period of a couple of years, repeated informal conversations with union leaders, and interviews with management officials and community leaders.

In the case of the metal workers' local the leadership group comprised 26 persons, of whom 20 were interviewed. There was no objective method, as was available in the steel local, to select an active group intermediate between the general members and the leaders, and so the stewards' body was chosen instead. A sample of 35 was chosen, of whom 24 were interviewed. Finally a 3 per cent sample of the rank-and-file membership yielded a list of 100, of whom 49 were interviewed. As with the steel local, interviewing ceased when no new patterns of responses were being obtained.

Among the plumbers there was no basis for selecting a group intermediate between the leaders and the rank and file, nor was any other ground apparent for dividing the general membership into two or more groups. The leadership group consisted of 14 officers or key committee members, of whom 10 were interviewed; these 10, however, included the business manager and 4 of the 5 business agents, the most active and important persons within the group. A 3 per cent sample was taken of the general membership from a list arranged alphabetically, excluding those who lived too far away. Of the 93 on this list a total of 34 were interviewed; interviewing was stopped at that point because the responses proved very similar.

In the case of the knitting mill there were 158 workers within the union's jurisdiction when the strike ended. For purposes of sampling, these were divided into four groups: (1) the leadership group, defined as all elected officers, executive board members, and stewards; (2) the rank-and-file group, defined as all, excluding leaders, who had joined the union prior to the strike and had remained members in good standing throughout; (3) the fence-sitters, consisting of those who joined the union prior to the strike and who subsequently withdrew and rejoined, plus those who joined for the first time during or immediately after the strike; and (4) those who went through the picket lines and who were still non-members when we conducted the field work.

There were 13 in the leadership group, all of whom were interviewed. Of the 82 in the rank-and-file group a sample of 41 was chosen. The first 16 whose names appeared on this list were interviewed, by which time it was apparent that the responses were very similar. A subsample of the remainder was taken and seven additional interviews held without obtaining any new patterns of responses. Of the 32 fence-sitters a sample of 16 was taken and 11 interviewed, with the responses again showing a high degree of similarity. It was hoped that interviewing among the 31 who crossed the picket lines could proceed as systematically as with the other groups, but the bitterness resulting from the strike was still so great that only 3 interviews could be obtained. We supplemented the material thus obtained with interviews with the company head, the union organizers, town officials, and leading citizens.

The local of coal miners had 10 persons in the leadership group, all of whom were interviewed. As with the plumbers, there appeared to be no basis on which a division could be made within the ranks of the general membership. Accordingly, a 20 per cent sample was taken of the rank-and-file members, arranged by clock number; this gave a sample of 55, of whom 39 were interviewed.

In the case of the telephone workers there was a leadership group of 11, of whom we interviewed 7. Our sample of the rank-and-file members—10 per cent of the operators and service assistants, 10 per cent of the equipment technicians, and a somewhat higher proportion of the clerical workers—came to 140, of whom we were able to interview only 30 before lack of time, combined with similar patterns of responses and difficulty in scheduling interviews, brought our field work to an end. Because of the far smaller proportion of telephone workers' interviews completed, we have less confidence in these results than in any of the other locals studied. The total number of union members interviewed in the six cases was 384, of whom 88 were in the leadership groups, 48 stewards or active members, and 248 rank-and-file members.

In only one case, that of steel, did we attempt a study of management opinion comparable to that made within the union. There were four significant levels of authority in the plant, consisting of top management, superintendents, general foremen, and foremen, and also a staff group of labor relations specialists. We took samples of each group except for the small top management group concerned with labor relations matters, where we interviewed every person. The interview guide was constructed to parallel that used for the union members in the plant. The analysis of the management interviews was completed with the aid of a grant from the company, and portions of the material published in an article, "Management Views the Local Union," that appeared in the April, 1953, issue of the *Journal of Business* of the University of Chicago. In the other cases no systematic study was made of management attitudes, though key officials were interviewed to check on collective bargaining history and other background material and to give us some management reactions to many of the matters covered in the interviews with union members.

In each case efforts were made to publicize the study by means of announcements at union meetings, notices posted on bulletin boards or carried in a union publication, or letters mailed to home addresses. In most cases we telephoned respondents at home to make appointments for interviews; in the cases of those who had no telephones we went to their homes to interview them then if possible or, if not, to make arrangements for a later visit. In the case of the miners we went to the mine entrance, contacting workers as they entered or left the pit.

Except for officers, who often were interviewed at the union headquarters if one existed, we interviewed workers at their homes unless they suggested another place. We avoided both union headquarters and company premises for interviews with rank-and-file workers lest they associate us with either union or company, in which case the content or tone of their remarks might be affected. Everyone was assured that the material would be held confidential, that no one would know that he had been interviewed unless he told, that his opinions would not be shown to union or management officials, and that nothing that appeared in print would permit his identification.

We had most difficulty in obtaining interviews with three groups— the Mexicans employed in the steel mill, the knitting mill employees who worked during the strike, and the women employed by the telephone company. With the Mexicans it was a combination of a language barrier plus evident fear on the part of some who had entered the country illegally that they might be deported; to cope with these difficulties, we obtained the assistance of an interviewer of Mexican origin. Some of the knitting mill workers were unwilling to be interviewed lest they bring to the surface again all the bitterness and tension aroused by the strike. The reluctance of a number of telephone workers to be interviewed was harder to explain; we had no difficulty obtaining interviews with the male employees but met with a number of refusals or repeated broken appointments with the women. We therefore know less about these three subgroups than any of the others covered in the study, and have the least confidence that those who consented to be interviewed are representative. In all the other cases there was only an occasional person who refused to be interviewed or who made and broke so many appointments that we abandoned the effort.

We opened our interviews by explaining the purpose of the study and pledging protection of the respondent's identity. Once we felt that we had gained his confidence, we asked the opening questions of the interview guide, usually taking out small notebooks and expressing the hope that he would not mind our taking notes. We wrote down the responses as fully as we could, word for word for the most important matters and key words and phrases for the remainder, and reconstructed the full interview as soon thereafter as possible. The notebook was put away in occasional cases where note-taking seemed to impede the interview. In the case of the most important interviews, as with a number of the leaders, we used a recording device, though for practical reasons we were unable to use this technique more extensively. The interviews with rank-and-file union members usually lasted from an hour and a half to two hours, and with officers from two to three hours and occasionally even longer.

The material was analyzed by single questions or by clusters of related questions, with the categories in all cases growing out of the data. We tried to discover both the major and minor patterns of responses on each subject, and the atypical as well as the typical reactions. In all cases we were concerned with the way in which major and minor themes varied as we went from one group to another within the same local or from one local to another where the question was comparable. For certain purposes, as for the development of the typology of union members, we analyzed the interview as a whole. We did little in the way of statistical analysis because we were more interested in qualitative analysis and because the limited number of interviews made it more meaningful to report our results in the form of majority or minority tendencies rather than as percentages.

The interviewing was supplemented by observation of local activities whenever possible. With several of the locals, we attended every type of formal or informal activity, such as local and group meetings, grievance committee meetings, and caucuses. Grievance meetings with management were also observed. All of this helped us to become sensitized to the characteristics and problems of each local, and also contributed to good relationships with officers and rank-and-file members. The fact that some of us had been union officers or members helped us to understand the locals and to develop rapport with their leaders and active members.

Interview Guide Used in Metal Workers' Study

1. How long have you been with the company?
2. What kind of work do you do? Job class and pay rate?
3. Do you like your work? Why do you say that?
4. In general, how do you feel about the company? Why do you feel that way?
5. Do you expect to stay at —— permanently? Why or why not?
6. Would you want your children to work at ——? Why or why not? (If no children, suppose you had?)
   a) What would you like your children to be?
7. How does your foreman treat you? Why does he treat you that way?
8. Has the union had any effect on how supervision treats the men?
9. Do you think you'll ever get a chance to be a foreman? Why do you think so?
10. Who gets such chances?
11. Would you like to be a foreman? Why do you feel that way?
12. Have you ever worked in a non-union plant? What was it like?
13. Did you ever belong to a union before you came here? What union? Were you ever active?
14. How did you happen to join? When was that? How did you feel about it?
15. Why do you think we have unions?
16. In general, how do you feel about the union? Why do you feel that way?
17. Has the union been able to accomplish anything? What?
18. *For those who don't mention wages in No. 17:* What do you think the union has done in regard to wages?
19. Is there anything you'd like the union to do that it isn't doing now? What?
20. Do you think the union should run social activities like picnics, parties, sports events, etc.? Why?
21. If members don't like the way the union is run, is there anything they can do about it? What?
22. How does the union get the non-members to join?
23. How do you think they should get non-members to join?
24. If persuasion fails would you favor a clause in the contract requiring every worker to join?
25. What should be done about non-members if persuasion fails and there is no union shop?
26. Why do you think some workers would rather not join?
27. *For inactives only:* Did you ever have a problem in the shop or the union? What was the problem?
    a) Whom did you talk to about it?
    b) If you had a problem whom would you talk to?

28. *For inactives only:* Does the union representative ever talk to you about what's going on in the shop or the union? What kind of things? Do you think he should?

29. *For inactives only:* How do you feel about *your* steward?

30. *For inactives and leaders only:* What do *you* think makes a good departmental steward?

31. How much interest do you think there is among workers in the plant as to what happens in the union? Why do you think that is so?

32. *For inactives only:* Do you ever go to regular union meetings?
    a) Why don't you go more often? *Or:* Why don't you go?
    b) Why do you go when you do go?

33. *For inactives only:* Do you (did you) ever say anything at local meetings? Why or why not?

34. *For inactives only:* Do you find out what's going on at local meetings when you don't go?

35. *For leaders and actives only:* Do many members attend local meetings?

36. *For leaders and actives only:* Do the people who don't go to local meetings find out what's going on? How or why not?

37. *For leaders and actives only:* Do many members attend departmental meetings? Why or why not?

38. *For leaders and actives only:* Do the people who don't go to departmental meetings find out what's going on? How or why not?

39. Can any member run for office in the union?
    a) *If no:* Why not?
    b) *If yes:* How does he go about doing it?
    c) *If yes:* What qualifications does he have to have?

40. Is it necessary to line up with cliques, caucuses, or factions?

41. How do you feel about cliques, caucuses, or factions? Why?

42. *For inactives only:* Were you ever more active than you are now?
    a) *If yes:* How come you used to be more active? What's changed?
    b) *If no:* How come you never became more active?

43. *For inactives only:* Do you ever go to departmental meetings?
    a) Why don't you go more often? *Or:* Why don't you?
    b) Why do you go when you do go?

44. *For inactives only:* Do you ever say anything at departmental meetings? Why or why not?

45. *For inactives only:* Do you find out what's going on at departmental meetings when you don't go? How or why not?

46. *For leaders and actives only:* How did you happen to become active?
    a) What keeps you active?
    b) What do you get out of it?

47. Have you ever picketed during a strike? How come?

48. Were there any strikes where you didn't picket? How come?

49. What do you think strikes have accomplished in this plant?

50. Under what conditions do you think the union should call a strike?

51. What do you think are the sacrifices of going on strike?

52. Why do workers, nevertheless, go on strike?

53. How do you feel about the amount of dues you pay? Why?

54. Does the union spend its money wisely? Why do you think so?

55. How do you feel about the dues checkoff clause in your contract?

56. Upon what basis are you paid?

57. If your rate was cut or the company added more work to your job, and wouldn't give you more money, what would you do about it?

58. *If grievance is mentioned:* Supposing you didn't get satisfaction on your grievance, is there any other action that you can take?

59. *If grievance is not mentioned:*
    a) *Strike:* How would you go about it?
    b) *Quit:* Why would you do that?
    c) *Transfer:* Why would you do that?
    d) *Slowdown:* How would you go about pulling it off?

60. *If slowdown is not mentioned:* Would you ever consider a slowdown as a way of getting action? Why?

61. *For actives and inactives only:* Have you ever voted in local union elections?
    a) How come you voted when you did? How come you didn't vote at other times?
    b) How come you don't vote?
    c) How come you do vote?

62. Are elections run honestly?

63. Would it make any difference to you if the union disappeared? Why or why not?

64. *For actives and inactives only:* Do you feel it's your responsibility to see that the union does its job and does it right? Do you do anything about it?

65. Does everybody get a fair break in the union regardless of his color, religion, or nationality? *If yes:* How do you feel about it? *If no:* In what way? How do you feel about it?

66. Do any union officers discriminate in any way? In what way? *Or:* Why don't they?

67. Does everybody get a fair break in the company regardless of his color, religion, or nationality? *If yes:* How do you feel about it? *If no:* In what way? How do you feel about it?

68. Do any supervisors discriminate in any way? In what way? *Or:* Why don't they?

69. Do you feel the union should be active in community affairs? Why? What kind of affairs?
70. Should unions be active in politics? Why or why not?
71. *For those who answer yes:* What kinds of political activities should unions engage in?
72. Do you feel there are any political activities unions should not engage in?
73. What do you think about PAC? Why do you say so?
74. Should labor have its own political party instead of supporting existing parties? Why or why not?
75. Besides talking to people, how do you find out what's going on in the union world?
76. Do you read any union newspapers? Which ones?
77. Does your local belong to an International Union? Which one?
78. What do you think the International does?
79. Do you find out what's going on in the International? How?
80. Are there any advantages in belonging to an International Union? (Use title if given.) What are the advantages?
81. Are there any disadvantages in belonging to an International Union? (Use title if given.) What are the disadvantages?
82. Do you feel the International should have a say in local affairs? How much of a say? *Or:* Why not?
83. Should the local go to the International for advice? On what sort of issues?
84. Would it make any difference to you if the International disappeared? Why or why not?
85. *Personal data:*
    Age
    Place of birth
    Sex
    Marital status
    Number and age of children
    Religion (also wife and children)
    Place of birth of father
    Place of birth of mother
    (Look for other minority status)
    Education—last grade or year completed
    What is (was) your father's occupation?
    Was father (mother) a union member?

Interview Guide Used in Coal Miners' Study

1. How long have you been a miner?
2. What kind of work do you do? Pay?

3. Do you like your work? Why do you say that?

4. In general how do you feel about the company? Why do you feel that way?

5. Are there any other members of your family who are miners? How far back?

6. When did you first start working in the mines? How come?

7. Did you ever leave the mines to work in any other industry?
   a) If yes: Why did you leave? Why did you come back to coal mining?

8. Would you want your sons to work in the mines? Why or why not?
   a) What would you like your sons to be?

9. Why don't more young men go into the mines?

10. Do you expect to stay at mining permanently? Why or why not?

11. Have you ever worked in a non-union mine? What was it like?

12. Did you ever belong to a union before you joined the UMW? What union? Were you active?

13. When did you join the UMW? How did you feel about it?

14. How did you first hear about unions? When?

15. Why do you think we have unions? (*If protection is mentioned:* What does the union protect you from?)

16. What kind of problems do you feel are most important to the miners?

17. In general, how do you feel about the UMW? Why do you feel that way?

18. What has the UMW been able to accomplish?

19. *For those who don't mention wages under No. 18:* What do you think the union has done in regard to wages?

20. Is there anything you'd like the UMW to do that it isn't doing right now?

21. *For inactives only:* Were you ever more active than you are now?
    a) If yes: How come you used to be more active? What's changed?
    b) If no: How come you never became more active?

22. *For leaders only:* How did you happen to become active?
    a) What keeps you active?
    b) What do you get out of it?

23. Can any member run for office in the local of the UMW?
    a) If no: Why not?

24. How does a miner get to be president of the district?
    a) How did this come about?
    b) How do you think this has worked out?

25. *For inactives only:* Do you ever go to regular union meetings?
    a) Why don't you go more often? *Or:* Why do you?
    b) Why do you go when you do go?

26. *For leaders only:* Do many members attend local meetings? Why? *Or:* Why not?

27. Do you read any union newspapers? Which ones?
28. If members don't like the way the UMW is run, is there anything they can do about it? What? *Or:* Why not?
29. Do you remember the three-day week in 1949?
30. Why do you think the union went on a three-day week in 1949?
31. How did you feel about it? (Did you benefit by it?)
32. What would you do if the union asked you to go on a three-day week now?
33. Have you ever worked as a pick-and-shovel miner?
34. Have your feelings about mining changed since working in a mechanized mine? Why? In what way?
35. It seems to me that mining is a dirty and dangerous job. Why do you stick with it?
36. What do you think strikes have accomplished for you as a miner?
37. How does the UMW go about calling a strike? How do you feel about it?
38. What say do locals have in calling a strike?
39. Under what conditions do you think your union should go on strike? How about during wartime?
40. How did you feel about how the radio and newspapers talked about the UMW strikes during the war?
41. Do you think the UMW should be active in politics? Why or why not?
42. *For those who answer yes:* What kinds of political activities should the UMW engage in?
43. Do you feel that there are any political activities the UMW should not engage in?
44. Should labor have its own political party instead of supporting existing parties? Why? *Or:* Why not?
45. Do you feel the UMW should be active in community affairs? What kind of affairs? Why? *Or:* Why not?
46. How do you feel about the amount of dues you pay? Why?
47. Would it make any difference to you if the local union disappeared? Why or why not?
48. What does the International Union do?
49. Are there any advantages in belonging to an International Union? What are the advantages?
50. Are there any disadvantages in belonging to an International Union? What are the disadvantages?
51. Would it make any difference to you if the International Union would disappear? Why or why not?
52. Does the UMW belong to the CIO, AFL, or is it independent?
53. What are the advantages or disadvantages in belonging to ———?

54. What do you think of John L. Lewis? Why do you think so?

55. Is there anything you would want John L. Lewis to do that isn't being done now? Why? What?

56. What do you think will happen when John L. dies?

57. *Personal data:*
Age
Where raised
Sex
Marital status
Number and age of children
Religion (wife, children)
Place of birth of father. Where raised
Place of birth of mother
Education—last grade or year completed
What was (is) your father's occupation?
Was father (mother) a union member?
When did you first join the UMW?

INDEX

Addes, George F., 93
Allen, V. L., 212
Amalgamated Association of Iron, Steel and Tin Workers, 66
Amalgamated Clothing Workers, Toronto District, shop-chairman system, 214
American Federation of Labor
    bargaining in telephone industry, 147
    Building and Construction Trades Department, 46
    Labor's League for Political Education, 181, 231, 263
    plumbers' union, 46
    political activities, 231, 234–35
American Federation of Labor–Congress of Industrial Organizations
    codes of ethical practices, 270
    Committee on Political Education, 243
American Telephone and Telegraph Company, 139–40, 147
Apprenticeship, craft unions, 205
Apprenticeship, plumbers, 44
Attendance at local meetings, 186–91
Autonomy of officers of United Mine Workers, 211–12

Bell, Alexander Graham, 139
Bell System
    average gross weekly earnings, 143
    collective bargaining units, 146–47
    description of structure, 139–40
    employee representation plans, 144–45
    fringe benefits, 144, 163
    wage policies, 143
Bell Telephone Laboratories, 140
"Big Steel," 68, 197
Building codes, 44
Building and Construction Trades Department, American Federation of Labor, 46

Building trades unions; see Plumbers
Business agents
    building trades unions, 48, 60, 169, 176
    corruption in unions, 47
    powers, 205

Carnegie-Illinois Steel Corporation, 67
Centralia (Ill.) mine disaster, 22
Chamber of commerce, 65
Checkoff of union dues, 67–68
Class A Telephone Carriers, 143
Closed shop in craft unions, 205
Coal miners
    attitude toward John L. Lewis, 30–32
    attitude toward union, 23–25
    company stores, 30
    wage cutting, 15
    wage rates, 17
    wildcat strikes, 36
    work stoppages, 36–37
Coal mining
    decline in bituminous production, 18
    decline in employment, 18
    Illinois fields, 15
    mine explosions, 22
    wartime strikes, 17, 33
Codes of ethical practices, 270
Collective bargaining
    American Telephone and Telegraph Company, 147
    Bell System, 146–47, 197
    coal miners, 197
    metal workers, 197
    Western Electric Company, 146–47
Committee for Industrial Organization, Steel Workers Organizing Committee, 66–67, 198
Committee on Political Education, 243
Communications Workers of America, 14, 139, 162, 218
    affiliation with CIO, 146
    attendance at local meetings, 186–87

Communication Workers of America—
Continued
  collective bargaining, 197
  community activities, 226
  election of local officers, 192–93
  picketing, 159–60
  political activities, 230, 232
  salaries of local officers, 149
  strike, 145
  telephone industry bargaining, 147
  union achievements, 156–59
  union social activities, 223
  union stewards, 149
  wage-policy disputes, 143
Communist activities
  factionalism, 211
  United Automobile Workers, 93, 95
  United Steelworkers of America, 70
Community activities of labor unions,
  224–27
Company stores, 30
Company unions, 145
Congress of Industrial Organizations
  affiliation of Communications Workers
    of America, 146
  organizing drives, 17
  Political Action Committee, 231, 263
  political activities, 230, 235
  telephone industry bargaining, 147
Construction industry; *see* Plumbers
Contractors, employers' associations, 47
Corruption of officials, 26
Craft unions
  closed shop, 205
  turnover in leadership, 205–6
Craftsmen's Club, 49

Dailey Committee, 47
Democracy in local unions
  decision-making bodies, 272–73
  elections, 200–201
  metal workers
    nominations for officers, 201
    recall of departmental stewards, 201
    requirements, 206–8
    structural factors, 202–6
    turnover in leadership, 203–6
Democracy in national unions, 211–14,
  216–19
Democratic party, 229, 233, 238–40
Departmental stewards
  recall, 201
  role in relation to new workers, 268
Discipline boards
  United Automobile Workers, 270
  Upholsterers' International Union, 270

Discrimination in employment, 73–74,
  81, 106
Dues inspection line, 69, 77–79

Elections of union officers, 192–93, 200–
  201
Employee representation plans in Bell
  System, 144–45
Employers' associations of contractors,
  47
Escalator clause in metal workers' con-
  tract, 104

Factionalism
  International Typographical Union,
    209–10
  metal workers, 95–96, 199, 209–10
  steel workers, 70–71, 199, 209–10
Factory system, 3
Fair Labor Standards Act, 120
Farm Equipment Workers, 92, 95
Farm equipment workers union; *see*
  United Automobile Workers
Federal Communications Commission,
  140, 143
Fringe benefits
  Bell System, 144, 163
  United Mine Workers, 17

General Motors Corporation, 145
Gompers, Samuel, 263
Government employees, 217
Government intervention in disputes,
  274
Green, William, 19

Health and welfare benefits of United
  Mine Workers, 28, 31
Herberg, Will, 213

Illinois Bell Telephone Company, 143
Immigration, 3–4, 64
Inactive union members, 194–95
Industrial Workers of the World, 74
International Association of Machinists,
  232
International Executive Board (UMW),
  35, 212
International Ladies' Garment Workers'
  Union, 13
  attendance at local meetings, 186–88,
    190–91
  community activities, 226
  contract demands, 124
  election of local officers, 192–93
  fence-sitters and non-strikers, 130–33

Management Engineering Department, 127
NLRB election, 123
organizing drives, 117–20, 123–24
picketing, 126, 128–29
political activities, 230, 232
strike, 125–30
strike benefits, 127
union achievements, 133–35
union social activities, 221–22
wage rates, 120, 124, 127
International Typographical Union
democracy, 217
election of national union officers, 215
two-party system, 209–10, 213–14

Jewish workers, 48
Jurisdictional disputes, 44, 46–47

Knights of Labor, 16, 47
Knitting mill workers; *see* International Ladies' Garment Workers' Union

Labor laws and legislation
Fair Labor Standards Act, 120
National Labor Relations Act, 1, 67, 145
New Deal, 17, 235
"right-to-work" laws, 269
Taft-Hartley Act, 69, 118, 205, 230, 235, 269
centralization of union power, 213
union-shop poll requirement, 263
"Labor monopoly" fears, 274
Labor movement
effect of Wagner Act, 1
factors in development, 2–4
Labor party formation, 237–40
Labor racketeering, 47
Labor union discipline, 213, 270–71
Labor union policy issues
discipline process, 270–71
informing membership of issues, 273
opposition political groups, 271
power of union leaders, 269
representative government in union, 272–73
union security, 269–70
Labor union problems
occupational environment, 259
political action, 263–64
social mobility hopes, 256–58
strikes, 262
union security, 262–63
white-collar workers, 265–66
young workers, 265, 267–69

Labor unions
community activities, 224–27
political activities, 227–33
rank-and-file workers, 5–11
social activities, 221–24
Labor's League for Political Education, 181, 231, 263
Leadership; *see* Local union leadership
Legislative investigation of labor racketeering, 47
Lewis, John L., 16, 17, 19, 75
attitude of union members, 30–32
autocratic control of union, 246
disputes with union leaders, 16
opposition to district autonomy, 211
Progressive Miners of America, 16, 246
provisionalism in UMW, 26–28, 212, 218
three-day week, 37–38
Lipset, Seymour M., 214
"Little Steel" strike, 67
Lobbying, 214
Local union leadership
bargaining committee members, 166
business agents, 169
characteristics of leaders, 170–72
differences between leaders and rank-and-file members, 178–82
election of officers, 192–93
executive board members, 166
factionalism, 180
full-time officials, 168–69
grievance committee members, 166
membership loyalty, 255–56
motivation to become leaders, 172–76
officers, 166–68
political machines, 169
relations with supervisors, 182–84
rewards, 168, 176–78
shop stewards, 165–66
turnover, 203–6
Local unions, 5–6
Lockwood Committee, 47
Longshoring industry, 206

McDonald, David J., 70
Maintenance of membership, 67–68, 91
Membership participation in union activities
attendance at departmental meetings, 191–92
attendance at local meetings, 186–91
committee membership, 193–94
election of union officers, 192–93

Membership participation in union activities—*Continued*
  factors affecting participation, 196–200
  informal activities, 195
Metal workers; *see* United Automobile Workers
Mexican workers, 4, 71, 73, 88
Michels, Robert, 213
Mitchell, John, 16
Murray, Philip, 19
Muste, A. J., 208

National Federation of Miners and Mine Laborers, 16
National Federation of Telephone Workers, 145–46
National Industrial Recovery Act, 66
National Labor Relations Act, 1, 67, 145
National Labor Relations Board, 67–68
National labor unions
  democracy, 211–14
  excessive power, 269
  powers of heads, 214–15
National War Labor Board, 67, 92
Negro workers, 3, 71, 73, 88
New Deal, 17, 70, 235

Occupational environment as a labor union problem, 259
Organizing drives, 17, 117, 123–24

Picketing
  knitting mill workers, 126, 128–29
  metal workers, 107
  steel workers, 84
  telephone workers, 159–60
Plumbers
  apprenticeship, 44
  attendance at local meetings, 186, 188–91, 196
  attitude toward union, 56–59
  building codes, 44
  business agents, 47–48, 60
  community activities, 224–26
  dually oriented members, 249–50, 258
  election of officers, 192–93, 201–3
  factionalism, 209–10
  "good" union members, 245
  independence, 55
  Jewish workers, 48
  jurisdictional disputes, 44, 46–47
  strikes, 56–57
  union dues, 58
  union initiation fee, 58
  union-management relations, 45–46

union social activities, 221–22
  wage rates, 49
  welfare fund, 49
Plumbers' Union, 13
Police attitude toward unions, 229–30
Political Action Committee, 231, 263
Political activities of unions, 227–33
  attitudes of workers, 263–64
  factors affecting action, 233–36
  opposition political groups, 271
Political machines
  corruption in unions, 47
  local union officers, 169
  national union heads, 215
Pot and Ladle Club, 49
Professional workers, 217
Progressive Miners of America, 16, 26, 246
Provisionalism in United Mine Workers, 25–28, 212
  constitutional provisions, 218
  Illinois District 12, 17
Puerto Rican workers, 4, 71

Racketeering, 47
Rank-and-file workers, 5–11
  expectations of employer, 260–61
  expectations of union, 260
  types
    card-carriers, 250–51
    crisis activists, 246–49
    dually oriented members, 249–50
    "good" union men, 244–46
    ideological unionists, 242–44
    indifferent members, 250–51
    "loyal but critical" members, 246
    unwilling unionists, 251–52
Rarick, Donald C., 70
Recall of departmental stewards, 201
Republican party, 233, 238, 240
Retail Clerks' Union, 127
Reuther, Walter
  factional conflicts, 93, 95
  labor party support, 237
  political pronouncements, 232
"Revolving door" plan, 270
"Right-to-work" laws, 269
Roman Catholic church, 65
Roosevelt, Franklin D., 76

Sexton, Brendan, 216
Shape-up in hiring of longshoremen, 206
Sheet metal workers, jurisdictional disputes with plumbers, 44
Shop-chairman system, 214
Shop committees, 96

Shop stewards, 165–66
Slowdowns
    metal workers, 107–9
    steel workers, 84–86
Social activities of labor unions, 221–24
Social mobility of workers, 234, 256–58
Socialists, 95
Steamfitters, jurisdictional disputes with plumbers, 44
Steel workers; *see* United Steelworkers of America
Steel Workers Organizing Committee, 66–67, 198
Stevenson, Adlai E., 233
Strikes
    coal miners, 17, 32–38
    knitting mill workers, 125–30
    leadership problems, 262
    metal workers, 94–95, 106–7
    plumbers, 56–57
    steel workers, 83
        1919 strike, 64, 66
        1937 "Little Steel," 67, 229
    telephone workers, 145

Taft, Philip, 212
Taft-Hartley Act, 69, 118, 205, 230, 235, 269
    centralization of union power, 213
    union-shop poll requirement, 263
Teamsters' Union, 127, 237
Telephone equipment technicians, wage rates, 142
Telephone workers; *see* Communications Workers of America
Thomas, R. J., 93
Turnover in leadership in craft unions, 205–6
Typology of union members, 241–54

Union members, types
    card-carriers, 250–51
    crisis activists, 246–49
    dually oriented members, 249–50
    "good" union men, 244–46
    ideological unionists, 242–44
    indifferent members, 250–51
    "loyal but critical" members, 246
    unwilling unionists, 251–52
Union security
    leadership problems, 262–63
    policy issue of unions, 269–70
    "revolving door" plan, 270
Union security clause, 68, 74, 91, 94
Union-shop poll, Taft-Hartley requirement, 263

Union stewards for telephone workers, 149
United Automobile Workers, 13
    attendance at local meetings, 186–88, 190–91
    Communist influence, 93, 95
    Detroit study, 233, 238
    discipline board, 270
    discrimination in employment, 106
    dually oriented members, 249, 258
    election of local officers, 192–93
    factionalism, 95–96, 199, 209–10
    inactive members, 194–95
    local structure, 96
    organization of local, 91–92
    picketing, 107
    political activities, 230, 232
    slowdowns, 107–9
    Socialist activity, 95
    strikes, 94–95, 106–7
    union achievements, 102–6
    union security clause, 91, 94
    union social activities, 221–22
    wage rates, 97
    wartime no-strike pledge, 92
United Electrical Workers, 95
United Labor Committee, 127
United Mine Workers, 13, 74
    achievements, 31
    attendance at local meetings, 186–87, 190–91, 197
    centralization of authority, 35–36
    collective bargaining, 197
    community activities, 226–27
    corruption of officials, 26
    election of local officers, 192–93
    formation of union, 16
    health and welfare benefits, 28, 30–31
    history of union, 16–18
    Illinois District 12, 16–17
    inactive members, 194–95
    International Executive Board, 35, 212
    leadership disputes, 16
    Lewis, John L.
        attitude of union, 30–32
        opposition to district autonomy, 211
    membership decline, 18
    occupational setting, 259
    organizing activities, 17
    political activities, 228, 230, 232
    provisionalism, 25–28, 212, 218
    strikes, 32–38
    three-day week, 37–38
    wage rates, 17, 28
    working conditions, 29, 31

United States Senate, telephone industry study, 147
United States Steel Corporation, 66–68
United Steelworkers of America, 13, 68, 70
   attendance at local meetings, 186–88, 190–91
   collective bargaining, 197–98
   Communist activity, 70
   community activities, 226–27
   election of local officers, 192–93
   factionalism, 70–71, 199, 209–10
   inactive members, 194–95
   picketing, 84
   political activities, 228–30
   slowdowns, 84–86
   strikes, 83
   union achievements, 79
   wage rates, 71
Upholsterers' International Union, 270

Wage cutting, 15
Wage policies of Bell System, 143

Wage rates
   coal miners, 17, 28
   knitting mill workers, 120, 124, 127
   metal workers, 97
   plumbers, 49
   steel workers, 71
   telephone workers, 142–43
Wagner Act; see National Labor Relations Act
Welfare funds, 49
West Frankfort (Ill.) mine disaster, 22
Western Electric Company, 140, 146–47
White-collar workers, obstacles to organizing, 265–66
Wildcat strikes, 36
Wisconsin Employment Relations Board, 128
Woll, Matthew, 210
Workers; see Rank-and-file workers
Working conditions of coal miners, 29
World War II coal production, 17, 22

Young workers, lack of involvement with union problems, 265, 267–69